*Praise for*

## The Good, the Bad and the Ugly...

"An informative, intuitive analysis of some of the most famous, and infamous, deals in recent private equity history. Through a series of detailed case studies, Sebastien Canderle offers a thorough review of the factors that can set apart successful deals from disastrous ones, as well as the behavioral traits that separate long term success from its opposite. Must-read for finance professionals."

**Philip Grant, Grant's Interest Rate Observer**

"By covering the many facets of private equity in a clear and rigorous writing style accessible to non-specialists, this book provides an invaluable and entertaining glimpse of this secretive industry."

**Thomas Mählmann, Chair of Finance and Banking**

**Catholic University Eichstätt-Ingolstadt School of Management**

"Sebastien Canderle takes readers on an engaging journey in the intriguing and impenetrable search for extraordinary private equity returns. A thrilling and masterly written story about ethics, accountability and death by debt overdose."

**Leila Pinto Campillo, Professor of Finance**

**University College London School of Management**

"Ambitious in intent, this is a balanced and insightful account of what makes a private equity deal 'good, bad or ugly'. The case histories bring this book alive and illustrate in an instructive way how transactions are either skilfully piloted, haphazardly navigated or end in shipwreck."

**James Sefton, Chair in Economics, Imperial College**

# THE GOOD, THE BAD AND THE UGLY

# OF PRIVATE EQUITY

# ALSO BY SEBASTIEN CANDERLE

*Private Equity's Public Distress*

*The Debt Trap*

# THE GOOD, THE BAD AND THE UGLY

# OF PRIVATE EQUITY

Success and failure in buyout land

SEBASTIEN CANDERLE

First published in 2018

Copyright © Sebastien Canderle

The right of Sebastien Canderle to be identified as the author has been asserted in accordance with the Copyright, Design and Patents Act 1988.

All rights reserved; no part of this publication may be reproduced, stored in a retrieval system, or transmitted in any form or by any means, electronic, mechanical, photocopying, scanning, recording or otherwise without the prior written permission of the Author. This book may not be lent, resold, hired out or otherwise disposed of by way of trade in any form of binding or cover other than that in which it is published without the prior written consent of the Author.

Whilst every effort has been made to ensure that information in this book is accurate, no liability can be accepted for any loss incurred in any way whatsoever by any person relying solely on the information contained herein.

No responsibility for loss occasioned to any person or corporate body acting or refraining to act as a result of reading material in this book can be accepted by the Author, or by the employers of the Author.

# CONTENTS

Figures and tables .................................................................................. viii

Prologue. A question of performance ................................................... 1

PART ONE – The Good: Lucky or talented? ...................................... 11

Chapter 1. Hilton Hotels: "the best leveraged buyout ever" ............. 13

Chapter 2. Mergermarket: The ideal LBO candidate ........................ 43

Chapter 3. A pragmatic blueprint for private equity best practice ... 65

PART TWO – The Bad: Cursed or reckless? ..................................... 85

Chapter 4. Univision: The telenovela of a corporate zombie ............. 87

Chapter 5. 3i: Mirror to the economic cycle and to human
psychology.. ........................................................................................ 119

Chapter 6. Toys "R" Us: Leveraging in retail is no child's play ..... 157

PART THREE – The Ugly: Greedy or wicked? ................................ 189

Chapter 7. Bhs: A roadmap to bankruptcy ..................................... 191

Chapter 8. TIM/WIND Hellas: The Trojan horse of leverage ....... 231

Chapter 9. Private Equity's C-words: Collusion, corruption and
conflicts of interest ............................................................................ 261

Epilogue. A matter of underperformance ........................................ 287

Acknowledgements ............................................................................ 317

About the author ............................................................................... 318

Index .................................................................................................. 319

Notes .................................................................................................. 327

# FIGURES AND TABLES

Figure 1.1 – Hilton stock performance versus S&P 500 and sector indexes from 2001 to 2006

Figure 1.2 – Hilton's revenue breakdown between four main divisions

Figure 1.3 – Hilton Worldwide stock performance in three years post-IPO vs. S&P 500

Figure 1.4 – Hilton's net debt and leverage ratio (2006, and 2008 to 2016)

Table 1.1 – Blackstone's investments in and proceeds from Hilton

Figure 2.1 – Mergermarket Group's revenue and EBITDA margin from 2003 to 2006

Figure 2.2 – Mergermarket Group's revenue and EBITDA margin from 2006 to 2013

Figure 2.3 – Mergermarket Group's revenue and cash EBITDA margin from 2013 to 2016

Table 4.1 – Change in ratings for the main US TV broadcasters in 2014, 2015 and 2016

Figure 4.1 – Univision's EBITDA and leverage ratio from 2006 to 2016

Figure 5.1 – 3i Group plc stock performance between July 1994 and December 1999

Figure 5.2 – 3i Group plc stock performance between January 1999 and December 2003

Figure 5.3 – 3i Group plc stock performance between January 2003 and December 2009

Table 5.1 – 3i Group's key performance indicators in 2000 and 2017

Figure 5.4 – 3i Group's net asset value and headcount from March 1994 to March 2017

Figure 5.5 – FTSE 100 index and 3i Group plc stock performance between January 1999 and December 2017

Figure 6.1 – Toys "R" Us's sales and EBITDA margin from 2000 to 2006

Figure 6.2 – Toys "R" Us's sales and EBITDA margin from 2005 to 2017

Figure 6.3 – Toys "R" Us's leverage ratio (Net debt/EBITDA) and interest cover (EBITDA/interest) from 2003 to 2017

Table 7.1 – Financial indicators for Marks & Spencer in 2004 and 2014

Table 7.2 – Financial indicators for Bhs in 2004 and 2014

Figure 7.1 – Taveta's net debt, operating profit and leverage ratio from 2006 to 2016

Figure 8.1 – STET/TIM Hellas's revenue and EBITDA margin from 2000 to 2005

Figure 8.2 – TIM/WIND Hellas's revenue and EBITDA margin from 2007 to 2010

Figure 8.3 – WIND Hellas's revenue and EBITDA margin from 2013 to 2016

# PROLOGUE

# A question of performance

*"Those who manage other people's money are more careless than when managing their own"*[1]

**Mervyn King, Governor of the Bank of England from 2003 to 2013**

The growth experienced by the world economy over the past four decades has been fed by an enormous injection of credit. Whether one looks at mortgages, credit cards, corporate borrowings or government debt, modern growth is heavily dependent on leverage. In America, total debt as a percentage of national GDP rose from 50% in the mid-1970s to 400% forty years later, while China saw total debt jump from 100% of GDP in the early 1990s to 300% in 2017.[2] Throughout, credit acted as an intravenous injection in the bloodstream of the world economy.

As a craving user of leverage, the private equity industry is one of the main beneficiaries of the financialisation of the markets. A fast-shrinking number of corporations, whether public or private, can now be deemed out of reach of buyout fund managers. Multi-billion-dollar transactions have become ordinary occurrences. Many household consumer brands like Dell, Heinz, Hertz and Toys "R" Us have experienced private equity ownership. Understandably, as PE firms grew in stature their performance and conduct came under scrutiny.

## Performance matters

Investors' overconfidence and unrealistic optimism are among the most common biases identified by behavioural economists to explain poor investment results. When asked, less than 11% of people consider themselves to be below average investors.[3] So called 'sophisticated' investors, like professional fund managers, also tend to exaggerate their investment skills. Private equity specialists suffer from similar delusion. Most believe (and report) that they are top-quartile performers.

What is perhaps more telling is the lack of performance consistency over time. More often than not, a fund manager that is a cut above for one vintage will not be for subsequent ones. This lack of 'persistence' in returns, as academics call the idea that a firm's future performance

is predicted or not by past results, has been demonstrated. In fact, it has gone worse during the short history of private equity. In the 1990s, slightly more than 30% of top-quartile PE fund managers remained so in subsequent vintages. In the 2000-04 period, that proportion fell to 28% before dropping further to 13% in 2005-09 and 12% in 2010-13.[4] Weak reliability of past performance is a point that will resurface throughout this book.

For investors keen to select top fund managers among a vast population of undifferentiated firms and individuals, this is not good news. But it is made even more challenging by the techniques used by fund managers to hide their true underlying performance. To back the contention that they are superior to their peers, PE firms will cut their performance numbers as necessary. For instance, a mid-market, US-focused generalist fund will select the worst performing fund managers in its category and rule out the best ones by using its own methodology: it might omit some of the star investment firms because they cover different sectors or geographies, or because they also handle turnarounds rather than exclusively buyouts. The opportunities to manipulate performance reporting are almost endless.

Logically, not all fund managers and not all leveraged buyouts (LBOs) can be top quartile or even above average. What this book attempts to highlight is the characteristics that distinguish first-rate investors and good deals from the bad or truly ugly ones. It also offers recommendations, informed by case studies.

## The PE model

Over the past forty years, private equity (in its purest definition restricted to leveraged buyouts, which is the area this book covers) morphed from a local or national activity operating below the regulatory radar, into an international and eventually global power base with considerable influence on political agendas and economic efficiency.

The current climate for a fundamental reassessment of the world of finance's contribution to the broader economy calls for research and analysis that clearly detail out how financial engineering creates or destroys value. Fund management has grown to such an extent that it can rightly be considered the new banking. Banks used to be the main providers of investment and lending services to businesses. They had traditionally granted income, in the form of interest, to capital providers (including individuals) in exchange for using the latter's assets as the banks saw fit.

In a market economy, you typically get paid if you let someone else use your capital. When you put your money into a savings account, you earn interest. If you rent out your apartment, you get compensated by the tenant. When you invest in a company, you commonly receive a dividend as a reward for getting your money tied up in a risky endeavour.

What is astonishing is that PE fund managers get paid for the privilege of using other people's money. Not only private equity firms do not pay investors – the fund providers, also known as limited partners or LP investors – they charge them an annual management commission that can be as high as 2.5%. Partly for that reason, private equity has faced brisk expansion.

In addition to this tremendous fee-earning potential, growth in private equity was driven by several unique factors: the investors' contractual obligations to commit capital in advance and for a set number of years, enabling fund managers to charge fees on these commitments rather than on the portion of capital invested; a lack of transparency and limited accountability; and, last but not least, full benefit of capital gains without much exposure to the downside (capital losses).

Not surprisingly, these extraordinary benefits are granted as a quid pro quo for expectations to yield returns on capital significantly better than would otherwise be earned from other asset classes.

## The bigger picture

At the risk of losing readers early on, this is a book for people unable to believe that unregulated free markets are the only viable option to run a capitalist economy. It is addressed to people who have taken stock of the performance volatility and value destruction potential of market bubbles and crashes such as those witnessed in 2005-10, if not of the earlier and equally wasteful dotcom craze and accounting frauds of 1998-2003.

Free-market theories were invented to serve two key purposes. For economists to attempt to satisfy their thirst for rationality, forcing into mathematical formulas what is essentially emotional human behaviour. And for the wealthy and the politically motivated to justify deeds that would otherwise be easily discredited in the face of overwhelming evidence in terms of structural inefficiencies, incidental or intentional side effects, and criminality.

# Prologue

Because this book raises concerns about the way capitalism is practiced in the early years of the 21ˢᵗ century does not imply that we should go back to the revolutionary stages of the previous century. Socialism and communism have demonstrated that they are not fit for purpose. But in view of the numerous financial crises recorded in the past hundred years, neither is market fundamentalism.

This book is part of a trilogy on the impact of leveraged buyouts on modern-day capitalist economies. One of the main criticisms expressed towards the first two volumes is that they only showed mistakes carried out by fund managers but did not provide sufficient guidelines about how the latter were expected to avoid failures. *Private Equity's Public Distress* and *The Debt Trap* made clear that PE investors were, at times, victims of their own ingenuity. *The Good, the Bad and the Ugly of Private Equity* offers more of a contrast between best-in-class investment practices ("the Good"), the unfortunate results of a trial and error approach as well as negligence ("the Bad"), and the occasional excesses that are part and parcel of any industry lacking proper governance and regulation ("the Ugly"). Examining these transactions and fund managers' practices will place the sector's issues in sharper focus. *The Good, the Bad and the Ugly* introduces suggestions to better assess the performance of leveraged buyouts and fund managers.

The goal of this exercise is the same as for the first two volumes: to help practitioners improve the way they carry out their trade, with emphasis on deal assessment, portfolio management and corporate governance. Where this book differs is that, with apologies to finance experts, it has been cleansed of its most technical and esoteric content in response to feedback received on the first two instalments. This should make the subject matter accessible to a wider audience without weakening the substance of the message: the fact that private equity would benefit from effective compliance and risk management.

Some of the individuals and firms depicted in the following chapters do not appear particularly talented or diligent. However, rather than picking on these characters, the industry needs to acknowledge that they are not isolated examples. Many of the mistakes mentioned in this book are ongoing. We can all learn from them.

## The search for best practice

The book is organised into three parts. Either through luck or by following best practice, fund managers can deliver superior returns. This is the picture presented in Part One. It highlights the positive outcomes of LBOs in terms of performance for fund managers, investors and corporate executives.

As chapters 1 to 3 indicate, occasionally PE fund managers can deliver tremendous performance. It is important to understand that this first section of the book does not concern itself with potentially negative effects that buyouts can have on third parties (what economists call externalities), during or after the period of PE ownership. Just because a private equity firm achieved great returns from an investment does not automatically imply that the transaction was an unmitigated success for employees, customers or other economic participants.

Any self-proclaimed sophisticated investor must strive continuously to improve his or her game. While PE fund managers spent the first three decades of LBO investing in a free and careless manner, the years following the financial crisis have seen various attempts to correct past mistakes. The first section of this book will look at the criteria specific to good private equity dealmaking. We will review important features of performance optimisation (Chapter 1 on Hilton), the example of an ideal LBO candidate (Chapter 2 on Mergermarket), and the determinants behind successful LBO investing and fund management (Chapter 3).

The aim of Part One is not to bring together the best in thought and practice from an official, industry standpoint. There is little public

# Prologue

information regarding underlying private equity performance, and information voluntarily disclosed by PE firms is generally heavily biased and fudged. After almost 15 years working for and with fund managers, I have gathered my own convictions of what represent best practice – thereby, Part One reflects personal opinions.

## The curse of malpractice

Thirty years ago, portfolio management and operational expertise did not matter. That sounds heretical, but it was partly due to the lack of experience among the body of buyout deal-doers. Also, there were so many candidates for corporate carve-outs and turnarounds that the industry's pioneers did not have to exert themselves looking for targets; they spent most of their energy sourcing debt financing. Today, bankers and private debt fund managers fall over each other to back leveraged buyouts, the most determined users of corporate debt in the economy. Equally, modern corporations are better run than their 1970s and 1980s counterparts were. The implications for PE fund managers is that they must resort to financial innovation as well as operational discipline to earn superior returns.

This book is about the PE value creation machine. While full of potential, at times key components of the engine get jammed. During my career as a fund manager, I was often struck by the widespread use of terminology that described the dangers associated with leverage. Terms like 'revolver' – a working capital facility – and 'bullet repayment' – the redemption of a loan at maturity rather than through an amortisation schedule – appropriately act as reminders that the use of debt is a precarious undertaking. Although LBOs are a forty-year old corporate finance practice, no one has yet broken the code. The approach adopted by all the fund managers remains essentially one of experimentation. Several of our case studies will point out that human fallibility can lead to disastrous consequences.

What Parts Two (The Bad) and Three (The Ugly) illustrate is that, in their search for extraordinary returns, fund managers often take inconsiderate risks. These stories will help us clarify how behavioural shortcomings work out at the micro, corporate level. Whether the disastrous results are due to unforeseen circumstances, negligence or wicked intentions is open to interpretation. What is not is the effect on underlying portfolio companies and the fund managers' own reputation. Part Three, in particular, exposes the worst aspects of the industry's practices.

By dividing the book into three parts, I do not imply that the contribution of the PE industry is neatly split into three equal portions: one-third producing good or excellent returns, another third delivering poor performance, and the rest destroying value. I have not conducted the kind of comprehensive research – nor has anyone else, as far as I know – allowing me to determine the proportion of successful LBOs, those that genuinely create economic value above and beyond the superficial and mechanical use of debt. In fact, there is overlap across the three sections. It is rare for a deal to be an unmitigated turkey or unequivocal triumph, or for a fund manager to be an unquestionable failure or superstar. What is important to keep in mind is that the transactions and investors featured in this book are simply used as background to bring home the main arguments of my thesis.

The aim is to offer a contrast between, on one side, deals that have gone well and fund managers who have, sometimes unwittingly, taken good care of their investors' money and, on the other side, deals or professional managers that became victims of human and institutional failings. The Epilogue offers solutions to the thorny issues behind underperformance and malpractice, showing how we can learn in equal measures from those who fail and those who succeed.

This book is an inquiry into the state of private equity. It is not intended to be a textbook or a manual. It is written to encourage everyone to think about how private equity actually works and what changes are on the way. Because changes are needed. I started this section by explaining the extent of the delusion under which practitioners operate. Behaviours and governance must improve significantly if the sector's participants wish to take their fiduciary duties seriously.

---

## TERMINOLOGY

*Throughout this book, the term limited partner, or LP, refers to the fund provider committing capital towards investment vehicles managed by general partners, or GPs. The latter are fund managers, commonly known as private equity firms, which invest the LPs' capital in the form of equity holdings in leveraged buyouts.*

*Examples of LPs are pension funds (such as California-based CalSTRS and CalPERS mentioned in Chapter 4), insurance companies, banks, sovereign wealth funds (like the Government of Singapore's GIC, discussed in Chapter 2), universities and family offices. This book also covers transactions completed by some of the largest GPs in the world: 3i, Apax, Bain Capital, Blackstone, KKR, Providence and TPG.*

# PART ONE

# The Good: Lucky or talented?

*"You are only as good as your last deal"*

**Wall Street saying**

*The following stories should not be seen as an unequivocal backing of all the methods adopted by their protagonists.*

*There are serious reservations, expressed by academics, trade union representatives, regulators and politicians, regarding the contribution of private equity to our economies. Many practices, even if they yield significant gains to the fund managers and investors, can have a detrimental impact on other economic participants.*

*Nevertheless, this section introduces key parameters behind value creation in leveraged buyouts. For that reason, several aspects of these transactions should help readers interpret success in private equity.*

# CHAPTER 1

## Hilton Hotels: "the best leveraged buyout ever"

*Hotel groups are curious LBO targets. On the one hand, their property-heavy business model offers great opportunities for asset-backed loans and other secured debt products. On the other hand, their cyclicality means that performance heavily depends on timing.*

*Logically, buying hotel assets when the economy is in a recession gives the investor a chance to ride the recovery and exit at a much higher valuation. Conversely, purchasing at the top, just when the economy is about to go into reverse, can be fatal, unless you are patient or lucky. In its buyout of Hilton, Blackstone was both.*

With due respect to the younger readers, the rise to fame of socialite and reality TV star Paris Hilton in the noughties did not put the Hilton name on the map. The hotel group traces its roots to Cisco, Texas. It is there that Conrad Hilton – Paris's great-grandfather – bought his first property, the Mobley Hotel, during the 1919 oil boom, upon learning that room occupancy turned over three times a day.[1]

It is only after World War II, on 31 May 1946, that the Hilton Hotels Corporation was created by consolidating all the various properties Conrad had acquired and developed over the years. The immediate post-war period saw tremendous growth in the business, with revenue doubling between 1943 and 1946, while earnings more than tripled. The business model was already well established and diversified: room fares only accounted for two-fifths of revenue in 1948; food represented almost one-third and beverage over 12%.[2] That same year the group launched its international operations.

By the mid-1960s Hilton had expanded across the United States and generated almost $200 million in revenue in that country alone. In 1966, with 79-year-old Conrad as chairman and his 39-year-old son Barron as president, the group prepared the disposal of the international activities in order to focus exclusively on the huge potential that the US hotel industry represented in the era of mass tourism and leisure consumption. Trans World Corp, the holding company of airline TWA, acquired Hilton International the following year, aiming to make the most of the nascent globalisation of the American way of life.

After Conrad's death in January 1979, the hospitality group decided to develop the upscale brand Conrad in its founder's honour. By now generating over $450 million in revenue and $67 million in net profit, the group had lost 'a pioneer in the highest sense of the word',[3] as his son wrote in the annual report, but was in the very capable hands of an equally ambitious man dedicated to serving people. Barron would spend the next three decades consolidating Hilton into a truly global name.

In the 1970s Hilton had acquired assets in various segments of the hospitality market. After purchasing a couple of Las Vegas casinos in 1970, it had bought the prestigious Waldorf Astoria in New York. Yet the group's acquisition spree truly picked up in the 1980s and in the 1990s. In particular, after the appointment of Stephen Bollenbach – a former gaming executive with the Trump Organization – as president and CEO in 1996, Hilton became the world's largest gaming company through the acquisition of Bally Entertainment. The hospitality-to-leisure conglomerate ended the decade with the acquisition of Promus, expanding its family of hotel brands to include Doubletree, Hampton Inn, Embassy Suites and Homewood Suites among others.[4]

After spinning off the gaming operations in 1998, the Hilton team kept oversight of the business: Bollenbach acted as chairman while Barron Hilton remained a board director. By 2005, following another series of acquisitions, the gambling activity was rebranded Caesars Entertainment; in March of that year, it agreed to merge with its rival Harrah's to form the largest casino operator worldwide.[*]

As a group exclusively focused on the hotel trade, Hilton was ready for its own transformative combination. A year after the Caesars-Harrah's deal, Hilton Hotels Corporation completed the $5.7 billion acquisition of Hilton International, the UK-based organisation that owned the Hilton brand outside the US. Almost four decades after the original split, the two entities were unifying the brand under one roof.[5] In truth, since 1997 the two entities had shared the same logos, promoted each other's activities and maintained joint reservation systems. But the merger instantly transformed Hilton into a globally integrated hospitality specialist.

As proof of its management's superior strategic skills, in the five years leading up to the purchase of the international activities, Hilton Hotels Corporation had vastly outperformed its peers, both operationally and on the stock market (see Figure 1.1). The year 2006 had been particularly stellar thanks to the synergistic aggregation of the group's international activities and the demerger of the casino unit.

## "That's hot!"

This strong display did not go unnoticed. In the first week of July 2007, the hotel group announced that it had received an approach from The Blackstone Group, the world's largest private equity group. The latter proposed to acquire the business for $26 billion,[6] in what was the

---

[*] For more information on the next chapter in the corporate life of Caesars Entertainment, please refer to *The Debt Trap* (2016)

eighth biggest ever buyout on a worldwide basis. Sixty-one years after listing on the New York Stock Exchange and adopting the role of market consolidator, Hilton had become the target.

**Figure 1.1 – Hilton stock performance versus S&P 500 and sector indexes from 2001 to 2006**

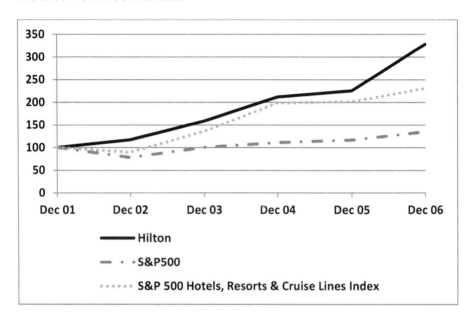

Note: *rebased to 100 on 31 December 2001 – Source: company filings*

Having joined in 1954, Barron Hilton was leaving the group founded by his father. It was certainly an emotional decision, though what would have made him feel better was the fact that he stood to make $1.2 billion out of the sale. Though his grand-daughter was unlikely to see much of it – Barron eventually declared his intention to pledge 97% of his fortune to charity.[7] Still, Paris probably didn't need the money. As she once said: "I get half a million just to show up at parties. My life is, like, really, really fun."

# Hilton Hotels

Despite the credit squeeze that had started in the spring, Blackstone remained eager to close mega deals: it was offering a 40% premium above the previous day's opening share price.[8] A $560 million termination fee to be paid by Hilton if it backed out effectively ensured that the transaction would go ahead.[9] In this management buy-in led by Christopher Nassetta, an experienced real estate executive, and financed with $5.5 billion in equity and $20.5 billion in borrowings, Blackstone completed in October 2007 the second largest transaction in its 22-year history.

Headquartered in the stronghold of capitalism, New York City, Blackstone had built a reputation as a savvy investor for the past two decades. Hilton was not its first transaction in the hotel sector. It already owned more than 100,000 hotel rooms in the United States and Europe, including La Quinta, a 575-hotel limited-service mid-scale chain, and LXR Luxury Resorts.[10] As it was preparing the delisting of Hilton, the PE group had orchestrated its own IPO only weeks earlier. The credit boom of recent years had helped engineer a liquidity event for its founders and senior partners. On 22 June 2007 Blackstone's shares had started trading. Valuing the investment group at $34 billion, the IPO was the largest in the US in almost five years. At the close of its first trading day, the stock valued chief executive Stephen Schwarzman's 23% stake at $8.7 billion.[11]

The hugely successful and visible listing raised issues around the special tax treatment of partnership shares held in buyout firms. Equally, some investors questioned the fact that Blackstone was selling 'partnership units' rather than traditional shares – there were limited voting rights attached to those units.[12] Clearly, it would have been naïve of prospective investors to think that they could exercise any sort of influence on Blackstone's management. Schwarzman and his senior team knew very well how much power investors with voting control can wield. In its capacity as controlling shareholder in portfolio companies, Blackstone regularly removed corporate managers not willing or able to execute the recommended strategy. By issuing partnership units without proper voting rights, Blackstone was only prepared to grant economic interest. Dividend distributions, not veto rights, were on offer.

Finally, and more importantly for corporations like Hilton looking for cash-rich owners, Blackstone was about to announce in early August the completion of the largest fundraise in PE history: a $21.7 billion buyout vehicle with a global scope.[13] In fact, 70% of that amount was already committed, and Blackstone had indicated its intention to soon go back on the fundraising trail.[14] The fact that, around that time, banks were struggling to syndicate hundreds of billions of dollars in LBO debt left the private equity group's management undeterred.

## Deal rationale

Despite the onset of the Credit Crunch, Blackstone had shown its mettle by closing a very complex and cycle-dependent hotel transaction.

By 2006 Hilton had spent an entire decade transforming itself from a single brand to a collection of nine separate identities serving a broad range of customer segments. From its original US-focused presence, management had built an international portfolio of assets. In the ten years to 2006, the number of properties had increased tenfold to over 2,900 and the number of rooms was close to half a million.[15] Shareholder value creation had been robust, growing by 240% over that period. The unique value enhancing potential of the reunited North American and international activities was probably a key reason behind the buyout. But one recent change to the Hilton business model would have attracted Blackstone's interest most particularly.

As evidenced in the 2006 annual report, the hotel group had been steadily moving to a more fee-based business model by adding new units, growing revenue per available room (RevPAR) at hotels, and selling previously owned assets while retaining management or franchise agreements. The fee activity had grown 51% in 2006 from a combination of jacking up RevPAR and absorbing Hilton International. Supplementing this expansion was the retention of management and franchise fees levied on hotels earmarked for disposal.

The Blackstone juggernaut, already the largest and best-diversified alternative fund manager in the world, knew all about fee-earning businesses. The investment group had itself developed a variety of commission-based financial products that had the benefit of offering more steady and predictable income streams than the more traditional performance-contingent revenue model.

Seeing Hilton apply a similar approach to property management would have instinctively registered as the ideal model for a cash-dependent leveraged buyout. Strategic focus on fee origination was what guaranteed the viability of modern-day fund managers and hotel managers alike, turning what were previously risk takers into rentiers. Better to leave the cost and risk of asset ownership to third parties and to retain the fee-earning management rights. It was partly this line of reasoning that Hilton's leadership had followed when choosing to divest its casino activities, although the oppressive regulatory framework specific to that sector was also to blame.

Blackstone was not the only party to have acknowledged Hilton's potential. In 2006, thanks to Wall Street's enthusiastic backing, the hotel group's stock had registered 46% in total return to shareholders, far outpacing the S&P Hotels, Resorts and Cruise Lines (+15%) and S&P 500 (+16%) indexes.[16] The acquisition of the international assets had provided an excellent growth story. Hilton was reaping the benefits of this combination. Blackstone's plan was to keep at it.

## Revival and survival

As 2007 came to an end, Blackstone's best deal of the year was neither the Hilton take-private nor the gigantic acquisition of Equity Office Properties a few months earlier. Rather, Blackstone had timed its own market listing to perfection. After floating in June on the back of strong earnings, in its first post-IPO report the business recorded a third-quarter loss of $113 million. Thankfully, some Blackstone employees had already cashed out part of their stake. After closing at $35 on the first day of trading, the PE group's stock traded at $22 by November.[17] Its downward trajectory was only just starting, and Hilton's difficult syndication and structuring would not help matters.

By the end of January 2008, the securitisation of $8 billion of Hilton's LBO loans still had not taken place. While some subordinated debt tranches had eventually found buyers in private placements, investors were not very responsive due to the growing impact of the Credit Crunch.[18] The debt markets were about to shut, preventing Blackstone from optimally structuring the transaction. But it soon would be the least of Blackstone's concerns. The Great Recession was to have a huge impact on hotel stays, hurting the underlying performance of the hospitality group.

Acquired with over $20 billion in debt, and with blended interest rate hovering around 5.7%, at the outset Hilton earned $1.7 billion a year in EBITDA.* With over $1.1 billion in interest payments and capital expenditure of half a billion dollars, there was little room for error. By February 2008 quoted comparable Marriott International had seen its stock fall by a fifth in the past eight months while InterContinental's shares had halved, implying that Blackstone's $5.6 billion equity ticket in Hilton was worth practically nothing.[19] A prolonged recession would

---

* EBITDA is a cash earnings metric that stands for earnings before interest, tax, depreciation and amortisation

likely impair Hilton's ability to meet debt commitments and impose tricky decisions on management and owners alike.

In March, as Blackstone's stock sat at $14, almost 55% down on its IPO price, its private equity division reported a fourth-quarter loss.[20] The stock halved again following Blackstone's pre-tax loss of over half a billion dollars in the quarter to September 2008.[21] The downfall of Lehman Brothers, the bailout of several too-big-to-fail financial institutions, and massive layoffs in the final months of the year affected business trips, holiday budgets and hotel occupancy. At Hilton, revenue per available room was now in free fall.[22] Management began implementing cost-cutting measures to play for time; perhaps the widely expected recession would be short-lived.

One factor played in Blackstone's favour. Executed at the top of the bubble, the financing package did not have onerous debt covenants and its loan maturities were years away.[23] Still, as the financial meltdown of 2009 spread and the economy fell off a cliff, the hotel group registered dwindling cash flows. Operating in a notoriously cyclical sector dependent on consumer and corporate spending, the group was at a disadvantage in a downturn. In the summer of 2009, refinancing options, including a debt-for-equity swap, were being discussed.[24]

Blackstone wasn't looking much healthier. Its stock had bottomed out below $4 a share in February 2009. It would spend the second half of the year fluctuating between $8 and $13, a humbling level when compared to its $31 introductory price twenty months earlier. PE groups Apollo and KKR, which had both contemplated their own listings in the summer of 2007 before the Credit Crunch compelled them to reconsider, were surely relieved that their performance was not getting the sort of publicity that befell on their rival. In the first quarter of 2009, Blackstone's net loss exceeded $230 million, only a slight improvement on the previous quarter.

Hilton was finding its debt pile a heavy load in the greatest economic crisis since the 1930s. After writing down the value of its investment by more than half,[25] Blackstone planned a massive capital restructuring by injecting fresh dollars to buy back some of Hilton's debt at a deep discount. Discussions with lenders were aimed at cutting up to 25% of the $20 billion debt package, extending maturity on the remaining loans, and converting the subordinated loans into equity. Blackstone's move was part of a countrywide endeavour to slash debt. Across America, $1 trillion worth of senior and subordinated corporate loans was maturing before 2015.[26] In a fight for survival, many PE firms were going through the very same exercise that Blackstone was attempting to impose on Hilton's lenders.

In February 2010 Hilton secured a deal with its debt holders to cut leverage by about $4 billion. Blackstone injected $800 million in fresh equity to buy $1.8 billion of the loan package, implying a 56% discount. Some lenders received just 35 cents on the dollar while others converted their debt into preferred equity, receiving shares to sell in an eventual public offering. This balance sheet cleansing, combining an equity cure with a debt-for-equity swap, also pushed back some of the maturity dates.

Unable to grow into its heavily leveraged structure, Hilton had had to refinance. And its lenders were taking a serious hit, including the New York Fed: the federal reserve bank had received $4 billion of Hilton's original LBO loans when taking on $29 billion in troubled assets from Bear Stearns, the distressed bank sold for a song to JP Morgan in March 2008.[27] As Steven Kaplan, professor at the University of Chicago, would later describe Blackstone's move: "It was like refinancing your mortgage when interest rates were low. They basically paid off their debt when it was very cheap to do so, because everybody was frightened and the price of their debt went very low."[28]

## Rebuilding from the ground up

One of the guiding aspirations of Hilton had always been to develop a super-luxury chain of hotels to rival Four Seasons and Mandarin Oriental. The group's Waldorf Astoria brand had never gained a meaningful share of the exclusive world of luxury hospitality. To remedy this injustice, in 2008 Hilton had hired a couple of executives from rival hotel group Starwood. The latter's W chain was to serve as model for what management presented as the Denizen brand, targeting 'citizens of the world'.

But the ex-Starwood executives who worked on developing the Denizen hotels were soon accused of industrial espionage by their former employer. In early 2009, Starwood sued them and Hilton, alleging that the Denizen project was based on thousands of documents, presentations and market research stolen from Starwood. It later transpired that at least 44 Hilton executives were aware of the trade secret theft. After a lengthy investigation and litigation, Hilton agreed in December 2010 to make a $75 million cash payment to Starwood and to be banned from creating its upscale boutique hotel chain as part of a settlement.[29] The group would have to satisfy itself with serving the masses of tourists and business travellers rather than the super wealthy. Yet this setback was not to have lasting impact on the group's fast improving fortunes.

Already in March 2011, accountants were reported to be poring over the books to bring them up to international reporting standards in anticipation of a stock market relisting.[30] Since the start of the year, hoteliers had become cautiously upbeat: room occupancy was up; tourists and corporate guests were back. After the previous year's recapitalisation, Hilton was in the best of shapes, ready to take full advantage of the economic recovery. In September, confirming that the group was once again in growth mode, Blackstone acquired Mint, a British hotel group that was then merged with Hilton's DoubleTree and Garden Inn families of hotels.

As further evidence that the group's luck had turned since its distressed refinancing, in February 2012 Jonathan Gray, the executive who had led the Hilton buyout, was elevated to the Blackstone board and rumoured as a possible successor to Schwarzman.[31] If Hilton had not been in rude health, it is unlikely that Gray would have received such an honour.

Early the following year, Hilton attracted significant buzz in banking circles as a possible relisting candidate for the second half of 2013.[32] In preparation for the float, the company needed to lick its balance sheet into shape. In August, it issued a $250 million loan for the timeshare division, Hilton Grand Vacations.[33] That same month, management lined up Wall Street banks to act as IPO underwriters. To help get the float away, in September it launched a renewed attempt at structuring $7 billion in commercial mortgage-backed securities, a transaction that had come to naught five years earlier as the credit drought was taking hold. Proving that the markets hadn't quite recovered fully from the crisis, in November the size of the issue was halved. But it was still the largest CMBS offering since the financial crisis. In tandem, Hilton issued a $7.6 billion seven-year loan, running alongside $1.5 billion in unsecured bonds.[34] It was essential for management to extend the company's debt runway as it was prepping itself up for a reintroduction to the stock market.

After six eventful years, Blackstone yearned to get out of the hotel group. Hilton had grown tremendously coming out of the Great Recession. After reaching a low point in 2009 with less than $7.6 billion in revenue – down 15% on the prior year, in 2013 it was on track to generate $9.7 billion. But margins had come under pressure. EBITDA was flat since the buyout, implying margin erosion from 20% to less than 18%. Yet, under Blackstone's tutelage, management had repaid or expunged 30% of its debt, cut costs, expanded internationally and focused on the more profitable franchise model. Predictably, to pretty up the IPO candidate, EBITDA was reported on an adjusted basis, taking out various expenses and losses deemed of a one-off nature. On that parameter, margin exceeded 22%.

# Checkout time

The business was reacquainted with the public markets on 11 December 2013. Proceeds exceeded $2.3 billion,[35] used to pay down debt further but also to repay investors that had converted their loans into preferred equity during the 2010 restructuring. The economic recovery coupled with Blackstone's negotiating skills had saved the business. As Robert La Forgia, the finance chief of Hilton at the time of its sale to Blackstone observed, "They almost lost the company, and might have without the debt restructuring."[36] Experts welcomed the relisting. A *Bloomberg* article applauded the outcome, marvelling at "the best leveraged buyout ever".

What the public was buying, at a pricey multiple exceeding 19 times EBITDA, was the expectation that the broader positive macroeconomic, travel and tourism trends would continue to drive longer-term growth in the lodging sector. The growing global middle class was meant to boost demand. The IPO prospectus explained that there was an imbalance between demand and supply in the US. It had contributed to a RevPAR annual growth rate of 6.8% over the three years to 2013. In addition, there was hotel under-penetration in most emerging markets, with countries like Brazil, China and India offering significant growth potential. Compared to the US, in China the hotel industry provided one tenth the number of rooms per capita, while in India it offered 75 times fewer rooms per head.[37]

The public would also invest in a business with lower earnings volatility. The shift towards fee-earning managed and franchised assets as well as timeshare activities improved visibility and lowered the unpredictability of profits. As this trend continued, fees were to contribute 90% of EBITDA by 2016.

Finally, to give the group sufficient runway post-relisting, management had refinanced $13.4 billion in mortgaged and secured subordinated loans on 25 October 2013.[38] The debt load, brought down from $14.6 billion to less than $12 billion, or 7 times EBITDA (see Figure 1.4), still promised to test the nerves of the public markets.[39] But Blackstone's Schwarzman was optimistic, noting: "When you can have that kind of growth in EBITDA with the kind of leveraged capital structure that is on, equity accretion is tremendous. You kind of want to let your winners run a little bit because you're accreting a lot of value for our shareholders every quarter."[40]

The listing gave the hotel group an enterprise value of about $33 billion, about 27% higher than for the LBO six and a half years earlier. Representing three-quarters of the equity, Blackstone's stake in Hilton was worth $16 billion. The PE group had invested over $5.6 billion in the 2007 delisting and $800 million during the 2010 refinancing, so it was on course to make 2.5 times cash on cash.

The down-to-earth, if slightly dispiriting, university professor Steven Kaplan remarked in a *New York Times* article, "This is a good deal if you're measuring it relative to the public market. But it's not a home run." With most buyout firms aiming for an internal rate of return of about 20%, spread over six years the investment in Hilton yielded about 16% per annum for Blackstone, the same article commented. Still, with Blackstone recording one of its most successful deals ever, Kaplan admitted: "In dollars, a $10 billion profit is a lot of money, even to them."[41]

It was vintage PE. But the stunning payoff was on paper; Blackstone had not disposed of any stock during the IPO. In private equity, as in all classes of investments, capital gains only matter if you bag them. Until your investment has been exited, your winnings aren't real. So, let's review in turn how Hilton executed its transformation under PE ownership and how Blackstone managed its way out of the hotel group.

## Outstanding results

What looked like a doomed overleveraged business in 2009, written down by as much as 70% in Blackstone's books,[42] had not just survived: it promised to yield great results for its PE backer. The recipe had been two-pronged.

*Redesigned business model*

Under Blackstone's guidance, the Hilton group did not initiate much operational improvement. Because of the economic crisis, operating margins fell from 15.6% in 2006 to a cycle low of 7.2% in 2010. Due to impairment losses, in 2008 the hotel group recorded an operating loss of $4.5 billion.[43]

Where the business was significantly remodelled is in its gradual but marked move away from the traditionally asset-rich property ownership strategy in favour of hotel management and franchising. Between mid-2007 and late 2013, as a result of the transformation spearheaded by chief exec Nassetta and his team, and despite the sharp industry downturn experienced during the Great Recession, the group:

- increased the number of rooms by 36%, or 176,248 units, and the number of hotels by more than 1,000 to 4,080 units,

- grew the number of rooms in the development pipeline by 60%, almost all of them within the higher-margin, capital-light management and franchise segment,

- increased the total number of rooms under construction by 133%,

- enlarged the geographic diversity of the pipeline, with rooms in development outside the US increasing from less than 20% to more than 60%, and rooms under construction outside the US increasing from less than 15% to nearly 80%,

- increased the average global RevPAR premium for all brands by approximately two percentage points to 15%,

- broadened membership in the Hilton HHonors loyalty programme by 88% between 2007 and 2012, reaching 39 million members by the time of the IPO.[44]

The key aspect of this growth is that, unlike traditional capex-fuelled hotel development, it did not require huge capital outlay. The management and franchise segment generated high margins and long-term recurring cash flows. By the time the group relisted, that division had grown by 40% in terms of number of rooms, representing 98% of the overall room growth, with virtually no capital investment by the group.[45] Third parties were the ones committing the funds while Hilton charged fees for the privilege of managing the properties. Hilton's capital-light operating model had seen the number of rooms and properties expand at a good clip while capex spend had gone down as a proportion of earnings and cash flows.

The most important transformation was indeed the pronounced shift in favour of the managed and franchise properties, from which the group derived 47% of its revenues in 2013 compared to 31% six years earlier. As Figure 1.2 shows, the trend continued after the relisting. This shift was the key reason behind the group's significant growth in profitability – between 2010 and 2013, EBITDA had grown by more than 40%. At the time of the IPO, the hotel group earned EBITDA margins of 23% at its Ownership division, but in excess of 30% at the Managed & Franchise unit, while the Timeshare activities yielded margins of 27%.

This conversion meant that the execution risk was outsourced to third parties: the franchisees were the operators responsible for delivering the guest experience on site. Franchise strategies had been very successfully carried out in the catering industry: witness many fast-food chains' global branding from the 1960s onwards. But this approach had never been attempted on such a scale in the hospitality sector. Through its portfolio of brands in each subsegment of the high-end hotel industry, Hilton had taken a chance. It had paid off.

Franchise operations depend on trust. It is one thing to place confidence in fast-food franchisees to deliver customer service over a period of time that rarely exceeds 30 minutes; it is another to ensure quality and reliability over the entire duration of a hotel stay.

**Figure 1.2 – Hilton's revenue breakdown between four main divisions**

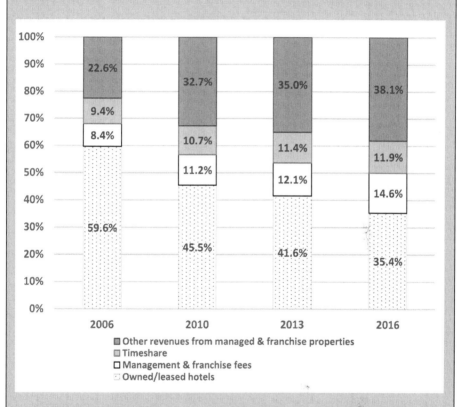

*Source: Company filings*

Not only did the group depend on outsiders to deliver great service, it also asked them to fund its expansion. At the time of the relisting, Hilton's pipeline included the construction of another 1,069 hotels (with 186,000 rooms), but only one of these would actually be operated by the group. Of the $40 billion needed to fund construction, the company's estimated spend was just $70 million.[46] By using third-party capital to finance growth, management had nailed the art of risk outsourcing. The deal was a feat of adroitly executed juggling between property portfolio diversification, disciplined cash monitoring and cost control.

*Deft debt restructuring*

There are three main reasons behind the Blackstone-backed Hilton's ability to refinance its debt pile in 2010. First, it was an updated, supersized version of J. Paul Getty's quote: "If you owe the bank $100, that's your problem. If you owe the bank $100 million, that's the bank's problem." When you owe lenders $20 billion and these same institutions are going through their own balance sheet restructurings – as they did in the midst of the Credit Crunch, the financial crisis and the Great Recession – your debt becomes the entire banking community's problem.

Blackstone's unwise decision to purchase Hilton in the summer of 2007, only weeks after the outbreak of the Credit Crunch, could have been fatal. What saved the hospitality group is not just Nassetta's remarkable expansion strategy and product shift. It is also the outright bankruptcy of the entire banking system, forcing Hilton's lenders to be a lot more accommodating than they would otherwise have been. Default on any tranche of the loans automatically granted the lending syndicate the right to repossess some of the Hilton properties used as collateral or to request higher interest and charge penalty fees.

With a syndicate including names like Bear Stearns and Lehman Brothers, two banks that crumbled in the prelude to the financial crisis, a borrower as large as Hilton was unlikely to be given an earful for taking inconsiderate risks. Instead, the lenders rolled over, offering fantastic leeway and bargaining power to PE-backed borrowers. It enabled repeat amend-and-extend procedures that no small company can pull through (as we will see in the case of TIM/WIND Hellas in

Chapter 8, these procedures frequently wiped out the subordinated, unsecured bondholders). This is not the kind of compassionate behaviour you would expect from mortgage lenders. The latter are often more than happy to repossess the homes of individuals who default on their mortgage repayments. Admittedly, a longer economic recession not counterbalanced with quantitative easing and historically low interest rates could have cost Blackstone its control over the hotel group.

The second reason behind the successful capital restructuring is related to the opportunity to purchase some of the group's discounted debt from distressed lenders. At the worst time of the Great Recession, Blackstone put up more than $800 million in additional funds to buy out the tranches of the debt that granted no security over Hilton's assets. The hotel group was also able to convert part of the subordinated loans into preferred securities.[47] Blackstone was cash-rich at a time when smaller fund managers were running out of money and needed to return funds to their investors. The borrower also benefited from a stroke of luck. Because the original lenders backing the LBO were never able to syndicate or securitise their loans, Blackstone and Hilton's management only needed to renegotiate and reschedule the debt package with a handful of banks and unsecured lenders, instead of the more frequent cast of hundreds of institutions typical of mega buyouts carrying multibillion-dollar loans on their books.[48]

Lastly, Blackstone carries out many transactions each year, and does so year after year. No bank or private debt fund manager wishes to upset such a firm or it risks being frozen out of future lucrative deals. That kind of bargaining power is unique to global PE groups. Blackstone made the most of it.

## Chronicle of the best LBO ever

At an enterprise value of 19.3 times EBITDA,[*] Hilton's IPO was priced above both Marriott (14.1x) and Starwood (12.8x). The sky-high valuation allowed the group to degear somewhat. Despite its size and price tag, the relisting was uneventful, institutional investors having acquainted themselves with the business during previous bond refinancings.

In the months that followed the float, the company's stock did not stick to a very steady pattern. That all changed after the release of strong quarterly results at the end of April 2014. With the stock finding a healthy trading range above the IPO price, Blackstone prepared its exit. In mid-June 2014, six months after the relisting, the firm cut its stake in Hilton from 76% to 67% and raised $2 billion. The sale took place at $22.50 a share, a 12.5% premium to the IPO price.[49] By late September, Blackstone was out of the lock-up period that followed the June offering. So, in November, in the second monetisation of its stockholding, it sold another 90 million shares at $25 each. The $2.25 billion in proceeds were a welcome addition to the PE owner's coffers.[50]

In May 2015, the deliberate quest for profits resumed. Blackstone again tendered 90 million shares as the hotel operator's stock continued to rally. In what would soon be dubbed 'Mother's Day Massacre' due to its timing and disastrous aftermarket trading, the $2.7 billion block sale – the biggest sponsor block on record – left the three underwriting banks nursing $90 million of losses when public appetite failed to materialise. The thin discount ensured that Blackstone achieved a strong price, but the general impression was that the sale had been priced too high, leading to poor aftermarket performance. This third

---

[*] After applying several judiciously chosen adjustments to earnings, Hilton's equity analysts came up with a more reasonable but less reliable valuation multiple of 14.9 times adjusted EBITDA

block sale since the IPO reduced the PE firm's stake to 46%.[51] A key selling point for the deal was the prospect that Hilton could join major stock indexes, including the S&P 500, because the free-float now exceeded 50%.

Although at the time Starwood, the owner of the Sheraton and Westin brands, was in play, Hilton did not show much interest. Its management preferred to stick to an organic growth plan, although given the Denizen espionage incident any expression of interest would likely have been spurned. It would also probably have led to a fall in Hilton's stock price, not a welcome distraction when the group's largest shareholder was in the process of checking out. Rather than acquiring one of its peers, in February Hilton had sold one of its landmark properties, the Waldorf Astoria in New York, while agreeing to a 100-year management contract. The $2 billion proceeds were redeployed to acquire five faster-growing hotels. The move provided a 20% boost to Hilton's stock price in just three months,[52] enabling its main shareholder to execute the May block sale at a premium. Though extremely helpful to engineer Blackstone's partial exit, the stock price jump was only temporary. By the end of September, the stock had lost over one-fifth of its value. By year-end, shares in Hilton — still Blackstone's single largest holding — had fallen a further 20%.

Logically, Blackstone's own stock was down markedly over the same period. When the NYSE-listed PE group reported that its quarterly results to 31 December 2015 had fallen short of projections, its stake in Hilton alone had stripped $2.6 billion in value.[53] The inability to replicate the level of proceeds achieved in 2014 had hurt the bottom line. After bringing in $4.6 billion from two block sales in Hilton stock in 2014, Blackstone had yielded less than $2.7 billion the following year. Its pre-tax profit had more than halved on the prior year.[54] Having opted out of the running in the auction for Starwood in order not to dilute its focused strategy and resilient share price, Hilton had nonetheless witnessed significant value adjustment, its stock reverting in December 2015 below the IPO price of $20 a share (see Figure 1.3).

## Demerger

Stuck with its stake and keen to convince the markets that the hotel chain, despite its billions of dollars in LBO debt, was worth more than what it was quoted, Blackstone worked hard to orchestrate its exit. The PE firm followed a dual track: (i) finding a trade buyer for part of its stake, which it could dispose of in a private placement, and (ii) splitting the various divisions of what was in effect a hospitality conglomerate. The aim was to enhance transparency and ultimately boost the valuation of each entity to facilitate Blackstone's definitive farewell.

**Figure 1.3 – Hilton Worldwide stock performance in three years post-IPO vs. S&P 500**

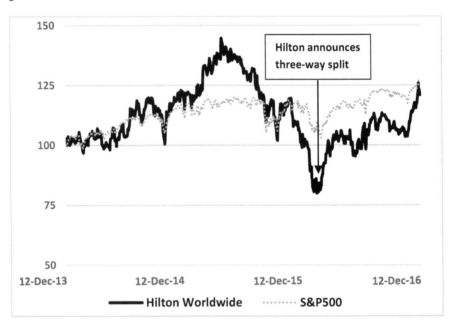

*Note: rebased to 100 on IPO day*

In February 2016, when announcing the full-year 2015 numbers, management relented to the pressure exercised by the public markets. Hilton explained that it would be splitting three ways in an effort to lower its tax bill and produce value for shareholders. The main operating company would incorporate the fee-earning hotel management activities, a real estate investment trust (REIT) would include the property assets (PropCo) and be saddled with the mortgage debt, while the timeshare business would form a third entity under the Hilton Grand Vacations (HGV) brand, managing holiday resorts and selling vacation ownership interests. Before the announcement, the hotel group's stock was trading 20% below its IPO level. In a bid to reignite the share price as quickly as possible, the demerger was expected to occur by year-end.

In August, Hilton asked lenders to do the company a favour by extending three-quarters of $4.2 billion in secured loans from 2020 to 2023. Management also issued $1 billion of unsecured notes to refinance existing subordinated loans.[55] Having earned the business further breathing space, in October Blackstone finally managed to find a strategic buyer. It sold a quarter of Hilton's shares to HNA, a Chinese conglomerate keen to capitalise on the hotel group's potential in Asia and other international markets. Proceeds of almost $6.5 billion valued Hilton's stock at $26.25, a generous 15% premium to the closing price.[56] The move reduced Blackstone's interest to approximately 21%. As part of the deal, the PE firm would continue to have two seats on Hilton's board, including one for Jonathan Gray who was to remain chairman. The latter had increased his influence within Blackstone: at the end of 2015, assets in the real estate division, overseen by Gray, had topped the $100 billion mark for the first time ever.[57]

The following month, Blackstone sold 55 million Hilton shares for $1.3 billion, cutting its stake below 16%.[58] Hilton topped off the year with another loan issuance, this time by HGV, the vacation rental division soon to be demerged. The latter was in the market for $300 million in senior debt to help fund its independence from the mother ship.[59] Managing nearly 50 club resorts in America and Europe, HGV was to retain use of the Hilton brand under a long-term licence agreement. Completing the reorganisation, and structured as a tax-efficient investment trust, Park Hotels & Resorts was injected with 67 of Hilton Worldwide's owned hotel properties as part of the latter's asset-light strategy. The freshly independent PropCo was valued at about $10 billion.[60]

The year had started with underwhelming trading, due to nervousness among the industry's corporate clientele in the midst of an uncertain political climate in the run-up to the US presidential election. But the 'Trump Bump' in the fourth quarter opened the way for the group's demerger and Blackstone's significant withdrawal from a 46% stake to less than 16% in Hilton, generating over $7.7 billion in proceeds.

What drove management's decision to split the group into three separate divisions was their very diverse growth and profitability profiles. While management stated in the 2016 annual report that Hilton was the fastest-growing global hospitality company on an organic basis, it was meagre consolation to shareholders who had seen no growth in the share price in the first two years post-IPO. The managed and franchised properties as well as the timeshare division grew more than 6% that year, but they were dragged down by the owned and leased activities, which had seen revenues decrease 2.5%. At the EBITDA level, the managed and franchise activities (the core Hilton Worldwide unit) and timeshare (Hilton Grand Vacations) had experienced growth of 5.6% and 8.2% respectively while operating cash flows from the PropCo (Park Hotels & Resorts) were down 3.3%. It still would not prevent many investors from taking the plunge with Park Hotels's separate listing. The key benefit of an investment trust is its intention to distribute at least 90% of its annual income to shareholders. The PropCo's dividend yield was expected to exceed 6%.

**Figure 1.4 – Hilton's net debt and leverage ratio (2006, and 2008 to 2016)**

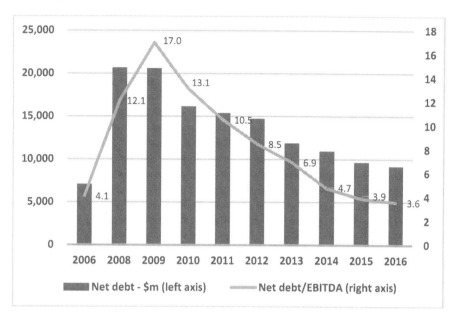

*Note: The 2008 and 2009 EBITDA numbers exclude $5.6 billion and $475 million of restructuring losses, respectively – Source: company filings and author's analysis*

By the end of 2016, Hilton had managed to repay over $5 billion of its debt pile post-IPO. Yet the group was still sitting on more than $9 billion in LBO loans (see Figure 1.4). It was taking an awful long time to sort out the LBO legacy, but the planned demerger and separate listings had re-energised the hotel group. Its stock had shot up almost 30% in 2016, outpacing both the S&P 500 (+9.5%) and the S&P Hotel sector index (+5.2%).[61]

Throughout 2017 the group's entities continued to restructure and reschedule their loans to support their respective stocks and help Blackstone exit. In March, Hilton Worldwide repriced $3.2 billion and extended $750 million of its term loans.[62] Three months later, Blackstone orchestrated a series of transactions to further reduce its exposure to a decade-long holding in the hospitality conglomerate. On 1 June, it priced 15 million shares in Park Hotels & Resorts for a total consideration just shy of $400 million.[63] A week later, for almost $990 million in proceeds it sold 15 million shares in Hilton Worldwide, bringing its ownership down to 10%.[64] Shortly thereafter, it was back to the trough with a block trade of almost 10 million Hilton Grand Vacations shares for $342.6 million. The sale left Blackstone with just a 5.4% stake in HGV.[65] That remaining stake was disposed of in September for $183 million.[66] A month later, in a $940 million block trade, the PE firm sold 14.6 million shares in Hilton Worldwide: management had chosen to repurchase nearly one million shares from Blackstone – not every selling stockholder can expect to receive that kind of support from portfolio companies. It probably was the best way to avoid a Halloween version of the 'Mother Day Massacre' witnessed two years earlier.[67] Rushing out the door, the PE group disposed of almost 17 million shares in Park Hotels & Resorts in early November,[68] yielding $500 million in proceeds.

## Table 1.1 – Blackstone's investments in and proceeds from Hilton

| Year | Transaction | $ billion |
|------|-------------|-----------|
| 2007 | Equity investment | > 5.6 |
| 2010 | Equity cure | > 0.8 |
|      | **Total investment** | **6.5** |
|      | | |
| 2013 | IPO | 0.0 |
| 2014 | Block sales | 4.6 |
| 2015 | Block sale | 2.7 |
| 2016 | 25% stake sale to HNA | 6.5 |
| 2016 | Block sale | 1.3 |
| 2017 | Block sales | 3.4 |
| 2018 | Block sale | 1.3 |
|      | | |
|      | **Total proceeds** | **19.8** |
|      | **Net proceeds** | **13.3** |

*Source: company filings and author's analysis*

After these sell-offs, Blackstone was left with less than 6% in Hilton Worldwide; it took a final bow in 2018 by pocketing $1.3 billion for that remaining stake. In total, as shown in Table 1.1, the private equity group generated $19.8 billion in proceeds. Not bad when compared to its original $6.5 billion investment.

## What went wrong for public investors

In the fiscal year 2016, Hilton sourced 90% of its EBITDA from the management and franchise divisions, the remaining 10% coming from owned and leased properties.[69] However, this steady cash-flow generation had become somewhat pedestrian – EBITDA had grown 3% in 2016. As we saw, this translated in disappointing shareholder returns. It was noticeable when compared to the group's main rival: between 12 December 2013 and 13 December 2016, Marriott International's total shareholder return exceeded 91%, the S&P 500 index's total return was 36%, while Hilton's total return was only 26%, or an annual rate just shy of 8% over those first three years of trading.

*Overvaluation*

It seems counterintuitive that a company that grew its top line by a fifth and its EBITDA by a third in the three years following its public listing would underperform its peers and the broader S&P 500. Nonetheless, there is a simple explanation.

Hilton Hotels listed in December 2013 on a price-earnings ratio of 48. Three years later, that ratio was below 15, while the group's balance sheet remained laden with debt. Even valued on an EBITDA basis (which takes out the impact of interest expense), Hilton's valuation multiple stood at about 12 times on 31 December 2016 compared to 19 times EBITDA upon relisting.

It is not obvious why investors thought the Hilton IPO was going to be a good deal at such a nosebleed valuation. Even at the peak of the real-estate bubble, in 2007, Blackstone had paid 15 times that year's EBITDA. Despite the business model shift, Hilton did not warrant such a generous valuation-multiple arbitrage.

*The necessary delay for RevPAR to catch up*

While EBITDA experienced double-digit growth between 2013 and 2016, revenue per available room only rose in the mid-single digits. Three reasons explain this situation.

First, by expanding at a much faster pace than the competition, the group needed time to fill its new hotels to capacity. While these new developments were probably going to pay off in the long term, the public markets took a more cautious view, preferring to wait and see until the new developments delivered on their promise.

The second reason behind the relatively slow growth in RevPAR was a direct consequence of the group's transformation into an asset-light hotel group. While owned properties typically generated RevPAR of $145, the managed and franchise properties yielded about $100.

In addition, expansion in the fast-growing markets of South America, the Middle East, Africa and Asia had a detrimental impact on revenue per available room. This key performance indicator was much lower in emerging countries. Again, in the long run, it was likely that new markets would deliver significant returns; for now, their RevPAR was 15% to 20% lower than at more mature US and European properties.

*Unexpected trend in short-stay flat sharing*

Millennials have already internalised the harsh reality that they will be poorer than their parents' generation. To them, splurging on hotel luxury would be seen as irresponsible. Hilton's IPO prospectus featured a long list of risk areas for potential investors to pay attention to. One main threat was missing though, showing how difficult it can be even for sector experts (perhaps most particularly for them) to anticipate disruptive change. There was no mention of a five-year old lodging platform called Airbnb. While Hilton has a strong focus on the business segment of hotel stays, its more affordable hotel brands like DoubleTree and Garden Inn might be exposed to the growing trend in favour of short-stay flat sharing.

The advent of Airbnb and other Internet-based unregulated flat-sharing and short-stay providers was a key unknown for any prospective investor. By early 2017 Airbnb offered access to 2.3 million rooms worldwide, more than the combined inventory of the three largest hotel chains Hilton, Marriott and InterContinental.[70] Crucially, Airbnb has more variable than fixed costs compared to traditional hotel groups; it should therefore be more resilient to economic slumps. That is assuming health and safety regulations and licensing laws don't spoil the party. At any rate, the new competitive environment invited public markets to remain cautious when assessing hotel stocks. Despite the sycophantic *Bloomberg* article reporting the fantastic performance of the Hilton buyout from Blackstone's standpoint, the post-IPO returns for investors were far from stellar. But then, that's a matter for the public to worry about.

The core message of the *Bloomberg* article was premature but ultimately accurate. Blackstone laboured to engineer its checkout. It was caught in the post-relisting apathy of the stock, but by orchestrating a three-way demerger in late 2016, Hilton's management finally extracted additional value for shareholders, key among them the financial sponsor that had enabled the senior executive team to make a fortune. Nassetta alone made $2 million in annual compensation out of his Hilton gig plus his holding of 7.6 million shares, worth over $150 million on IPO day. After an eventful ten-year PE-backed adventure that included extensive balance sheet restructuring and a complete business model redesign, Hilton had earned its tag as the best leveraged buyout ever.

## INTERPRETATION OF PRIVATE EQUITY SUCCESS

*To reiterate, it is dangerous to reach definitive conclusions from one very profitable LBO. Success can be derived from skills, hard work, luck, or a combination of these factors.*

*Blackstone is a diversified fund manager supposed to deliver superior returns. Yet, in the decade following its June 2007 listing, the company's stock failed to provide much upside to shareholders. After listing at $31 a share, the Blackstone stock was priced at $32 in December 2017. Despite Hilton's success, Blackstone itself was not a good investment, in part because of the high volatility of its earnings, as the case illustrates, but also because most of its revenue was redistributed to employees.*[*]

*Blackstone staff derived almost $30 billion in annual compensation and capital gains in the first decade following the group's IPO. That equated to 85% of the group's management, advisory and performance fee income over the period. Staff remuneration was based on short-term returns achieved on leveraged investments while holders of Blackstone stock needed consistent, long-term performance. The group's assets under management had grown from less than $90 billion in the summer of 2007 to $390 billion at the end of 2017. Yet shareholders had little to show for it. Fortunately, in its IPO prospectus Blackstone had warned that its "common units are not an appropriate investment for investors with a short-term focus." The very long term will have to do.*

---

[*] Some argue that Blackstone's underperformance is due to its partnership status. If it was a corporation, the firm would see its stock automatically included in stock indexes, which would boost liquidity. It feels like a cop-out when assessing an investment firm offering a supposedly compelling business model

# CHAPTER 2

# Mergermarket: The ideal LBO candidate

> *Few companies successfully transition from the start-up stage to the growth development phase – where they expand organically by launching new products and services – and go on to establish market leadership – when they can morph into buy-and-build platforms capable of assimilating a series of bolt-on acquisitions in existing and adjacent sectors. Mergermarket achieved all this, becoming in the process the perfect candidate for a leveraged buyout*

The finance industry's appetite for information is well-nigh bottomless. Information does not only convey power to its holder; in finance, it often leads to riches. Which is why fraudulent trading remains so prevalent, decades after the introduction of insider-trading prohibition laws. Academic research, based on equity option activity before M&A announcements, reveals that about a quarter of deals show abnormal volumes and excessive volatility likely to involve insider trading. Less exhaustive investigations suggest that public companies issuing profit warnings see their stock drop the day *before* the announcement in two-thirds of cases; similarly, takeover announcements are *preceded* by increases in the target's share price in 70% of cases.[1] The statistical rule of normal distribution dictates that, in an efficient market, stock prices should rise and fall in equal proportions ahead of the public disclosure of any new piece of information.

For individuals and institutions keen to deliver superior returns, lawful access to information ahead of the crowd is therefore very valuable. Many market participants are prepared to pay for it, whether they trade public stocks or invest in private companies.

I first came across Mergermarket's eponymous and flagship product in 2005, as I was using the financial database to screen acquisition targets for one of my portfolio companies. Back then, I was working for private equity firm Candover. By the time I was considering the acquisition of the Mergermarket Group, in the first half of 2006, I had moved on to another employer, media specialist buyout shop GMT Communications Partners.

Mergermarket, a data provider of live M&A transactions, had been put up for sale by its venture capital backers, though its three co-founders – chief executive Caspar Hobbs, Editor-in-Chief and product innovator Charlie Welsh, and finance director Gawn Rowan Hamilton – were still running the show.

To state that I was keen to close that deal would not be excessive. I was confident, from what I knew about the product's characteristics and the business model's fundamentals, that Mergermarket was a fantastic buyout candidate. It was a high-growth, high-margin business with predictable and recurring revenue and cash flows.

When at Candover, I had worked on two deals that fit the same description: pan-European financial information provider Bureau van Dijk (BvD), and global oil and gas specialist Wood Mackenzie. Both were data analytics and publishing companies with strong barriers to entry, valued sector specialisation and great cash-flow profiles backed by healthy renewal rates and multi-year contracts.

The way I was proposing to structure the transaction was by paying £100 million upfront, 40% financed with bank debt. The sellers wanted me to include an additional £40 million of deferred consideration, due only if management achieved its very bold growth plan. After weeks of negotiations with the vendor's advisers and Mergermarket's founder-entrepreneurs, I was left in no doubt that GMT Communications would be granted exclusivity if we were prepared to table an offer of £100 million plus performance-based ratchets for the senior executives leading the management buyout.

While Mergermarket was a smaller business, it offered much better growth prospects than BvD and Wood Mac did. All that remained was for me to convince my colleagues at GMT Communications that this transaction had the potential to turn our fund into a top-quartile performer. Even though the partners leading this investment firm had expertise in the media arena, my mission would prove an impossible task.

The valuation I had put on the business translated into a last-12-month EBITDA multiple of 16 times and a forward multiple of 13 times, excluding deferred consideration – Candover had bought Wood Mac and BvD on forward multiples of 12 times and 12.8 times respectively. Mergermarket was pricey, but the business's annual revenue growth had averaged 80% in the previous three years. The sales forecast for 2006 showed a growth rate nearing 50%. EBITDA margin had shot up from 17% to 27% between 2003 and 2005 (see Figure 2.1). I knew, from my experience with BvD and Wood Mac that profitability was likely to rise as more customers came on board. These two companies delivered EBITDA margins of 35% to 40%.

The beauty with online database publishers is that information costs the same to produce whether you sell it to one user or a multitude of them. The economies of scale are almost unrivalled. Certainly, no print publisher could match that sort of operating leverage and competitive advantage.

And that was more or less the issue. The senior partners at GMT Communications had years of experience in the communications industry, but most of these had been spent investing in traditional media. Such knowledge was all but irrelevant at a time when the industry was being remodelled by the Internet. For people not familiar with the new-media sector, the sheer momentum that could be gained from network economies was sometimes hard to fathom. When, in mid-2006, GMT's investment committee chose to walk away from the quasi-exclusivity status I had painstakingly secured, I reacted with theatrical yet crestfallen frustration. As you are about to read, the committee's decision was a huge missed opportunity.

**Figure 2.1 – Mergermarket Group's revenue and EBITDA margin from 2003 to 2006**

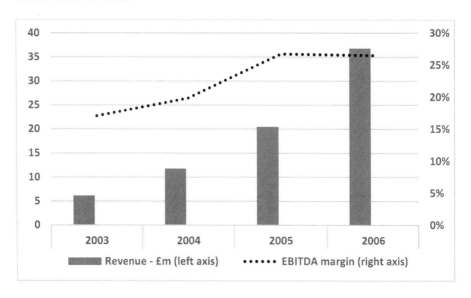

*Source: company filings and author analysis*

## Small data

Ingeniously conceived as both a newswire and a database publisher, in a matter of six years Mergermarket had built a monopoly in the deal intelligence sector. Its journalists did not care about reporting PR-sponsored news items. The eponymous mergermarket product was

## Mergermarket

after M&A scoops, moving as far upstream of the deal process as practical. Accuracy, relevance and timeliness were of the essence. Ideally, sources needed to breach non-disclosure agreements to provide inside information that mergermarket would then publish for the benefit of its clients. The intelligence had to be practically useful, almost predictive, enabling customers to generate ideas and new business opportunities.

Founded in late 1999, the company had expanded its subscription-based product offering to the credit markets, with the launch of Debtwire, and to event-driven intelligence for traders and hedge fund managers with its dealReporter solution. During the due diligence process, management had also revealed that they were developing or about to launch other services. Importantly, while the firm had established a strong market position in its home region, Europe, it offered tremendous international growth potential in the Americas and Asia. Management intended to develop the firm's presence in these geographies by leveraging its European customer base: many of Mergermarket's clients in Europe were American banks, private equity firms, hedge fund managers, law firms and advisory boutiques.

The event-driven information segment was poorly served, which offered the London-headquartered group a strategic advantage. The addressable market was worth hundreds of millions of dollars a year, spread across thousands of clients. The diversity of the customer base ensured that no client would represent too large a chunk of the group's revenue.

Mergermarket had star qualities. It developed a portfolio of proprietary products in financial information. It was impeccably positioned to build a solid market leadership without the fear of being outgunned by any of the largest financial media groups. Unlike Bloomberg or Dow Jones, Mergermarket covered private transactions, which represented a fraction of the opportunities derived from public capital markets. Bloomberg et al were unlikely to find the revenue potential of private

M&A data of much value. That was the sort of competitive advantage that a player can earn by simply operating below the radar or in a niche segment. The low-hanging fruit of private markets was valuable to a growing company like Mergermarket but not to media titans making billions of dollars in sales.

Way before the latest tech craze came up with its own set of buzzwords, from 'big data' to artificial intelligence, the world of business had recognised the significance of proprietary knowledge. The City of London is full of stories where dealmakers with advanced knowledge of an important event make a killing by trading on such information. The one example that keeps being bandied about is that of Nathan Rothschild speculating heavily in government bonds upon learning, thanks to an unequalled network of messengers employed by his family bank, of Napoleon's defeat at Waterloo in 1815 several hours before even the British Government's War Office was informed.

As the speed of information increased over time, other fortunes were made by service providers like Reuters, established in 1851 by German-born British entrepreneur Paul Julius Reuter at the London Royal Exchange. Reuter earned a reputation as the first to report news scoops from abroad thanks to the commercial application of a recent invention: the electric telegraph. In the early 1980s, the information service set up in New York by its eponymous founder, former Salomon Brothers partner Michael Bloomberg, built on the age-old practice of dispatching timely information on price-sensitive events.

Offering intelligence on anything from political news to economic indicators and financial updates, newswires and data publishers provide fantastic tools to make money. Their declarations are surely less bombastic than those of AI-obsessed geeks, yet their journalists know the true value of a scoop and its skilful delivery to people with deep pockets. Individuals benefiting from this sort of information need to trade carefully in order not to be found guilty of both insider trading and market abuse, although reading bestsellers like *Flash Boys* and *Black*

*Edge* will convince many of us that professional investors are never short of imagination to make a fast buck by taking trading positions ahead of the crowd.

Beyond the dissemination of business intelligence, what made Mergermarket such a compelling buyout candidate was the progressive scaling up of the company's proprietary network of users. It fed the swelling cash flows that, in turn, could be used to pay down LBO debt and subsidise organic and external expansion.

Yet, despite the cash-flow generation potential, the market growth opportunities, the diverse customer base, the cross-selling capabilities, the strong fundamentals of electronic trading and financial services, the clients' growing need for market-moving intelligence to gain a competitive advantage, and a long list of compelling arguments in favour of a leveraged buyout in 2006, not a single PE firm ended up submitting a binding offer for the Mergermarket Group. Initially, my colleagues at GMT Communications had been guardedly receptive to the deal. In fact, due to my persistence GMT was the last financial sponsor involved in the process and, by withdrawing, left the field wide open for strategic bidders.

## Steady does it

While the co-founders of Mergermarket would have preferred to lead a management buyout and replace their VC backers with PE owners, the lack of risk appetite from financial sponsors left the executives little choice but to seek a buyer elsewhere. As a quid pro quo for their investment in Mergermarket back in 2000, the venture capitalists could try to force a sale by dragging the three entrepreneurs, but equally, it was difficult to sell the business without the cooperation of the management team. De facto, the VC investors needed to get the senior execs on their side in order to successfully exit.

Several corporate buyers had been involved in the bidding process from the outset, but few could demonstrate the necessary strategic fit. One party soon earned preferred bidding status due to its obvious synergistic benefits and industry relevance. After weeks of negotiations, on 8 August 2006 The Financial Times Group, a division of media conglomerate Pearson, acquired Mergermarket for £101 million. The deal structure also included up to £40 million of deferred bonuses contingent upon future performance. It was eerily similar to the terms I had negotiated, proof that my proposed bid had been spot on. The transaction enabled the target's VC backers to make a 14-times return on their investment.[2]

The Mergermarket acquisition was just the tip of the iceberg for Pearson. As a standalone, it was a great deal. It complemented the FT's traditional news service with early-stage intelligence on potential corporate activity. There was the glaring potential of cross-selling Mergermarket's products to the Financial Times's client base, although the young company already covered a fairly broad range of blue chip clients. Its customers included 29 of the world's top 30 investment banks, 18 of the top 20 law firms and 25 of the top 30 private equity houses.[3]

In 2005, Mergermarket originated less than one-third of its top line from outside Europe. With Pearson's backing, it spent the next few years building a global presence. During the sale process, the roll-out in Asia had been mentioned as a great opportunity. The Middle East and Latin America were also untouched territories. That was all up for grab.

On top of the cross-selling and international upside, the group would spend the following years developing its existing products. For instance, in 2006 Debtwire was only serving the corporate and LBO loan markets; within two years it launched an asset-backed securities product, followed by a municipal bonds offering four years later. Expanding the product portfolio also meant creating new solutions in different verticals. In the first four years after its acquisition by

Pearson, the company developed business intelligence services in pharmaceuticals, international trade as well as online deal sourcing and matching.

As a buy-and-build platform, Mergermarket proved a world-class opportunity. Pearson used the company as a vehicle to consolidate the highly fragmented business information segment. In September 2007 Mergermarket acquired Infinata, an information and analytics provider to the life science and high technology industries.[4] The group then went through a series of small add-ons. In early 2010 it acquired loan and bonds data specialist Xtract Research to strengthen its offering in fixed income. Two years later, infrastructure sector specialist Inframation Group joined the group. Mergermarket's shopping spree confirms that, at the transactional level the company was a marvel. Its well-knit M&A road map for growth showed that it was fairly simple to cross-sell products and services to clients, especially when the latter are price-insensitive.

Thanks to the transformation that the group went through, in the first six years of Pearson ownership the compound annual rate of growth in revenue and EBITDA averaged 19%. By 2012 revenue exceeded £100 million, and while the company had focused on growth rather than profit maximisation, at 27% EBITDA margins were on par with the ones achieved in the year of acquisition (see Figure 2.2). Yet, the Mergermarket's corporate ethos had not gelled with the Pearson's more conventional culture. In mid-2013 Pearson took the decision to divest.

The integration of the Mergermarket publication assets with the FT Group should have boosted cross-selling and collaboration – the two divisions' journalists could deliver a more comprehensive and compelling product to clients – but the unequivocal view from Mergermarket staffers is that the degree of integration remained very low throughout the period of ownership. The two entities were so aloof that the proposed demerger was unlikely to create much friction.

On the contrary, it was welcome by both Mergermarket's and the *FT*'s senior teams. For *Financial Times* lifers, the upstart represented a somewhat dumbed-down approach to providing financial information to its sophisticated clientele. The upstart's database publishing activities were not as noble as the more intellectually stimulating journalistic prose. To the *FT*'s award-winning correspondents, the Mergermarket Group employed hack writers masquerading as data sleuths, whereas to Mergermarket's industrious deal intelligence specialists, the *FT*'s public-relations-driven journalistic approach belonged to a different era.

Pearson had held onto the company for seven years and, despite the testing financial markets, the investment was a success. Figure 2.2 shows that there was a dip in revenue in 2009, directly attributable to the Great Recession, but it is important to note that there was an incentive-related reason behind the revenue fall.

When the business was sold to Pearson in 2006, management had negotiated a two-year incentive plan partly based on top line growth and profitability. To maximise their deferred bonus, Mergermarket's senior executives negotiated two-year commercial deals with clients in order to maximise revenue recognition in 2007 and 2008. When these multi-year contracts expired in the second half of 2008, many clients did not renew or used that time to negotiate better terms while the financial crisis was in full swing. It contributed to an 8% revenue decline in 2009.

Yet, when one considers that Mergermarket's client base was comprised primarily of banks, private equity firms, hedge funds, lawyers and other institutions heavily dependent on the health of the M&A markets, the fact that the revenue drop was only in single digit is further evidence of the resilience of the Mergermarket Group's business model.

**Figure 2.2 – Mergermarket Group's revenue and EBITDA margin from 2006 to 2013**

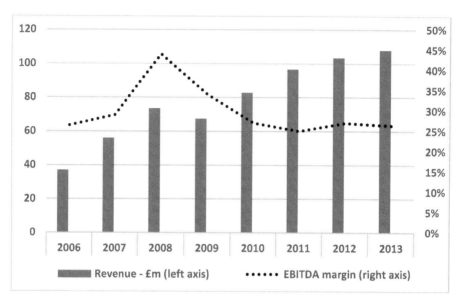

*Source: company filings and author analysis*

## The group's long overdue LBO

After a very competitive process that saw numerous bidders vie for the target, on 29 November 2013 Pearson agreed to sell Mergermarket to London-headquartered buyout house BC Partners. The latter valued Mergermarket at £382 million, including £245 million in LBO debt sliced into a £150 million seven-year secured loan, a £70 million eight-year note, and a $40 million working capital facility. The transaction closed in February 2014 on a valuation multiple of approximately 13.5 times prior-year EBITDA, while leverage sat at 7 to 7.5 times earnings.[5]

At this point in the group's history, it is worth revisiting the objections that mid-market PE firms formulated back in 2006. Otherwise, it would be difficult to understand why BC Partners was happy to pay

THE GOOD, THE BAD AND THE UGLY OF PRIVATE EQUITY

such a good price for an asset that buyout fund managers had shunned seven years earlier.

In 2006 Mergermarket was what is called a growth capital play. It was at a stage of development comprised between early-stage and maturity. Such transactions focus more on the growth potential of a target than on its earnings. For that reason, future profitability and cash flows were difficult to predict. There is a natural trade-off between revenue expansion and profit margins as investing in growth usually requires increasing the cost base, which impacts earnings, at least in the short term, when corporate overheads, sales and marketing expenses go up. That explains why I had only managed to negotiate a 40% leverage ratio with lenders back in 2006 whereas BC Partners was able to fund its LBO with more debt.

The higher risk profile of Mergermarket in 2006 scared off mid-market LBO fund managers, even though development capital deals are supposed to be their bread and butter. An issue that often crops up with mid-market transactions is the fact that the target companies can be vulnerable to new entrants with deeper pockets. I had tried to convince my colleagues that Bloomberg, Reuters and the like were not interested in the smallish private markets when the opportunities in public debt and equity could bring billions of dollars in revenue. My colleagues had countered that Google might be a threat. Never mind that the search firm only operated in the business-to-consumer arena. My impression was that if Google was going to enter the business-to-business markets, and more specifically the financial sector, targeting the tiny private M&A data segment wasn't going to move the needle for their top line. They were more likely to go after Bloomberg than after Mergermarket. Never mind that Google operated a search engine, not a newswire. Never mind that Google made money through mass advertising, not through the sale of subscription-based, exclusive, niche information. Never mind that Google was a data aggregator, not a data producer.

Beside concerns around commercial threats, there was the mistaken view shared by many prospective buyers that Mergermarket's co-founders were going to make a fortune by selling out (they owned over one-third of the business), thus their heart and drive might no longer be into it. Instead, they would presumably be preparing for their retirement. Because the three co-founders were aged 40 or less, had readily agreed to roll over 70% of their proceeds into the LBO vehicle and would therefore retain close to 40% of the PE-backed business, my opinion was that they would actually retain significant skin in the game. I was quietly confident that I could ask them to increase their reinvestment.

While I am not at liberty to disclose the nature and content of the GMT Communications investment committee's proceedings, I eventually recognised that my arguments would not sway the debate. This inability to identify Mergermarket's strong competitive position, together with a general lack of understanding of the full potential that electronic data publishing represented in what was only the second decade of the Internet, explains why GMT and other PE firms failed to identify Mergermarket as a fantastic opportunity in 2006. By contrast, seven years later BC Partners had to fight off stiff competition to clinch the deal.

## Market consolidator

Under Pearson's ownership, growth was primarily driven by new client wins and price increases. Mergermarket was still very much at a development stage, where organic improvement plays a strong role. Acquisitions had played a part in the second half of the investment period as the company's runaway growth had cooled down, but the business remained small-scale – a point made by agency Moody's in January 2014 when rating the company's LBO loans as very speculative.[6]

Nevertheless getting more mature, with the full backing of BC Partners, Mergermarket was getting ready to follow a fervent buy-and-build scenario. In June 2014 the company acquired Perfect Information, a workflow solution and filings provider with 17,000 users in 42 countries. In September 2015 it purchased venture capital publications AVCJ and Unquote from Incisive Media. Two months later, risk intelligence and data provider C6 Intelligence was added to the portfolio. In January 2016 the firm bought Creditflux, an information provider on credit funds, as a great complement to Debtwire's existing offering. Finally, in May 2017, for about £30 million Mergermarket absorbed Tim Group, a specialist in the electronic delivery of equity trade ideas and investment recommendations.[7]

Not surprisingly, this energetic deal activity helped boost the top line, as Figure 2.3 testifies. At the same time, it brought down BC Partners' blended entry earnings multiple as many of these bolt-ons were completed at valuations much lower than the one paid for the Mergermarket Group. It would have a positive effect on the returns the PE firm could expect to generate on the way out.

Speaking of exit, after more than three years of ownership BC Partners decided to put out feelers to test the market's appetite for its portfolio company. Throughout 2016 the buyout group had received several unsolicited approaches for the asset. Mergermarket had shown strong top line growth and earnings improvement. The product and international roll-outs coupled with horizontal consolidation via acquisitions in segments such as equities, fixed income, M&A and compliance had created a very compelling portfolio. But it was unclear what all this was worth without getting feedback from the outside. In the spring of 2017, BC went on a search for bidders.

**Figure 2.3 – Mergermarket Group's revenue and cash EBITDA margin from 2013 to 2016**

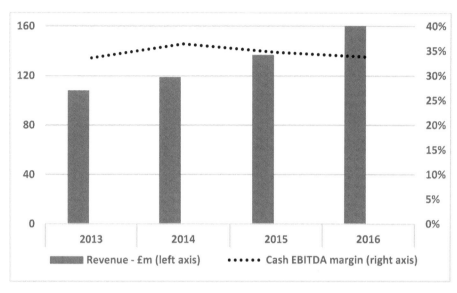

*Note: cash EBITDA adjusts normal EBITDA with deferred income – Source: company filings and author analysis*

## Performance drivers of a great buyout

They say data is the new oil. Once you have found an abundant and fertile reservoir, the product will gush out faster than you can reinvest the cash proceeds. Mergermarket turned out to be the perfect candidate for a leveraged transaction. Value creation and preservation was derived from multiple sources:

- The ideal LBO is **boring, plodding and predictable**. Mergermarket was not quite dull enough, but it did its best at delivering reliable performance. The high visibility of revenue was subscription-based, and the quality and accuracy of the data kept annual contract cancellation rates below 5%, even if they rose somewhat during the financial crisis.

- **Fast revenue and earnings growth** continued apace. The penetration of Mergermarket's products was still limited back in 2006. As we saw earlier, even as the rate of organic growth was falling in Europe, the publishing group was planning to roll out its offering in new geographies and to complement its portfolio via add-on acquisitions, a two-pronged strategy tenaciously implemented under Pearson's ownership.

- **Steady and predictable cash-flow generation** was amplified by **limited capex needs** and the lack of seasonality, reinforcing cash conversion.

- Not only was there no seasonality but **working capital requirements were negative** as clients paid one year in advance. As explained, some clients even accepted to sign multi-year contracts (a habit I had noticed during my buyout of oil & gas information provider Wood Mackenzie). Thanks to these payments, Mergermarket and other database publishers supply huge sums of deferred revenue, making it easier to assess, months ahead, whether and with how much headroom debt covenants would be met, thereby enabling renegotiations and recapitalisations with lenders.

- **High cash conversion** was primarily driven by a factor common to all database publishers: **economies of scale**. When one report or news item is produced, it costs the same whether it is delivered to one client or to one million of them. As Mergermarket grew its number of customers, every marginal revenue dollar fed straight to the bottom line, this operating leverage seamlessly converting into cash. **The network effect** (the same product delivered to an ever-growing customer base) explains why profitability expanded. Operating margin for the core mergermarket product shot up from 26% in 2005 to 53.6% in 2008. It was still 50% in 2015 despite intense competition.[8] By 2016 consolidated cash EBITDA margin stood well above 30% (as seen in Figure 2.3), which was less than the 50% achieved by the core product, but group reporting included traditionally lower-margin activities like event management and print publications.

- **High renewal rates**: the vast majority of specialist database users tend to renew their subscriptions. The contract renewal rate typically exceeds 90%, reinforcing the predictability and recurrence of revenue already discussed. At Mergermarket, renewals were often conducted with price increases, showing that the company's products offered opportunities to optimise pricing.

- The main reason behind that high renewal rate is not that Mergermarket products are 'must-haves' – a point that was advertised by the company's management and advisers. While this might be true for some customers, I suspect that most PE and hedge fund managers as well as corporate financiers and lenders would be able to perform their job without getting access to the publisher's products, even if the latter could be described as 'nice-to-haves'. No, the reason for the high renewal rate is that **clients are price insensitive**, particularly at the larger end. This low price elasticity of demand is due to the relatively small expense (tens of thousands of dollars) that the subscription to these products represent for financial institutions managing hundreds of millions if not billions of dollars in assets.

- Mergermarket's client base was **fully diversified**. The information group was not dependent on one or two key clients, which is usually a big warning sign for PE investors. In cases of high revenue concentration, the loss of one major customer can immediately wipe out a huge portion of a company's top line, putting its earnings and cash flows at risk. None of Mergermarket's clients represented more than 5% of total revenue, so the low

> impact of any one customer loss provided visibility in revenue and cash production, enabling predictable debt redemption.
>
> - Given its established position in the financial information and research sector, all the group needed to do was to add products and services to its portfolio and to sell those to existing customers. This is a synergistic strategy that the company pioneered under VC ownership (until 2006) on an organic basis, and that it pursued assiduously while under corporate (2006-13) and then PE ownership (post 2013) by spearheading a very aggressive **buy-and-build programme**. Both Pearson and BC Partners were more than happy to let management expand the product portfolio as long as it remained a normal extension to Mergermarket's proprietary business intelligence platform.

## The way out

Recall that, back in 2006, I had secured some debt to fund the target's buyout. The banks I had spoken to were only willing to provide 40% of the enterprise value in the form of loans, leaving the rest to be funded by equity. It might seem surprising that such a cash-generative business would not earn a better leverage ratio. Let me explain.

Unlike Hilton, Mergermarket was not an asset-rich company. In 2006 its tangible assets were non-existent, and its only valuable asset was its database. The brand was quite low-value back then, even if it had built its notoriety as an expert in the financial services sector. Ten years later, when BC Partners was considering an exit, intangible assets represented over a quarter of the group's total assets while goodwill (the accumulated premium on book value paid as part of various acquisitions since inception) accounted for another 56% of total asset book value. Tangible assets were still negligible, but the company's predictable cash flows made it a reliable borrower. Lenders were likely to queue up at the door to keep Mergermarket as a client.

In July 2017 the company launched a £500 million dual-currency dividend recapitalisation.[9] Also in the early summer, BC Partners went through a partial secondary buyout by selling a 30% stake in Mergermarket to Singapore's sovereign wealth fund GIC. The latter paid an earnings multiple of 14 to 16 times, based on various definitions of EBITDA.[10] The debt refinancing comprised £380 million of existing loans alongside a £50 million revolving credit facility. The deal also included £295 million for BC Partners through a full redemption of shareholder instruments and cash dividends. In parallel, GIC was making a £175 million preferred stock injection. Leverage was at 8.6 times according to Standard & Poor's, or 7.2 times on an adjusted basis according to Moody's.[11] Despite its growing size, the company's concentrated revenue stream in the financial services industry raised its risk profile from a credit rating standpoint. The two agencies retained their very speculative grades, but it was now acknowledged by investors and lenders that the business had become a first-rate LBO candidate.

BC Partners was following a familiar scheme adopted by some of its PE peers in recent years. Rather than fully exiting or going through a complex dividend recapitalisation that required stressful negotiations with lenders, it was easier to execute a partial exit with one of its core LP investors (i.e. GIC) while retaining a majority stake in the company. On the secondary partial exit, BC Partners returned to its investors more than twice their original cash-out and kept a 60% stake in the newly rebranded media group Acuris.

The great advantage of selling out to sovereign wealth funds and other LP investors* is that they have lower target returns than traditional financial sponsors. While a PE fund manager like BC Partners is after 15% to 20% annualised returns, institutional investors like GIC would be happy with 10% to 12%. Both parties can agree to a higher

---

* A reminder that the term 'LP investors' refers to fund providers that allocate capital to private equity firms and other asset managers

valuation multiple without either side having to compromise. GIC had also helped The Carlyle Group partially exit its investment in British roadside recovery group RAC in September 2014. The deal between BC Partners and GIC followed the same template. A year later Carlyle had sold the remaining controlling stake in RAC to buyout group CVC. Exiting in two stages gave Carlyle the chance to secure a partial realisation similar to an IPO (always good from a time-value-of-money standpoint) while staying involved one more year to benefit from further upside. BC Partners was taking a similar approach with Mergermarket.

A goodly number of mid-market buyout shops had reviewed the opportunity back in 2006. More than 30 mid-market fund managers had received the information memorandum. Yet none of them had recognised the target's outstanding value indicators. At the time, several PE firms, including some with a media expertise, were incapable of identifying Mergermarket as one of the most promising growth companies in publishing. It is worth noting that any of these mid-market financial sponsors could have made more than 4 times their money had they invested back in 2006. By following the route taken by Pearson and selling out seven years later, conservatively assuming no repayment of debt or dividend recap during the holding period, the LBO would have earned an internal rate of return of 25%.

Such a home run would have guaranteed GMT Communications a smooth fundraise for its subsequent vintage GMT IV. Instead, after three years on the road, in 2017 the GMT team gave up on the new fundraising exercise and was forced to wrap up a liquidity process for Fund III, allowing investors to sell their holdings or recommit to a secondary vehicle housing three remaining portfolio companies.[12] Sometimes the deals you don't do are the ones that hurt the most. Dejected, I had left the firm long ago, in the summer of 2008.

## GROWTH AND PRIVATE EQUITY PERFORMANCE

*Companies in a development phase are great candidates for leveraged buyouts. There is usually significant growth potential, both organically and externally, for mid-market buyouts to yield superior returns without having to resort to the sorts of financial engineering techniques we will witness in Parts Two and Three.*

# CHAPTER 3

# A pragmatic blueprint for private equity best practice

*There is no such thing as the 'best fund manager.' There are many ways to achieve great investment results. Every investment team has its own skill set, its own idiosyncrasy, and its own weaknesses.*

*Yet, while the light-touch regulatory environment the PE industry benefits from explains the lack of reliable information about performance, some tools and techniques can be considered best practice.*

This chapter is not trying to offer new management theories. It is about investment practices that should deliver consistent and better returns. It attempts to sketch out the primary features of a private equity investing business model, where the word 'model' should be read both as a representation of the investment process on a smaller scale than real life, and as a standard to be imitated.

PE fund managers are not known for their fastidiousness. Deal-doing is a dynamic, creative and intoxicating activity that gives bragging-rights to those who close the most inventive and record-breaking transactions. But I would argue that a best-in-class PE firm should not be a trailblazer. Instead, it should demonstrate an uncanny discipline in handling growth and managing assets. Chances are most readers will not find any of the points in this chapter revolutionary. Performance in

## It's all about management

Private equity owners have earned a bad reputation as asset-strippers for the way they ruthlessly execute reorganisation plans, at times including sweeping rounds of layoffs. Often, staff cuts affect senior management.

Although there is limited public data on this point, it is estimated that between two-thirds and three-quarters of corporate executive teams running a portfolio company on behalf of PE owners will be reshuffled, or rescaled (meaning that one or several executives will get sacked) during the period of ownership.

The challenge for a private equity investor is to identify the best management team to implement a business plan capable of coping with a leveraged capital structure that often leaves little room for error. The execution risk of a buyout is at its greatest when the leveraged company is poorly run. A fast-growing company will require senior managers able to accelerate growth. Another business that has been neglected by its previous owners might need a turnaround plan, in which case a team focused on operating efficiency might be best suited.

It is no coincidence that LBOs were originally termed 'management buyouts'. Even if transactions can now be completed by bringing in managers exclusively from the outside (in a deal confusingly called a 'management buy-in') or by asking incumbent executives to work alongside new managers brought in for their expertise, there is no question that the managers running a portfolio company are essential to the success of a leveraged buyout. That explains why PE firms do not hesitate to be brutal in their selection of the investee's senior team. Yet there is no secret formula. Over time, after many hits and misses fund managers learn to identify corporate executives with the right blend of doggedness and flexibility to adapt the business to whatever obstacles and economic conditions it will face during the life of the transaction.

## The danger of going native

If corporate managers are so vital to the success of a buyout, the corollary is that a weak management team is often the main reason behind LBO failures. Several case studies in this book will highlight the consequences of behavioural failings. Managing other people's money is a difficult trade, one that requires a high degree of rationality throughout the decision-making process. Sacking individuals is a very emotionally loaded decision.

The biggest test that a fund manager faces when backing incumbent managers or selecting new candidates to run a company is to decide how much time to allow these individuals to deliver on a business plan. At which point must private equity owners determine that a management team is no longer the right one and must go? One must not act too early. Pulling the trigger without giving the chief exec and his colleagues sufficient time would be counterproductive, sending the message across the organisation that the owners are unrealistic in their expectations. But not making a decision is equally damaging.

Failing to act at all is what we call 'going native'. Because humans tend to select individuals who resemble them most (we will discuss this concept of 'homophily' later), they are frequently incapable of taking the harsh but indispensable decision of firing people who have not delivered on their promises. Procrastination will not only impact investment returns. It will also send the message to employees of the portfolio company that underperformance is tolerated, with the risk of institutionalising failure.

## Doing one's own due diligence

Before closing a deal, a conscientious investor must do a thorough preliminary analysis. A fund manager's success over the years might legitimately be due to luck. But as Benjamin Franklin once wrote, "diligence is the mother of good luck."[1]

Fund managers do not carry out due diligence to satisfy their own curiosity. They do so because, without professional inspection, they would not be able to raise debt to finance their acquisitions. A leveraged buyout makes economic sense if it is funded primarily with loans. These sums are borrowed by the target from bankers and, increasingly, private debt fund managers who expect private equity firms to provide due diligence reports covering every risk element of the transaction: macroeconomic situation, market landscape, competitive positioning, financial performance, litigation and other parameters that could endanger the cash-flow generation, and thereby creditworthiness, of the target.

Thus, lenders are behind the demand for due diligence. For proof, fund managers like venture capitalists that do not borrow heavily to finance the acquisition of assets, and are not under pressure from lenders to demonstrate their thorough understanding of the company they plan to invest in, do not perform extensive investigations.

What often happens is that the ceaseless toil of due diligence becomes more superficial when the economy and the M&A market become bullish. Research shows that between 2014 and 2017, due diligence times dropped from an average of 7.4 to 6.1 months.[2] While there are various reasons behind such a trend, including the adoption of M&A insurance and the rise in pre-deal analysis, the main factor is increased competition during the auction process.

During the rampant 2006-08 period, many transactions, including the acquisition of Dutch banking group ABN AMRO by its rival Royal Bank of Scotland, were completed after only weeks of negotiations, not giving the acquirer sufficient time to perform a thorough assessment. What also became prevalent in those days was the production of vendor-instructed due diligence reports (meaning that the seller was analysing its own business!), which were in some instances heavily doctored. Similarly rushed practices appeared in 2017 and 2018, proving that many PE investors were once more prepared to throw caution to the wind as the markets got frothier. While proper due diligence cannot guarantee strong returns, cursory analysis often leaves many blind spots and can be a precursor to failure.

## Slow and steady wins the race

Fund managers must deliver dependable performance. We will see in later chapters that fund providers stay away from a private equity firm offering unpredictable or poor returns, choosing to reduce their allocation to future vintages, or to withdraw further commitments entirely.

During sporadic booms, fund managers tend to show a frustratingly common taste for short-termism. Whenever a rally develops into a full-blown bubble, investing sangfroid usually makes room for deal-doing hubris. Here are key features of companies or markets that should offer better odds of success to PE firms prepared to keep a disciplined approach to investing.

- *Revenue recurrence, cash flow predictability*

Because companies undergoing a leveraged buyout are exposed to years of compounding interest and, ultimately, the repayment of the loans they borrow, they need to produce a regular stream of cash flows. The best way to secure such a stream is by embracing a business model where the recurrence of revenues and cash flows cannot be jeopardised.

Software as a service (SaaS) is better than the delivery of software or hardware on its own since the SaaS provider offers solutions over time, not just a one-off product sale. Smartphone manufacturers are not just hardware or software developers. They provide application platforms that attract app developers and make their offer stickier with the end user. Once smartphone users have downloaded multiple apps on their phone, their apps sit in the cloud and are transferable from one phone to the next, but only for devices of the same brand or operating system. The fact that app developers are independent, usually self-employed, contractors also reduces the risk profile of this revenue model (from the app platform's standpoint). Apps follow a blockbuster profile, meaning that very few of them are winners. If Apple had to develop all apps in house, the fact that many of them are worthless would create an uncertain flow of revenue while staff costs would be fixed.

So, the value is no longer in the single product sale but in the recurring platform access. This business design around solutions rather than products is what General Electric introduced in the 1980s under Jack Welch's leadership. From selling fridges or aircraft engines, GE became a supplier of options, accessories, maintenance and even financing solutions. Offering a complete, integrated solution makes cash flows more predictable because the switching cost for customers goes up. Logically Apple and General Electric are great LBO candidates, particularly the latter for a break-up strategy. Only their size protects them from the claws of private equity firms...for now.

Subscription-based and fee-based revenue models, like the ones espoused by Mergermarket and Hilton respectively, are better than blockbuster projects (like video games or movies) because they provide good visibility. Similarly, businesses with an installed base offer predictability – the example discussed as a case study at most business schools is Gillette and its famous razor-and-blade bundled offering that ensures customer stickiness. Looking at more modern versions, social networks like Facebook and search engine Google also benefit from the network effect, a modern version of the installed base principle. In summary, businesses with recurring revenues and variable (or outsourced) costs are great LBO targets.

- *Fragmentation of customer and supplier base*

One way to protect cash flows is to trade with a large enough base of suppliers and clients. We saw that Mergermarket benefited from a diverse set of customer segments. During the financial crisis, while investment banks and private equity firms reduced their information budgets, lawyers and traders were probably less affected by the economic downturn, helping Mergermarket to weather the storm.

Inversely, being dependent on one or only a handful of key service providers or clients is risky. Companies with that sort of sourcing or sales profile are not generally good candidates for an LBO. We will see in Chapter 4 that Univision was heavily dependent on one key content provider, which affected its performance.

- *Cyclical vs cycle agnostic*

To state the obvious, cyclical companies are not reliable sources of leverageable assets. Sectors like retail, especially fashion retail, as well as transaction-based industries like investment banking, air travel, commodities trading, and advertising-dependent segments are best avoided. That makes Chapters 4, 6 and 7 of this book all the more fascinating.

There is a dangerously complacent phrase in the investing world. People sometimes refer to businesses that are supposedly 'recession-proof'. Let's just say that no company is truly safe from the negative effects of a downturn, especially if it is overleveraged. Nonetheless, subscription-based models (e.g., Mergermarket), food & beverage manufacturing (a key staple of many private equity firms) and businesses that operate on long-term contracts (such as airport and toll-road operators) are more resilient than others and should therefore be of interest to buyout investors.

- *Asset efficiency*

For asset-rich businesses, the key question a fund manager must answer is how to get more out of the assets. Asset intensity, that is the ratio of assets to revenues, can be a drag on earnings.

Private equity fund managers, traditionally seeking businesses with unencumbered assets to use as security, are nowadays eager to lighten the asset load of a portfolio company. An asset-intensive business requires regular upgrades or investments to replace obsolete equipment. As witnessed in the Hilton story, management contracts can give conventional property managers like hotel groups a way to maximise return on equity without the burden of capital expenditure on cash flows better used to redeem debt or distribute dividends.

In part to make itself less cycle-dependent, Hilton transformed its model from asset-rich to fee-based, making the group less sensitive to volatility in asset valuations and the frequent extravagance that affects property markets.

Of course, the danger of following an asset-light strategy is that when the business hits a roadblock, it cannot resort to selling part of its property or equipment to generate cash urgently. It might thus be forced into liquidation. When its accounting fraud came to light in 2001, Enron could not cope. Management had spent years morphing the business from an asset-based gas pipeline operator to an asset-poor trading platform. With liabilities three times the size of its asset book value, Enron had no alternative but to file for Chapter 11. Even if they do not get that creative on the accounting front, highly leveraged buyouts could find it difficult to face a downturn or market disruption if they follow an asset-light model.

- *People businesses*

Traditionally, a sector like advertising was not a good source of LBOs as it relied on creative people, a fickle lot. But now that ads are automated, advertising platforms like Facebook and Google are fantastic targets; that is if their founders ever considered financial engineering worth their time. At present, they'd rather focus on real growth and value creation via product and service innovation. But that could change.

A business like EMI Music showed during its failed buyout in 2007-11 that its recording unit, dependent on artists and repertoire staff, was too volatile for a leveraged transaction. The publishing catalogue was more predictable and a good target for securitisation, as KKR demonstrated with its 2009 investment in BMG Rights, a publishing joint venture with German media group Bertelsmann. For less hair-raising buyouts, it is best to stay away from people businesses.

- *Popular culture vs. tech culture*

For years, apart from corporate turnarounds provoked by down-cycles, LBO fund managers focused almost exclusively on value plays, that is on sectors and companies with long product cycles that grew sales and cash flows unremarkably, yet steadily. These businesses rarely experienced large shifts in performance. The tech revolution that started in the business-to-business sectors of the economy and gradually infiltrated the consumer world over the past thirty years has changed the structure of many industries. Companies that were expected to adapt to popular culture, with trends measured in multi-year or even decades-long product life cycles, today face a much more dynamic boom-and-bust, fad-oriented market.

The digitalisation of whole swathes of the economy, from information to retail, and from entertainment to leisure, shortened product upgrades to one year, sometimes a few quarters for the most ephemeral video games. As noted in some of our case studies (Univision and Toys "R" Us, in particular), the consequences of technological disruption on companies trying to deliver predictability to service debt can be traumatic.

To avoid being caught flatfooted, a private equity fund manager must identify those sectors exposed or likely to get exposed to the tech culture, and refrain from investing in them.

## Not all performances are created equal

Any rate of return must be assessed on a risk-adjusted basis. A fund manager might be able to deliver extremely high returns by taking inconsiderate risks.

Risk assessment is not an exact science. It requires intellectual honesty as much as expertise that can only be acquired through time, a painstakingly methodical approach that does not tolerate shortcuts. As a rule, however, a company with high business uncertainty is not a good candidate for a leveraged buyout. The financial risk that LBO loans add to an investee rarely mix well with market shocks such as economic recessions, technological disruptions or regulatory pressure.

In addition, the nature of the uncertainty may vary. Risks that can be deemed equivalent on a risk-return scale might be derived from various sources. While Apollo and KKR are known for their financial prowess, they have honed those skills over many decades with the abnegation of passionate artists. A new fund manager applying the same degree of leverage to its portfolio might not have the negotiating power or nous to extricate itself from an overstretched investee facing a downturn or other market challenges, as is bound to occur occasionally.

Similarly, distressed and turnaround specialists take bets that require significant expertise, the sort that cannot be improvised. These operational engineers bring in a set of skills that involves restructuring an organisation. But the nature of the risk they face is not financial, it is business specific. On a risk-adjusted basis, their returns might well be compared to those of financial engineers, but they have strictly nothing in common.

Failing to clearly identify (or underestimating) the kind of risk that a target company is facing can prove fatal for a private equity firm, as we will see when we discuss the Toys "R" Us story in Chapter 6.

## Upside takes care of itself, downside kills deals

Whether voluntarily or under duress, many fund managers will at some stage in their history be confronted with the need to enhance efficiency. This is certainly where they face their greatest challenge. Typically, senior professionals at private equity firms are financiers, many of them coming from the banking and accountancy worlds. They rarely focus on operational matters as a priority. Yet producing better results than the competition requires to supplement financial skills with other types.

Long ago, PE firms started hiring operating partners when their portfolio companies struggled due to structural or cyclical factors. But operating efficiency was generally an after-thought, not a core consideration during the pre-deal due diligence process. There is anecdotal evidence that the most successful buyout firms are those that have integrated operating tools into their value-creation processes alongside more traditional techniques like leverage. While efficiency improvements alone are unlikely to make a deal a success, they might well save the business when the going gets tough.

What is also certain is that when markets are pricey, as they were in 2006-08 and again in 2017-18, operational controls are usually needed to preserve and, in some cases, enhance value. Naturally, not all management tools will apply to every LBO situation. Merger integration is very relevant in a buy-and-build strategy, supply chain optimisation or outsourcing will help a manufacturer, and channel or logistics upgrades matter to a distributor.

The danger for a fund manager is to confuse process quality improvements with cost controls. Slashing expenditure on a wide scale generally has a negative impact on the long-term viability of a business, especially when coupled with a reduction or elimination of capital expenditure since the latter is required to boost growth. Private equity firms have showed that they do not necessarily care about the long-term well-being of a business. They are preoccupied with value enhancement during their period of ownership, with the goal of maximising returns on investment at the time of exit. That explains why cost-cutting is the practice that has hurt the sector's reputation most over the years.

## Exit first

While PE firms try very hard to portray themselves as business builders, the truth of the matter is that they are essentially traders. The proof lies in one of the quintessential rules of private equity investing. A key condition for a fund manager to invest in a business is to identify at the outset, before completing the buyout, a clear route to exit. Without a well-defined disposal strategy, a diligent financial sponsor should not invest – note that some fund managers often fail to heed that rule and are prepared to leave the exit stage in the hands of fate.

One of the most controversial practices of the last bull run were club deals of very large buyouts, as we will review in Chapters 4, 6 and 9. The key challenge of these multibillion-dollar transactions was not just how to add value to a leveraged business showing flat or negative growth; it was also how to identify a viable route to exit. Except for RJR Nabisco in the late 1980s, few large corporations had been the subject of an LBO until the 2004-08 era. While RJR had been a great candidate for a carve-out strategy, not many of the clubbed transactions of the credit boom could be sold piecemeal, which made their disposal far from straightforward. In that respect, their private equity owners were somewhat sloppy.

Still, the necessary corollary is that if devising an exit plan at the outset is considered best practice, it follows that private equity fund managers are very much short-term business merchants rather than long-term builders. But every rule has exceptions. Buy-and-build strategies aim to counteract the worst trading tendencies.

## Buy and build

While journalists like to describe private equity firms as investors that acquire struggling companies with the aim of turning them around, this image is not a true reflection of today's marketplace. It is correct that, when it all began in the 1970s, buyout candidates were very often non-core corporate carve-outs that had been starved of cash and management attention for a while – and thereby were in need of urgent and intense restructuring efforts.

But management practices have improved considerably over the past four decades. Distressed candidates are a small part of the deal flow that PE firms review each year – despite the growing number of zombie buyouts overgeared by their financial sponsors.

The implication is that the low hanging fruit of cost reductions, offshoring and operational improvements have sometimes already been harvested by previous owners, especially when the latter were themselves private equity fund managers.

Instead, the most common way to create value in today's environment is by using a portfolio company as a platform to make add-on acquisitions, taking an active role in industry consolidation, as the Mergermarket case proved. When completed at a lower entry valuation multiple than the price paid for an investee, bolt-ons can be accretive before synergies are even factored in. Not to mention that they are a nobler way to create value than excessive leverage will ever be.

## The limits of financial innovation

Innovations are rarely about superior performance. In their initial stages, they are about experimentation. And all new experiments breed their fair share of miscarriages.

Institutional lenders and private equity fund managers have greatly benefited from increased regulation of the banking industry. In the past fifteen years, they have grown their share of the corporate debt market through trials and errors, yielding a lot more of the latter. While the start-up world is familiar with the concept of trying out small and failing fast, this is hardly a possibility with buyouts. When a fund manager raises a vehicle for a ten-year term to invest in leveraged structures, failing might be a slow, bleak drudgery rather than a fast, exhilarating endeavour.

Field-testing is not an option in private equity. You're either in or out. When they experiment with new debt products and aggressive structuring techniques, PE deal-doers rarely anticipate the long-term effects.

## Handle leverage with care

Given the extraordinary impact that financial leverage has on equity returns, PE fund managers have spent the past forty years sharpening their use of debt funding. It is the area where the industry has witnessed the most innovation.

With its systematic use of debt, private equity is unbeatable at the yield game. To avoid getting too technical, I will simply state that leverage is the principal means through which PE fund managers maximise returns. But it is an exceptionally risky one. That helps explain the troubles suffered by TIM Hellas, Toys "R" Us and Univision, three companies that we will review later in the book.

There is little differentiation between leverage optimisation and maximisation. But the risk of default on debt obligations for many leveraged buyouts is usually high. Lengthy renegotiations with lenders to amend covenants and extend maturities are just the start. It can also lead to bankruptcy if the borrower cannot meet its commitments, as was the case with TIM Hellas and Toys "R" Us.

The golden rule is to keep debt as a proportion of total funding at a manageable level – up to 60% seems to work for most sectors, unless they are subject to sudden regulatory changes, technological disruption or fierce cyclical downturns, in which case leverage ratios should be set much lower.

Buyout firms tend to be aggressive deal makers in search of superior returns while lenders only seek to protect themselves against any downside. That creates a lot of tension during negotiations between deal sponsors that wish to borrow as much as possible and loan providers that want to make sure they will recoup their capital plus interest. But many private equity firms have become so large that they exert undue influence on lenders, especially during cyclical peaks when there is significant disequilibrium between supply and demand in favour of the latter (as was the case in 2004-08 and again in 2016-18). When there is too much capital in the financial machinery, borrowers are often granted exceedingly generous terms, including the ability to draw interest-only loans (meaning that the principal is only repayable upon the sale of the business or when the loans reach maturity) or without the need to meet strict financial ratios (what is called debt covenants in financial lingo).

In 2017, based on my discussions with bankers, over 90% of buyouts with an enterprise value above $100 million were financed with covenant-lite bullet loans, meaning that the debt raised was not amortised but only repayable in full upon maturity or change of control, giving the borrower years to operate without constraint from its lenders.

One way that, on the back of the 2008 financial crisis, PE fund managers have tipped the scales further to their advantage is by developing in-house credit activities. Indeed, some of the largest buyout firms in the world are also among the largest corporate lenders: Apollo, Bain Capital, Blackstone and KKR all play on both sides of the capital structure. That allows them to do two things: first, they can use their private debt divisions' ability to provide LBO loans as a bargaining tool when negotiating terms with third-party lenders; second, they can acquire companies on the cheap by buying the debt of distressed companies at a discount, with the option of taking full control of the leveraged business if the latter default on its debt.

As a case in point, in 2014 KKR's credit arm renegotiated the terms of the loans held by European vending machine operator Selecta. The latter had been the subject of a buyout by Allianz Capital Partners seven years earlier. A year after the refinancing, KKR took equity control of Selecta at what observers described as a bargain price. This type of lender-led buyouts gained in acceptance during the Great Recession and thereafter.

In summary, leverage is central to the success of any buyout, but if applied in excess or too creatively it can also be its downfall.


## The perils of diversification

Another area where private equity firms have experimented (more like improvised) is diversification. The way a fund manager convinces investors to part with their cash to commit to new products, in adjacent fields where it has no prior experience, is by insisting that its investment and management techniques are best-in-class, replicable and adaptable to non-PE specific realms of the alternative investment world. However, because they operate in a private (read: opaque) and under-regulated sector, PE firms do not disclose what these techniques are.

A Pragmatic Blueprint

Prospective investors must trust that a fund manager aiming to diversify does indeed possess superior controls and methodologies that are transferable. The track record of most LBO groups would indicate that this is not the case. To start with, most buyout firms have not demonstrated consistency in performance to warrant the trust of investors when it comes to raising capital for non-PE activities. The 3i case study in Chapter 5 will serve as exhibit 1.

Another bad sign about innovation in private equity is that decisions to launch new products generally come from the top. Financial institutions tend to follow a top-down, often autocratic management style, while start-ups generally apply a flatter, sometimes bottom-up philosophy to be more dynamic and adaptable in a fast-changing environment. Finance is not fast changing; but it does evolve nonetheless. When innovation takes place, it is because the participants perceive that changing is less risky than the status quo. On the heels of the financial crisis, PE firms devised new products primarily to diversify away from the cyclical buyout trade. They often poached talent from the competition (banks, hedge funds) to create more ways to generate fees. They were not pushed to innovate by their LP investors. Few among the latter approached PE fund managers asking to buy real estate or hedge fund solutions from them.

There is no evidence that this one-stop shop approach yields higher returns for investors that accept to become more dependable on their fund managers. In this instance, innovation gives more bargaining power to PE firms. A diluted investor base grants fund managers additional influence while a broader set of investment assets increases the predictability of their fee-earning potential. They also smooth out the fluctuations in capital inflows and outflows, thereby providing better performance visibility.

This is the dilemma with innovation in financial services. It might be crucial for the long-term survival of a fund manager, but it might not be in the interest of investors as it is likely to lead to inferior returns.

For LP investors, the systematic diversification policy increasingly implemented by the largest private equity groups is likely to be detrimental. Just like consumers will not necessarily find the best currency exchange or mortgage rates with the bank offering the most generous savings accounts; and just like a life insurer will not automatically provide the most compelling car or home insurance products; there is absolutely no reason to believe that a fund manager that built a solid track record in leveraged buyouts should deliver strong performance from its hedge fund or real estate strategy.

Anecdotal evidence strongly vouches for a cautious approach when dealing with one-stop alternative asset managers. Carlyle's foray into the world of hedge funds repeatedly ended in failure, including in a set of lawsuits brought against the firm in 2010. One of the lawsuits was launched by the liquidators of Carlyle Capital Corporation (CCC) in the wake of the March 2008 collapse of this $22 billion mortgage bond trading vehicle. The suit alleged breaches of fiduciary duties, wilful misconduct, recklessness and negligence.[3] Whether the various suits were with or without merit won't change the fact that CCC had to be shut down.

In November 2006, CCC's offer memo had promised "superior risk-adjusted returns from investments in a diversified portfolio of fixed income investments." The same memo offered "net returns of 14.1% and a projected net dividend yield of 12.5%" by the end of the following year. Instead, the vehicle keeled over within 16 months before making a single dividend payment. Carlyle had chosen to finance its investments with debt, irrespective of the fact that the investments themselves were debt products: supposedly triple-A rated mortgage assets.[4] We will see in Chapter 5 why it is not a good idea for a fund manager to use leverage to finance investments in debt instruments or in assets that are themselves leveraged.

The same Carlyle had other disappointments in its diversification strategy. It eventually sold its stake in energy sector expert Riverstone after a major 'pay to play' scandal that we will discuss in Chapter 9. In February 2016 Carlyle also discontinued its fund of funds business. And in 2017 it divested part of its hedge fund business, taking a $175 million impairment charge.[5]

Carlyle's missteps were only made visible because the group manages separate investment vehicles and hires specific teams for each product segment. Other investment firms use all-in-one global vehicles and allocate capital on an opportunistic basis. Their failures being blended with their successes, they do not get the same public exposure.

After being taught by their business school professors that diversification is a good thing, some readers might object to this view on a practice that is pervasive in asset management. Yet, while diversification is a great thing to reduce volatility (and hedging against volatility is the service that diversified groups like Blackstone and KKR offer), it only improves returns if the investor or asset manager ventures into areas where it holds similar expertise to the one exercised in its existing activities.

Because it is very challenging for any one party to become an expert investor in all asset classes, diversification generally translates into dispersion and dilution rather than outperformance. For well-intentioned LP investors, a veteran private equity fund manager with a narrowly focused remit in terms of deal size, geography and industry, should be a better investment proposition than the fee-hungry one-stop shops that saw the light in the years post-financial crisis.

## THE RELATIVITY OF PERFORMANCE

*To provide case reviews of fund managers and transactions that followed best-practice is a risky endeavour. Anyone who has read books by management gurus, with upbeat titles like* In Search of Excellence *and* Built to Last, *will know that companies that are presented as exemplars rarely hold onto their leadership position. It is even truer since the recent tech revolution gained momentum.*

*The key takeaways of Part One do not specifically and exclusively relate to fund managers or the transactions they are associated with. Few deal targets meet all the criteria to qualify as perfect LBO candidates. Hilton operates in a cyclical sector, but management skilfully reinvented its business model. Even a fantastic cash-flow generator like Mergermarket lacked, in its early years, the maturity that would have convinced buyout shops that the company was ready for a leveraged structure. For those reasons, practitioners must embrace investment and management discipline that can weather the test of time.*

# PART TWO

# The Bad: Cursed or reckless?

*"It's a good idea to review past mistakes before committing new ones."*[1]

**Warren Buffett, chairman of Berkshire Hathaway**

---

*Leverage is an alchemist's stone for turning operating cash flows into PE gold. It energises the animal spirit of modern-day capitalism. But history has often demonstrated the lethal potential of overindebtedness. As much as any other single factor, leverage is responsible for the desperately long list of distressed companies that plagued the Great Recession. Even in the absence of bankruptcy, the costs of financial distress can be significant.*

*A second issue raised in Part Two is the prevalence of malpractice despite everyone's best intentions. Repeating past mistakes does not just lead to uncannily similar outcomes, it is also an inexcusable practice when managing other people's money.*

# CHAPTER 4

# Univision: The telenovela of a corporate zombie

*Business-to-consumer media companies can be cyclical. A large proportion of their revenue is usually derived from advertising. The latter tends to be the first budget item slashed by corporations when entering a recession.*

*This cyclicality makes media assets tricky buyout candidates. Their performance depends on timing. Univision did not just suffer from the fact that it was bought just before the credit bubble popped; it was also served with a full plate of market disruption and a re-rating of old-media assets.*

As it was going through a strategic review in early 2006, Univision Communications Inc. was America's foremost Spanish-language media company. It controlled about 80% of the US Spanish-speaking TV market and a long list of radio, music recording as well as digital assets.[1]

The group had seen the light in Los Angeles in the early 1960s under the name Spanish International Network.[2] S.I.N. was an agglomeration of various independent Latino stations orchestrated by American entrepreneur Rene Anselmo and Mexican radio and TV broadcasting executive Emilio Azcárraga Vidaurreta. After going through various owners in the 1980s and 1990s, Univision started trading on the New York Stock Exchange in September 1996 under the stewardship of former artist manager and TV and movie producer Andrew Jerrold Perenchio.

In addition to the flagship Univision brand, the group owned the TeleFutura network and the Galavision cable channel. Since purchasing Hispanic Broadcasting for $3 billion in 2002, it was the leading Spanish-language radio broadcaster in the country.

In February 2006 Univision's board, led by Perenchio for the past 15 years, voted to explore strategic options. The stock price sat 25% below the level of late 2003, so the general sense was that the markets failed to fully appreciate the company's true worth. In fact, the whole media sector had been ignored for some time. While the S&P 500 index was up 20% in the previous two years, the S&P Broadcasting & Cable TV sector index was down 25%.[3] Although Univision was described as the fastest-growing media company in the United States and had a leading position among burgeoning Hispanic audiences,[4] between December 2001 and mid-2006 its stock price had aligned itself with its peers and fallen almost 15%.[5]

Within two months of announcing the strategic review and launching an auction, Univision attracted serious interest from corporate raiders. Mexican telecoms billionaire Carlos Slim purchased a 2.8% stake in the NYSE-listed company. Televisa, the dominant Mexican producer of Latino soap operas called telenovelas, already owned an 11% stake in Univision. But America, the land of free-market advocacy and unfettered capitalism, was oddly protectionist when it came to its broadcasting industry. Realising that the media held so much power and could easily manipulate public opinion, the US Government was not prepared to let non-Americans become a source of propaganda. For that reason, in 1985 Rupert Murdoch had switched his Australian citizenship for an American passport. The move had enabled him over the ensuing decades to build a media empire around the 20th Century Fox Film Corporation. As a foreign entity, Televisa was prevented by US laws from owning more than 25% of an American broadcasting company. At best, it could be a sizeable minority shareholder.

Despite speculative interest, the auction failed to attract bids from major media companies. Regulatory issues were partly to blame. American broadcasters were prohibited from owning TV stations that, when combined, accounted for more than 35% of the nation's audience. That ruled out News Corp, CBS and General Electric's NBC, for instance, as each already covered more than 30% of TV households.

The cap equally affected the valuation that Univision could fetch. Management had sought bids at $40 a share, but the price seemed ambitious given the dearth of strategic bidders.[6] One strong contender was the Televisa-led consortium, which in addition to Venevision Investments, a unit of the Venezuelan Cisneros Group, included a who's who of PE firms: Bain Capital, Bill Gates-backed Cascade, Blackstone, Carlyle and KKR.[7] Televisa, Venevision, and Carlos Slim Domit, a member of Televisa's board and Carlos Slim's son, together owned about 19.5%. To many observers, that gave their bid a crucial edge on the competition.

Yet, after months of negotiations, another bidder made the cut. Blackstone, Carlyle and KKR had unexpectedly pulled out of Televisa's front-running team, which prevented the Mexican group from tabling a compelling offer.[8] On 27 June 2006 Univision announced that it had instead agreed to be acquired by Broadcasting Media Partners, a Delaware holding company set up by a PE consortium comprised of Madison Dearborn, Providence Equity, Texas Pacific Group (TPG), Thomas H. Lee, and media specialist Saban Capital. Representing over 16 times forward EBITDA, the enterprise value stood at $13.7 billion. It was universally seen as excessive, although the winners had only outbid Televisa's team by 50 cents a share, or 1.4% of the total market capitalisation.[9]

## Priced for perfection

No one was surprised that two private equity consortia had been the only credible bidders for a multibillion-dollar acquisition. The enormous glut of capital that had found its way in the buyout markets during the effervescent first years of the new millennium needed to find a home. The real challenge was to find appropriate targets. A business like Univision, with a strong franchise, a leading market position and favourable growth prospects, seemed like a no-brainer.

Based in Los Angeles, Saban Capital was the investment vehicle of Haim Saban, a gifted Israeli-American multitasker who had, at various stages of his life, made a living as a media proprietor, investor, musician, not to mention record, film and TV producer. He had made his fortune when selling his TV and music empire to Walt Disney for $5.2 billion in 2001, the year when he set up Saban Capital.[10] He made another good bet when, in August 2003, he acquired a majority stake in the largest private German television broadcaster, ProSiebenSat.[11] He would eventually make more than 3 times his equity on that deal. Given his operational and sector know-how, Saban was taking on Univision's chairmanship, whilst Perenchio was stepping down, at the age of 76, pocketing about $1.35 billion from his 11.5% stake in the business.[12]

Saban had not partnered with some lightweights. TPG would top the LBO league in 2006 by closing $100 billion worth of deals globally.[13] It was officially the fourth largest buyout firm in the world, raising a combined $30 billion of capital in the ten years to 2007. Providence Equity commanded strong authority in the media microcosm, where it had built deep expertise since its creation by CEO Jonathan Nelson in 1989. Though it had less firepower than TPG's, by gathering $20 billion in the past decade Providence was the world's tenth largest private equity firm. Its influence would no doubt benefit Univision, particularly because Nelson was joining the board of directors. By the same fundraising criteria, Thomas H. Lee – an investor in the $19 billion buyout of outdoor advertiser and radio broadcaster Clear Channel in late 2006 – and Madison Dearborn were ranked 12th and 19th respectively and still warranted proper consideration.[14]

Expectations were high that the collaboration of these big hitters would coalesce into significant value generation. The ownership table looked like this: TPG, Thomas H. Lee and Madison Dearborn each held 23.31%; Providence Equity owned 20.45%; and Saban Capital was left with 6.74%. The five PE investors and their battery of advisers knew that, given the $10 billion the company was borrowing, the slightest hiccup in financial performance would have a cascading negative effect.

After receiving regulatory approval in the early days of 2007, the company launched its debt syndication process. Even if unusually large, the loan package was plain vanilla for those heady days: a covenant-lite $7 billion term loan, a $450 million delayed-draw term loan, a $500 million asset sale bridge loan, and a $750 million revolving credit facility.[15] It also issued $1.5 billion in high-yielding eight-year, non-cash interest-bearing, senior notes.[16] In short, the usual blend of secured and unsecured debt instruments.

At 12.1 times EBITDA, the $10 billion of loans put leverage at 75% of the capital structure.[17] The very steep debt-to-equity ratio forced the company to offer a generous 9.75% interest on its bond in order to attract investors. Another consequence of the stiff leverage was the decision by rating agency Standard & Poor's to cut Univision's corporate credit rating down five notches below investment grade, showing a real possibility of default on some portions of the LBO debt. The outlook was set as 'negative', indicating that additional cuts were likely over the next two years.[18] As one analyst presciently articulated:

> *"Leverage will be one of the highest we have seen. [It will place] a significant burden on a company that is otherwise quite healthy. Management will certainly have increased pressure to perform with little room for error."*[19]

But others were bullish, even if at times confusing in their views. One insisted, in an oddly circular and inverted logic: "It's very levered, but the leverage is actually manageable and supported by the enterprise value of the company." In truth, an enterprise value does not support leverage; the opposite is more common. The higher the leverage, the higher the valuation, essentially because a greater proportion of the deal is funded at the lower cost of debt. That brings down the weighted average cost of capital, which in turns justifies paying a higher price for an asset. A lower cost of capital implies a lower required return on capital.

## Deal rationale

Regardless of the flawed logic in the analysts' thinking, there were other solid arguments in favour of the transaction.

### Market position

Univision held a strong position in the media sector. Its assets included the namesake network, ranked as the fifth largest TV network in America regardless of language, as well as dozens of free-to-air and cable television stations, 73 radio stations, record labels and Web operations.[20] The company was the undisputed leading Spanish-language broadcaster, dwarfing its closest rival Telemundo. Univision's audience was more than four times Telemundo's at the time of the buyout.[21]

### Demand growth potential

The Hispanic population was the fastest growing in America. Between 1980 and 2000 the number of Hispanics had grown from 15 million to 35 million, seeing their share of the country's population rise from less than 7% to 12.5% over the same period. In the 1990s the Hispanic population in America had seen a rate of growth approximately seven times that of the non-Hispanic population.[22] By 2005 Hispanics accounted for 14.5% of the US population.[23] At the time of Univision's LBO, this trend was widely expected to continue. And these projections proved correct. According to the US Census Bureau, the Hispanic proportion of the population reached 17.6% in July 2015.

*Media consumption expectations*

The target audience was split between 14 million US Hispanics who were Spanish-dominant consumers and 36 million who alternated between Spanish-language and English-language channels.[24] Not only was this core audience expected to keep growing in line with the rise in the number of Hispanics in the country, but the consumption of TV content was also projected to grow as this audience was getting richer.

Between 1980 and 2000 the median annual household income of the Hispanic population across the US had increased from $36,700 to slightly more than $45,700. As the buying power of Univision's audience rose, Hispanics would consume more entertainment, as typically occurs with better-off consumers. The popularity of Spanish-language programming was forecast to continue.

*Loyal target audience means advertising revenue growth*

In the media world, advertisers are looking for a captive audience. Univision's predicted growth in viewership was to drive demand from advertisers. The broadcaster ranked as the fifth network in primetime among all key demographics, but in the 18-34 age group it out-delivered ABC, CBS, NBC or FOX 40% of the time.[25]

For the past 15 years the company had been run by Perenchio and his COO Ray Rodriguez. Both had huge experience in the entertainment industry. Their talent had helped to create Univision's ever-changing content and to build a very loyal audience. But leveraged buyouts need that little bit extra: operational adaptability coupled with a neurotic devotion to cash maximisation. The PE consortium's explicit course of action was to monetise Univision's content by boosting advertising revenues. Upon Perenchio's exit from the business, in February 2007 the financial sponsors announced that they were bringing in a CEO with a formidable career in advertising: Joe Uva, head of OMD, a media buying agency owned by advertising giant Omnicom.[26] His goal was to convert Univision's high ratings into an advertising gold mine.

*Profitability and predictability mean leverageability*

In the five years leading up to the buyout, the company had recorded EBITDA margins in the low- to mid-30s. Bankers love lending to such corporations. The ideal borrower must demonstrate predictability and steady cash flow generation to service its debt, a point made in Chapter 3.

*Deregulation*

The PE owners were not just interested in the target's cash flows. For years, lobbying by media groups had tried to influence the American Government into raising the ownership and coverage caps. In 2003 the industry's regulator, the Federal Communications Commission (FCC), had considered raising the coverage cap from 35% to 45% of the country's households, but the proposal was struck down by the Court of Appeals.

Saban's consortium was hoping that an upcoming change in ownership laws – allowing foreign groups to hold more than 25% of a domestic broadcaster's stock – would create a great uplift to Univision's valuation. That was pure speculation, but in effect it was a free option. Deregulation could simply bring in a positive valuation-multiple arbitrage upon exit.

## If you won't join them, sue them

At the time of the auction, many had expressed surprise that Televisa lost out. Rejecting an invitation by the winning consortium to embark on this promising LBO adventure, Televisa announced in July 2006 that it wanted to sell its 11.4% stake, before declaring that it might in fact counterbid.[27] The synergies between the Mexican company and Univision should have allowed the former to outbid the Saban-led team. For a start, Televisa provided the bulk of Univision's prime-time programming.

Acknowledging that fact, the winning consortium considered granting Televisa the option to increase its ownership in Univision to 19.9%. Eventually, the Mexican group chose not to. Instead, it elected to pocket $1.1 billion by selling its minority stake in April 2007,[28] at what it probably considered a very good price. Then, after the rough-and-tumble of the auction, Televisa proceeded to sue its business partner, arguing that Univision had breached the programme licensing agreement that tied the two broadcasters for another ten years. Allegedly, the defendant had failed to include $700 million of ad sales in its contractual reporting to the Mexican broadcaster.[29]

Adding to Univision's misfortune, the Credit Crunch started taking its toll. In the summer of 2007 the $7 billion covenant-lite term loan, Univision's best secured notes, traded at 93 cents on the dollar. By January 2008 it was 10 cents below par.[30] Cash had to be produced urgently, if need be by disposing of non-core assets.

Despite the slowing economy, the first quarter of 2008 saw trading continue to edge up, with revenues and EBITDA both rising 6% year on year. But in the face of a weakening advertising market, the company's liquidity suffered. Rating agencies Moody's and Standard & Poor's decided to downgrade the debt. By now, Univision's term loan was trading at a 15% discount.[31]

In April, management was compelled to draw down $700 million from the $750 million revolving credit facility, a short-term facility aimed at dealing with pressing cash needs. In the tight credit environment, management preferred to take out its committed bank financing. As one banker expounded:

> *"If a company loses access to the capital markets, it is going to drown slowly. But if it loses access to liquidity, it is like a bullet to the head. They can't fund their operations and they would be forced into bankruptcy."*[32]

Yet that meant the company's leverage was now 12.8 times larger than its EBITDA. The markets were anticipating trouble ahead, with Univision's bank loans trading at a 25% discount by May. That month the company sold its music division, receiving $150 million for it, about half what analysts had predicted.[33] The prevailing Credit Crunch was not the best time to fetch good prices for second-tier assets.

Results soon flagged. In the quarter to 30 June 2008, earnings were down 11% on the prior year, raising the debt-to-EBITDA ratio above 13.2 times.[34] Not surprisingly, given the prevailing economic environment, for the third quarter of 2008 trading continued to underwhelm. Univision reported EBITDA of $218 million in the quarter to September, down 7% year on year. Weak advertising market conditions explain why, by November, the company's unsecured bonds were trading at distressed levels: about 20 cents on the dollar.[35] Even the bank debt wasn't safe. In October, Standard & Poor's downgraded the secured loans' recovery rating, indicating that lenders could lose 30% to 50% of their money.[36]

Through the year the ongoing litigation with Televisa had acted like a 'Sword of Damocles', putting significant pricing pressure on Univision's bonds. In September, Televisa had demonstrated its market power by granting Mexican premier-league home soccer games to Telemundo, Univision's main US competitor owned by General Electric. Thanks to its hard-ball tactics, in January 2009 Televisa won concessions valued at more than $600 million from Univision to settle a case over the sharing of ad revenue. Televisa had alleged that Univision excluded certain programmes from a 25-year deal that called for Univision to share its advertising revenue with Televisa, even from shows that weren't made by the Mexican company. The concessions also included a new licensing agreement granting Televisa annual free air time. Upon the settlement, Univision's bank loans traded up but were still quoted at 50 cents on the dollar.[37]

The economy was not kind to Univision. In the first quarter of 2009 revenues fell 12% year on year. The radio broadcasting division experienced a major market correction, losing more than a quarter of its sales. But at group level, earnings benefited from advertising revenue recognition related to the new Televisa contract. Management hadn't remained idle either and cost-cutting had played its part. EBITDA was up 3.5% that quarter.[38] Acknowledging the company's travails, Providence wrote down its stake in Univision to 50% of cost while TPG marked it down to about 70 cents on the dollar.[39] But within months these valuations looked optimistic as Univision depreciated its assets by more than $5 billion, leading industry insiders to value the business at $9 billion, slightly less than the debt it owed.[40] For all intents and purposes, the equity portion was worthless.

With the litigation risk dealt with, the company decided to roll over part of its subordinated loans by postponing interest repayment.[41] When these 9.75% yielding loans had been issued two years earlier, an investor had expressed doubt that Univision would ever need to use the roll-over clause, adding that it was "a stable, even growing, business."[42] In the worst recession of the past 70 years, however, advertising-based media companies did not fare so well. To preserve as much liquidity as possible, management had little choice but to trigger the clause. Leveraged to the hilt – its total debt-to-EBITDA multiple was roughly 14.8 times for the 12 months ended 31 March 2009 –[43] the company was in survival mode.

As evidence, in June 2009 it reached an agreement with lenders to amend the senior credit facility (the part of the debt package that was best rated because most secured). In exchange for a consent fee, the leverage covenant was relaxed and a new $545 million tranche was issued to refinance existing notes. That gave the business some welcome breathing space, but it came at a hefty price – the new tranche had to offer a 14% annual yield to attract risk-wary investors.[44]

The new economic conditions were no longer about growth. Rather, they called for damage limitation, operational restructuring and financial re-engineering. That wasn't much fun for a commercial mind like Ray Rodriguez, President and COO of the media group. In August, he threw in the towel and announced his retirement. A native of Cuba, before joining Univision 19 years earlier Rodriguez had been the worldwide manager of well-known entertainer Julio Iglesias. Some of the decisions he was not a fan of involved headcount reductions: 300 staff had been let go in 2009.[45] The traditional, paternalistic management style was making room for more hands-on cash maximisation and debt management techniques. Rodriguez would have preferred to leave Univision on a higher note, but he knew that if the business was ever going to turn around, it would take years. It also required dealing with one of the most complex of ownership structures, reporting to five overbearing PE firms. His departure would be the first of many at the top echelons. A lot more pain was to come.

Market competition noticeably intensified. Rival broadcaster Telemundo launched a joint-venture cable channel aimed at Mexico and Latin America as part of its 16-month-old alliance with Televisa. Telemundo was reaping the benefits of the tense relationship between Univision and Televisa. In America, Telemundo still trailed in terms of ratings, but it had increased its share of the Spanish-language market in the past year from 23% to 30%.[46] By contrast, for the second year in a row, in 2009 Univision's revenues were down. Even though efficiency improvements helped boost EBITDA margin, in mid-2010 TPG admitted writing down by two-thirds its $837 million of equity deployed in the business.[47]

## If you can't beat them, join them

The advertising downturn provoked by the Great Recession eventually opened the door for Univision and Televisa to bury the hatchet and to extend and expand their licensing agreement. In October 2010 Televisa offered to pay $1.2 billion for an initial 5% stake in Univision, a chunk of 15-year debt convertible into an additional 30% equity stake, and an option to buy 5% more. Valuing the company's equity at $2.3 billion,[48] it crystallised an equity loss of $1.4 billion, or almost two-fifths of the $3.7 billion invested by the PE quintet.

Televisa had made $1.3 billion by selling its 11.5% stake to the financial sponsors back in 2007, only to reinvest three and a half years later for slightly less than 40% of the business. The Mexican group had had a lucky escape when it was outbid by Broadcasting Media. Sometimes the bitter taste of failure turns into the sweetest smell of success.

In exchange for paying higher fees to its Mexican business partner, Univision would get rights to use Televisa's Spanish-language soap operas and sports programming across all distribution channels, including via the Web. The agreement would both reduce production costs and increase ad revenue. After years of hostility the two media groups' agendas had finally dovetailed.

For the PE owners, already four years into the deal, locking in Televisa and more of its content could accelerate Univision's recovery. The use of Televisa's cash injection to trim the company's expensive loans as well as the maturity extension of three-quarters of the debt by 2.5 years reassured Moody's, which upgraded the group's outlook to stable.[49] Since leverage was still stuck at 10 times EBITDA, boosting the top line was not a luxury but the only hope to ever make a profit from this investment. With a strategic partner now acting as a cornerstone shareholder, for the first time since the buyout, Univision presented promising prospects.

The media group's refinancing process continued unabated during the last quarter of 2010, with two tranches of bonds raising a total of $1.25 billion to repay a portion of the shorter-dated loans. It was quickly topped up with a $315 million add-on in the first days of 2011.[50] The incessant financial restructuring was taking its toll on management. In March 2011 Univision announced that CEO Joe Uva had decided not to renew his contract. While the company's debt burden was eased by Televisa's recent capital injection, after four years at the helm Uva believed that there was more upside elsewhere, declaring: "The team is strong and I have decided the time is right for me to capitalise on other opportunities."[51] Chief Operating Officer Randy Falco, who had joined the Spanish-language network just three months earlier, was soon kicked upstairs as market pundits believed an IPO could take place within a year.

A New Yorker of Italian-American and German extraction, Falco was under pressure to prove his credentials to run the country's leading Hispanic media group. To critics, he quipped: "I speak the language of television. I speak the language of culture."[52] Regardless of his limited grasp of Spanish, he was taking over at a time when Univision was turning a corner thanks to the fast-recovering economy. His mandate included accelerating talks with distributors about so-called 'over-the-top' deals to get Univision's shows online to cable TV and Netflix subscribers. The debt-heavy company needed to lift cash flows to meet ongoing liabilities.

Within weeks of Uva's departure, the company cleaned up its balance sheet by launching a new high-yield bond of $600 million aimed at repaying another tranche of short-dated notes due in 2014.[53] Management was in a race to buy itself some time, pushing its debt wall as far back as possible. It was becoming self-evident to all parties that the LBO sponsors and lenders were in it for the very long haul.

For that reason, management spent the following three years rearranging the company's capital structure. In the first eight months of 2012 Univision pushed out more of its near-term maturities by issuing two tranches of secured notes worth a total of $1.2 billion.[54] Leverage remained high and a key preoccupation, with net debt still worth 9.7 times EBITDA. Then, in the first half of 2013, the group extended its debt maturities once more by issuing fresh term loans of $1.5 billion and a 10-year note worth $500 million to eliminate the remaining tranches scheduled to mature over the next three years.[55] Finally, in January of the following year the company launched a covenant-lite $3.4 billion loan to redeem its remaining short-dated debt.[56]

## Seeking a way out

In mid-2014 it was reported that Univision was up for sale with a $20 billion headline price. CBS and Time Warmer were the obvious buyers, though the suggested valuation was a bit rich. But the timing seemed right. Advertisers had returned following three years of budget cuts. Univision's focus on the Hispanic community was proving a strong angle for advertisers, which had somewhat failed to appreciate the economic potential of this demographic. TV advertising spending was in a robust recovery, helping the company's revenues in the first quarter of 2014 to rise 10%.[57] For the full year, the top line also recorded double-digit growth while EBITDA margin reached 42%, its highest level since the LBO.[58] In late December, Moody's upgraded Univision's enchanted labyrinth of debt, easing the path to a stock market float.[59] The broadcaster's media rights for the soccer World Cup that year had been a boon.

Yet, one ongoing market development promised to pile up woes for the media group and to affect its valuation. New outlets for programming were cropping up all the time: early 2013 had seen streaming media and video-on-demand provider Netflix enter the content-production segment. Web giant Amazon soon followed suit.

In 2015 Univision was due to 'celebrate' its ninth year under private equity ownership. It was intriguing that despite numerous loan maturity extensions, covenant amendments and earnings adjustments, the group had retained the same chief financial officer. That all changed when Andrew Hobson, CFO since the buyout, unexpectedly resigned in February of that year. With the group for the past twenty years, Hobson had dealt with Univision's first IPO in 1996 and was widely expected to lead the relisting of the media broadcaster. Despairing that Univision would ever emerge from its bout of debt-induced fever – the company had tapped the debt markets six times in the past three years – or running out of patience as the IPO was repeatedly delayed due to market headwinds, the finance chief was just another casualty of a distressed leveraged buyout well past its sell-by date.

Nevertheless, within weeks of his departure, Goldman Sachs, Morgan Stanley and Deutsche Bank prepared the ground for the listing, aiming to facilitate a $1 billion capital raise at a $20 billion valuation. With EBITDA of $1.2 billion on $2.9 billion of sales in the year to December 2014, the 16 times earnings multiple looked ambitious, at about twice industry comparables. But it also implied that the original $3.4 billion poured in by the PE consortium eight years earlier had tripled in value. An exit at that price would be an astonishing achievement, though TPG was a little more circumspect in its expectations, valuing its equity ticket up a third, to $1.14 billion, in a quarterly report.[60] Such a valuation yielded an anaemic yearly rate of return of only 4.2%,[61] before applying the firm's management fees.

Despite the finance chief's untimely departure, the company carried on with its endless capital restructuring, issuing in April over $800 million in high-coupon debt, only two months after completing another $1.25 billion bond refinancing.[62] By rescheduling these loans Univision's shareholders and corporate executives were buying time to fulfil their growth plan and orchestrate an exit in an economy that was getting ever more bullish.

## Bruised and battered

Unexpectedly, despite the brighter conditions, things got very political. In June 2015 Univision became embroiled in a legal battle with Donald Trump, the Republican presidential candidate. After dropping coverage of the Miss USA Pageant, which Trump partly owned, following incendiary and vinegary remarks the presidential candidate had made about Mexican immigrants, Univision became the subject of a $500 million lawsuit by The Trump Organization for breach of contract.[63]

Regardless, in July, five months after changing its CFO, the company registered for an IPO.[64] The owners were ready for the next episode of the PE saga: heading for the door. To offer adequate visibility on its medium-term performance, the group signed a five-year extension of its licensing agreement with Televisa. In exchange, over $1.1 billion of the latter's debentures, invested in 2010, were converted into common stock, granting the Mexican group 22% of Univision's voting rights, plus the conversion of warrants post-IPO.[65] In its listing prospectus, the company showed a balance sheet that was still bloated with debt.[66] The note conversion by Televisa reduced Univision's debt-to-EBITDA ratio to 7.8 times, down from 9.0 times,[67] but Moody's improved credit rating was still a full five notches into junk territory.

The company had the bulk of its loans due between 2018 and 2020, though the unsecured and secured bonds had maturities that stretched as far as 2025, almost 20 years after the LBO! Instead of taking the keys off the PE owners, the lenders had elected to earn fees in exchange for amending and extending the loans. The debt load cost the company $550 million a year in interest expenses and an additional $55 million on rate swaps to hedge the interest risk, so the creditors were richly rewarded for their gracious understanding.[68]

For the relisting to occur, Univision needed to deliver stable operating performance for a couple of quarters. Unfortunately, the third-quarter was negatively impacted by the unfavourable prior-year comparable numbers, which included advertising revenues related to the soccer World Cup.[69] Looking at full-year numbers, the broadcaster reported a 2% drop in revenues, partly impacted by the abnormally strong 2014 financial results and by the fact that 2015 was not an election year, which reduced the amount of political ad revenues. The persistent underperformance of the radio unit – a phenomenon that affected the entire industry as audience continued to migrate online to access ad-free music downloading and streaming platforms – led to $140 million of impairment charges.[70] On 4 December 2015, in the face of poor recent performance from media stocks, Univision pulled the plug on its proposed relisting.[71]

The year 2015 would have been ideal for Univision's PE owners to exit. The fact that the media group had the media rights to the 2014 World Cup had boosted revenues the previous year. Since Univision did not plan to carry the World Cups in 2018 and 2022, no such uplift could be expected further out.[72] Accordingly, in May 2016 more realistic valuation expectations were broadcast, although the suggested enterprise value of $16 billion represented an EBITDA multiple in excess of 12 times – 50% above market comparables. The PE owners still hadn't internalised the significant value correction media stocks had registered in the past decade.

To make exit plans more plausible, Univision was active on the M&A front throughout 2016. In January it absorbed a 40% stake in satirical news site The Onion; three months later it bought ABC's 50% stake in The Fusion network, a loss-making joint venture Univision had launched with ABC to specifically cater to millennial viewers; and in

August it got the green light to acquire six Gawker Media sites for $135 million.[73]

But all this corporate activity was hiding an uncomfortable truth: Univision was losing market share in its mainstream TV segment, which represented about 90% of revenues. Telemundo had gradually gnawed at Univision's audience, beating the PE-backed broadcaster in primetime viewership among their core demographics: the 18-to-49-year olds. As can be gathered from Table 4.1, Univision suffered from double-digit audience erosion to a degree much greater than any other major broadcaster had. Importantly, Telemundo's ratings had gone up appreciably in both 2015 and 2016.

**Table 4.1 – Change in ratings for the main US TV broadcasters in 2014, 2015 and 2016**

|  | 2014 | 2015 | 2016 |
|---|---|---|---|
| ABC | -4% | -1% | -8% |
| CBS | -7% | -1% | -7% |
| NBC | +19% | -9% | +12% |
| FOX | -10% | -8% | -5% |
| Telemundo | -5% | +10% | +5% |
| **Univision** | **-17%** | **-15%** | **-24%** |
| Average | -2% | -5% | -3% |
| Hispanic Average | -14% | -7% | -13% |

*Source: Bloomberg, Nielsen Live + 3 Day Prime Time Ratings, CreditSights*

In November 2016, amid a persistent drop in ratings – in the previous four years Univision had lost nearly half its primetime audience – management announced another round of layoffs, cutting 250 jobs.[74]

Yet, overall 2016 had been a strong year. Revenues had grown more than 6% thanks to political advertising for the presidential election campaign. EBITDA margin was now at 46%, its highest level ever, as the fall in sales and administrative expenses offset the rise in programming costs. With such strong operating performance, the company was able to reduce its leverage, with the debt to earnings ratio falling below 6.5 times for the first time since the buyout a decade earlier (see Figure 4.1).

Figure 4.1 – Univision's EBITDA and leverage ratio from 2006 to 2016

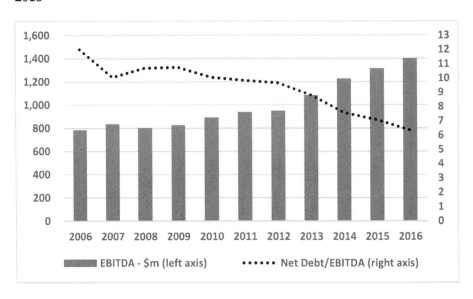

*Source: Company filings and author's analysis*

## ¡Ay, caramba!

It looked like the group was heading in the right direction, but the healthy earnings numbers reported by management were in fact the product of wishful accounting. On an unadjusted basis, the picture wasn't so rosy. In 2006 the last full financial year before the PE consortium took ownership, Univision had recorded operating margin of 30.8%. Ten years later operating margin was in the low 20s. In every single year between 2010 and 2015 Univision had recorded significant impairment losses, restructuring charges and various extraordinary expenses. They exceeded $1.3 billion over that period. When they occur on a yearly basis, restructuring charges can no longer be treated as exceptional. So, what went wrong?

*Increasing competition for Hispanic audience*

Between 2006 and 2016 Telemundo's primetime viewership doubled to 1.7 million; over the same period Univision's audience halved to 1.75 million.[75] Telemundo attracted more viewers in the sweet spot for advertisers — viewers aged 18 through 49 — in part because of its strong offering of sports events, in particular soccer, a big draw for Hispanic viewers. Univision relied for too long on Televisa's supply of telenovelas, but these mushy, over-the-top Cinderella love stories were upstaged – Telemundo's ratings beat Univision's on four occasions during the 2014–15 television season on nights when the former aired sports events.

In addition, Telemundo unashamedly provided a wide range of soap operas aimed at competing with its rival's core product. It launched the 'Super Series' telenovela format, more action-oriented and using the model common with English language drama series: multiple seasons, shorter episodes, and the incorporation of storylines more relatable to American audiences, a welcome improvement on Univision's Mexican sourced content. Unsurprisingly, in response to Telemundo's inroads and new products targeting Hispanics by the Fox and Discovery networks, Univision launched several new cable networks alongside its free-to-air channels. It started to Americanise its programmes and its fastest growing outlet was the sports-dedicated Univision Deportes.

The competitive threat was constantly evolving. As a case in point, on 18 January 2017, two days before President-elect Trump's inauguration,

Mexico's richest man Carlos Slim announced that he was launching a new US channel 'focused on Mexicans, made by Mexicans and transmitted from Mexico'.[76]

## Digital trends

Many blamed Univision's plight on the fickle millennials, specifically their infinite taste for social networking, self-promotion, user-generated content, and the ensuing fragmentation of audience. For sure the march of technological disruption had been relentless; the loss of young viewers was precipitous. Between 2010 and 2015 the number of those aged 18 to 34 who watched Univision's prime-time schedule dropped by 45%.[77] Without a stable audience, earnings and cash flows were under pressure, endangering the heavily indebted company. Nothing, not even Univision's unique brand, could escape the corrosive chaos of digital disruption.

Univision's audience dwindled partly because of the fundamental shift in consumer tastes in favour of online offerings. Pure Internet players had disrupted the field. Following its success in short, TV-style content, Amazon launched its film-production activities Amazon Studios in early 2015, two years after Netflix had unsettled the world of TV broadcasting with its political thriller series House of Cards.

Although Univision retained strong TV businesses, its online activities were almost irrelevant. It attempted to distribute more of its content online through partnerships, including with online video platform Hulu in 2011, but the gradual shift of audience to the Web turned into a veritable tsunami that threatened Univision's traditional TV-based ad revenue model. The ham-fisted 2016 acquisitions of The Onion and Gawker were meant to seed an online portfolio, particularly to reach a younger audience. Yet they raised a few questions. Could a traditional media broadcaster buy its way into online success? And were these assets compatible with Univision's existing offering? Questions that would take time to address, but time was a luxury the PE owners could ill-afford, as their holding period gingerly passed the twelve-year mark.

Despite its Internet portfolio, Univision does not have the algorithmic, network-based intelligence of an Amazon or Netflix. And that is an issue for advertisers palpably keen to ensure that their money hits the bull's eye. If they feel that their advertising spend is wasted, they will move it to online platforms best able to profile and segmentalise viewers and consumers.

*Margin squeeze*

One of the consequences of online competition was rising programming costs. In principle, it should have provoked a consolidation of the sector as media companies sought to capture synergies and efficiency derived from running larger operations. But regulators did not move swiftly enough, failing to acknowledge that their traditional view of content broadcasting and the limits they set on market share of TV audiences was no longer applicable in a world where Internet service providers were producing and distributing third-party content as well as their own.

*Contentious relationship with main supplier Televisa*

Another factor that was always going to represent an unwelcome risk for Univision was its heavy dependence on Televisa. The latter supplied over one-third of Univision's television programming and more than half of its content across other platforms. As a general rule, the best candidates for LBOs are companies that do not rely on one or several large suppliers or customers. Being so reliant puts future cash flows at risk since it weakens a company's bargaining power vis-à-vis business partners. As we saw with the Mergermarket case study, future cash flow visibility is one of the most valuable drivers of success. It offers a form of security to lenders. Univision was being held hostage by its main content supplier. Value migrated from Univision to Televisa.

Televisa proved an unreliable partner, selling its 11% stake in 2007 before choosing to repurchase a 5% stake plus options three years later. It initially tried to walk away from its exclusivity agreement on content development before reverting course. It is certain that it could have hurt Univision's operations if Televisa had decided to stop providing content. In the end, it used Univision's stressed balance sheet as an excuse to negotiate better terms for itself. And it offered Telemundo access to proprietary content for competing programmes to demonstrate its negotiating power.

## Layoffs

At the end of 2006, Univision employed 4,233 people. Ten years later, the group had approximately 4,000 employees.[78] Over the same period, net revenues rose 50%. Univision's operating efficiency had come at the expense of its workforce.

Perforce, the multi-pronged strain of digital migration of its young audience, pricing pressure from Televisa and a heavy debt load led management to introduce retrenchment initiatives. In early 2009 Univision fired 300 staff. In the spring of 2014 it cut dozens of workers as part of the restructuring of its radio division. In November 2016, up to 250 layoffs were announced as the company reported a third-quarter net loss of $30.5 million and an 8% drop in revenues. In 2017 the company went through another round of layoffs, including several of its programming executives and news anchor journalists.[79]

## Economic slump

Perhaps the greatest negative impact on Univision's growth came from the Great Recession. Advertising spend is very cyclical. Advertisers cut their budgets when the economy goes through a down cycle. From 2008 to 2010 America experienced its worst recession in eighty years. Among other factors, the collapse of the auto industry, one of television's biggest advertisers, hurt revenue.

*Buying at the top*

For the first quarter of 2006, the last one Univision reported on before announcing the buyout, the company had seen profit rise 21%. Univision was on its way to record a fantastic second quarter thanks to the programming of the soccer World Cup.[80] Univision was riding high as the economy was at boiling point.

It was not just the economy that was at its peak. The credit markets were also frothy. In a world where combative overconfidence is a badge of honour and the size of one's deals is a matter of pride, the period going from 2005 to 2007 had seen a rush to close ever larger LBO transactions. Hugely dependent on debt, mega deals the size of Univision could only be completed in a hot credit environment. But they sported extravagant valuations.

The Univision buyout was priced for perfection. It assumed booming demand, not the toughest economic environment in three generations. It conjectured for television to endure as the main broadcasting and creative medium, with the Internet remaining an essentially passive advertising platform. Mobile videos were not even born yet, so they never came on the radar as a potential competing channel.

Reality had been far from perfect. When the economy flatlined, Univision rested on rickety foundations. TV broadcasting licenses were no longer the barriers to entry they once were. Perhaps the best indication that the price had been excessive was the decision taken by KKR and Blackstone, traditionally pretty aggressive bidders, to walk away from the auction on valuation grounds – although their move was partly due to the degree of management control Televisa requested.[81]

*Complex investment consortium*

In order to claim the crown of the LBO Hall of Fame, the largest private equity firms did not choose to partner lightly. Although they preferred to lead transactions, every now and then, especially for large transactions, the likes of TPG and Providence needed to find other firms to ally with. It had the dual benefit of reducing exposure to one single deal and of eliminating competitive tension. This idea that it was better for all bidders to combine forces rather than compete would eventually lead to a full SEC investigation (as discussed in Chapter 9). In truth, the main drawback of setting up deal consortia is that it made decision-making less fluid, a very important point when an investment turns sour.

### Regulatory hurdle

The hoped-for deregulation had not materialised in the first decade of what must have been an intensely painful experience for management. Regulatory clearance remained a stumbling block for M&A. This was partly to blame for the failed trade sale process in 2014, leaving an IPO as the only credible exit option for existing shareholders – after the rough road travelled by the business since its 2007 LBO, no private equity firm would be valiant enough to have a go at a secondary buyout.

On 4 January 2017 the FCC announced that the mandatory ceiling applied to foreign ownership of US media outlets might be raised from 25% to 49%.[82] If the change was implemented, Televisa would be able to increase its stake in Univision, making an IPO exit scenario less of a necessity. Through its stock holding and warrants, the Mexican media group owned 38% of Univision on a fully diluted, as converted basis. But it was not allowed to hold more than 25% of the voting rights, limiting the appeal of making a bid for Univision.[83] Equally, the latter's strong dependence on Televisa's content made an acquisition by CBS, Fox or any other American network a long shot. Sadly, for the PE owners, the lack of M&A alternatives could only negatively impact their portfolio company's valuation.

> *Borrowing to excess*
>
> With a 12 times EBITDA multiple at the outset, the LBO loan package was at the top end of what is permissible for corporations with excellent credit and perfect market conditions. No other major media company in the US had a debt multiple in excess of 8 times.[84] Four years after the transaction, Univision's leverage still stood at 10 times earnings. The lack of progress on cash generation made the compounding effect of interest untenable, hence the numerous refinancings. As the US economy slowly recovered trading improved, with EBITDA growing from $900 million in 2010 to $1.3 billion in 2015, bringing the company's leverage down to a still punchy 7 times cash earnings in that last year.

## A new story line?

At the time of the LBO, one of Univision's most popular shows, appropriately produced by Televisa, was the soap opera 'Amarte es mi Pecado' (Loving You is My Sin), in which the naïve heroine is sold by her stepmother to the richest man in town, attempts suicide, is rescued, and falls in love with her rescuer...all in the first handful of 95 episodes. The Univision LBO went through as many twists as a telenovela, which wasn't helped by the on-and-off relationship with Televisa.

The cost of private equity's unrequited love for credit had been a series of corporate lows and financial downs, layoffs and management reshuffles, covenant breaches and loan extensions. It turned out like so many love stories, overwhelmed by the drudging routine and obligations of life commitment. After more than a decade of meticulously servicing its LBO debt, Univision was stuck in a strained financial intercourse, unable to escape its cruel condition of corporate zombie. But once it has turned into a zombie, an LBO is like nuclear waste. No one wants it in its neighbourhood, let alone in its own backyard. Hence the difficulty to dispose of it.

Struggling to meet debt payments, Univision cut back on programming. Logically, that led to audience loss,[85] which impacted revenue and earnings. According to a report prepared by the North American labour union UNITE HERE, the compound growth rate of Univision's EBITDA from 2006 through 2015 was 0.36%.[86] The same report indicated that the PE consortium charged more than $570 million in management and monitoring fees in the first nine years of ownership. Ahead of its expected IPO in July 2015, the consortium was paid $180 million for allowing Univision to terminate the contract.[87] Yet this kind of goose-plucking is standard practice in private equity.

In its resilience and ability to absorb a decade of PE abuse, Univision is a testament to the enduring and growing influence of Latinos in America. Each year between 2009 and 2015, the group's revenues topped the previous year's numbers. Thanks to the growing economic influence of its target audience, the broadcaster reached viewership parity with the five major English language television networks and remained, as advertised by its promotional slogan, 'The Hispanic Heartbeat of the United States.'

In 2017, as a new President entered the White House with an agenda that could hardly be described as pro-Latino, what with Trump's numerous provocative statements towards Mexicans and the Cuban regime, more than ever the Hispanic community across America needed a strong Univision, something that billions of dollars in LBO debt could only hinder. The travails of the economy during the Great Recession, the relentless digitalisation of media content and distribution, to say nothing of a POTUS hostile to the company's target audience, showed how fragile success could be in private equity.

## Double vision

If all you know about Univision is what you have read in these pages, you might think that it was difficult to predict such a lousy outcome. This is where remembering the past can come handy. Believe it or not, this was not Univision's first foray into the thrilling world of leveraged buyouts.

The company's first debt-fuelled experience took place during the previous LBO bubble, of the late 1980s. In a strange case of venturing too far from your core expertise, in November 1987 Hallmark Cards, one of America's largest manufacturers of greetings cards, partnered with the venture capital arm of First Chicago Corporation to acquire Univision, at the time already one of the nation's largest Spanish-language television broadcasters. In a $300 million buyout, the owners then merged Univision with ten Spanish-language TV stations they had acquired the year before. Three years later, unable to meet the upward ratchet of loan commitments in the face of a sudden economic downturn, the company was on the verge of bankruptcy.[88] How do you say *déjà vu* in Spanish?

After long and arduous negotiations by Hallmark Cards to repurchase parts of the LBO loans from the company's lenders, Univision avoided what could have been an embarrassing spell under Chapter 11.[89] The company was eventually sold in April 1992 to Hollywood producer Andrew Jerrold Perenchio and Emilio Azcárraga Milmo, the latter being the son of Univision's co-founder Emilio Azcárraga Vidaurreta.[90]

Fifteen years later, Univision's commanding market position gave private equity bidders the misguided notion that the company could grow its way out of a stretched capital structure. Instead, the valuations of traditional media assets greatly suffered in the years following the financial crisis, with advertisers reallocating their budgets to more flexible platforms, essentially because consumers moved online, preferring the convenience of on-demand content to the pre-set scheduling of a TV broadcaster.

Where the tale takes the turn of a real-life telenovela is in the identity of the owner and CEO of Televisa. His name is Emilio Fernando Azcárraga Jean III, the grandson of Emilio Azcárraga Vidaurreta, the latter a co-owner of Univision from the early 1960s until 1987, when he had been coerced by the American Government into disposing of his majority stake to Hallmark and First Chicago on the grounds that, by law, as a foreigner he could not own more than 25% of a US broadcaster.[91] Thirty years later his grandson was trying to reclaim what he felt was rightfully his.

## Blurred vision

Televisa had sold its stake in 2006 after its bid had been rebuffed. It then spent the next few years undermining Univision's economics by suing the TV broadcaster and renegotiating the terms of their content distribution agreement, before finally reinvesting at a much lower valuation when the company was at its weakest. Similarly, Perenchio had shown uncanny skills in his timing by buying Univision at the bottom (during the 1992-93 recession) before selling at the peak in 2006. Supposedly savvy fund managers had been taught an expensive lesson in terms of timing one's investment by two less 'sophisticated' strategic investors.

In retrospect, the PE investors' decision to pay in excess of 16 times EBITDA for a business that had come within an ace of bankruptcy 15 years earlier seems foolhardy, speculative and careless all at once. In their classic ebullient style, the financial sponsors had overcooked it. The private equity model dictates that portfolio assets should be exited within four to five years. Due to the time value of money, any asset stuck in portfolio beyond that timeframe hurts returns, penalising the entire vintage fund. Companies like Univision that stay in-house for more than a decade are literally life threatening for any fund manager wishing to raise a subsequent investment vehicle.

TPG had invested in Univision via its fund V. The same vehicle was used to participate in other ill-judged LBOs, including ultimately bankrupt casino operator Caesars Entertainment and energy group TXU. Some of TPG's largest LP investors were massively exposed to the fund. Retirement-plan manager CalSTRS had committed $1 billion and its peer CalPERS was on the hook for $600 million. With an annualised rate of return of 4% to 5%, TPG Partners V was a bottom-quartile performer.[92] Predictably, both CalSTRS and CalPERS passed on the opportunity to commit to TPG Partners VII, raised in 2015.

Thomas H. Lee managed to raise its seventh fund in 2014, even though its previous vintage of 2006 – impacted by the long holding periods of its two media assets Univision and Clear Channel – had yielded a third-quartile performance. Burnt on the 2006 vehicle, CalPERS again opted out of the new one.

Madison Dearborn and Providence Equity had made the school-boy error of investing into Univision via not just one but two of their funds. Accordingly, their performance was doubly affected. Madison's funds IV and V, raised in 2000 and 2006 respectively, delivered second- and third-quartile returns, and long-time backer CalPERS elected not to participate in the fund VII raised in 2014.

Providence Equity V (vintage 2005) and VI (2007) showed internal rates of return of less than 4% and 6% respectively,[93] failing to beat the public stock markets. In fairness to Univision, it was not the worse asset in Providence's portfolio: in 2010 the PE firm had lost hundreds of millions of dollars when the film studio Metro-Goldwyn-Mayer went bankrupt, and five years later another investee – security screener Altegrity – also went under in the face of fraud allegations, wiping out $800 million of the PE firm's equity.[94] Both Providence's vintages delivered bottom-quartile returns.

Unsurprisingly, Providence Equity was at pain to raise a subsequent fund, but eventually it secured $5 billion for its seventh vehicle in 2013, significantly less than the $12 billion committed to Fund VI before the financial crisis. CalSTRS and CalPERS, two of Providence's largest investors in vintages V and VI, chose not to invest in the subsequent fund. The well-worn phrase goes: once bitten, twice shy. Presumably the maxim also holds when bitten twice.

Like its co-investors, Saban Capital must be cursing the day it laid its eyes on Univision. Yet the collateral casualty of this transaction is the broadcaster. Twelve years into its second leveraged buyout, it was still trying to shake off the stultifying effects of private equity ownership.

---

## LEVERAGED BUYOUTS AND CORPORATE ZOMBIES

*Leverage has a mechanical effect on equity returns. During periods of growth, it improves performance irrespective of the fund manager's talent, which is why it is so tempting for PE firms to apply it to excess.*

*Univision is just one example of an LBO turned into a corporate zombie, exposing the operational and financial consequences of overleveraging when market conditions worsen. The financial crisis and the Great Recession created an amazingly large cohort of debt-laden PE-backed companies artificially kept alive by central banks' easy money policies.*

# CHAPTER 5

# 3i: Mirror to the economic cycle and to human psychology

*Few industries are suited to all economic seasons. With its glaring lust for – and heavy reliance on – debt, private equity is no exception. Asset management is an inherently cyclical activity. The business model is dependent upon a strong economy and even stronger financial markets to raise funds, produce fees and generate value for investors.*

*Over the years, fund managers have tried everything to diversify away this intrinsic cyclicality. As the undisputed pioneer in the field, UK-headquartered 3i Group attempted and failed, repeatedly, to build a smooth and steady ride. That makes it a fitting case study to portray the trade's major shortcomings.*

Immediately after World War II, Great Britain found itself in a precarious position. The country was on its knees and the Labour government of Clement Atlee was looking for a way to re-energise the economy. The main challenge that Atlee's team faced was to create new jobs for the many service men and women involved in the war effort and with no occupation to go back to. One way to do so was to set up a financing programme for entrepreneurs and small companies.

## The Macmillan gap

In the 1930s the British economy had suffered in the wake of the Great Crash. Between November 1929 and July 1931, the government looked into the economic and social impact of the stock market collapse by forming the Committee on Finance and Industry. Chaired by Hugh Pattison Macmillan, a member of the House of Lords, the Committee identified a chronic shortage of long-term investment capital for small and medium-sized enterprises (SMEs).[1] It recommended the formation of a company to bridge what came to be known as the 'Macmillan Gap'. This company would serve as an intermediary between lenders and underserved corporate borrowers. Despite the findings of the Committee, in part due to differing views about the reality or importance of the 'gap', nothing had come of these findings by the time the country was dragged into a fresh military conflict.

The destruction brought about by World War II compelled the government to encourage better cooperation between finance and industry. On 19 May 1945, as Britain was setting itself up for a major reconstruction project, the Finance Corporation for Industry (FCI) was founded with £25 million of capital and borrowing powers of four times that amount. Share capital was subscribed roughly in equal portions by insurance companies, investment trust companies and the Bank of England, with the deliberate mission to provide funding (principally in the form of debt) to facilitate the rationalisation and restructuring of key sectors of British industry.[2] FCI's aim was to restrict its investments to a small number of large companies.

In July of the same year, the Industrial and Commercial Financial Corporation (ICFC) was formed by the Bank of England to serve SMEs through the provision of long-term and permanent capital. Typical investments ranged between £5,000 and £200,000. ICFC was exclusively funded by the major English clearing banks, the Scottish banks and the central bank, with a pot of capital of up to £45 million. In its early years, ICFC provided 60% of its capital as long-term loans, often at fixed rates and repayable over 10 to 20 years. The remaining 40% were equity investments, frequently in the form of redeemable preferred stock.[3]

These two corporations provided strong assistance to economic growth during the ensuing decades. In the 1950s ICFC expanded in the British regions, first in Birmingham, later in Manchester, Edinburgh, and eventually across most of the country. By 1972 ICFC had 29 regional offices.[4] Two years later, FCI and ICFC merged to form another acronym – FFI, Finance for Industry. Incorporated as a public entity, the latter acted as a holding company, 85% controlled by clearing banks, 15% by the Bank of England. By then, these initiatives had helped more than 3,000 different companies finance their growth.[5]

## Expansion

Their success in backing national enterprises made FFI's senior executives confident that they could replicate their ingenuity abroad and across business lines. So, they launched activities in stock underwriting, early-stage venture, plant leasing, real estate and shipping finance. The financial conglomerate opened offices in Boston in 1982 and in Paris and Frankfurt the following year,[6] even if its priority remained the development of British industry. FCI provided medium-term loans of £1 million to £25 million to large companies such as the Scottish drinks company Distillers, glassmaker Pilkington, engineering specialist The Weir Group, and Associated Biscuit. ICFC continued to offer much smaller tickets.

In the first 40 years of activity FFI and its previous incarnations committed £2.8 billion towards the development of British industry and commerce.[7] They regularly raised funds from the public, usually as fixed-term, interest-bearing debt instruments. They continued doing so after FFI's rebranding to Investors in Industry, or 3i, in 1983.[8] As a sector-agnostic investor, the firm occasionally participated in the technology scene, including through successful investments in Bond Helicopters and Oxford Instruments, the pioneer of magnetic resonance imaging. The Boston office even evolved into 3i Ventures, dedicated to early-stage deals.

With the growing impetus for globalisation and deeper integration among the largest economies, management spied a chance to build a presence in continental Europe and beyond. Eager to slake its ambition for market domination overseas, after the office openings in Boston, Paris and Frankfurt, Investors in Industry put soldiers on the ground in Italy and Spain and set up an Australian subsidiary as well as an Indian joint venture.

Simultaneously, thanks to its versatile expertise as an investor in private companies, the firm was ideally positioned to participate in a new kind of financing. In the late 1970s management buyouts emerged in the United States and slowly made an entry into Britain. By 1985 Investors in Industry was already an experienced sponsor of buyouts, having closed 98 of them in 1981, 95 the following year, 78 in 1983, 79 a year later, and 70 in 1985. The firm's adverts appearing in the press at the time portrayed uncomplicated vignettes of dealmaking under the guidance of expert financiers. The ads promoted the new capital structuring methods of management buyouts. They were designed to appeal to business executives eager to take the plunge into entrepreneurship but short on specialist knowledge in corporate divestitures and debt issuance. Although the firm's three decades of venture capital experience gave it acknowledged credibility, in reality, like all its buyout peers, 3i's investment team was making it up as it went along. By 1987 the firm had closed over 600 leveraged transactions, representing over half the management buyouts done in the UK over the previous five years.[9] With such a market share, Investors in Industry was the undisputed leader in LBOs in the country, adding this crown to the one it held in early-stage financing.

Also in 1987, discussions emerged between the firm and its shareholders about an introduction to the stock market. The investment group was reported to be worth about £600 million. The idea of flotation was initiated by Midland Bank, an 18% shareholder strapped for cash and casting around for disposals.[10] It would be a great way for Investors in Industry to access external funding. By now the firm held £2.2 billion worth of assets in 2,500 separate investments, managed by 725 employees operating through 25 regional UK offices and five overseas.[11] Its headcount and office footprint made it not just the most influential early-stage and buyout investor in the UK and Europe; it was the largest globally. Listing on the London Stock Exchange would raise its public profile further.

However, the fierce stock market correction in October of that year forced IPO discussions to be postponed indefinitely. The crash also disrupted the syndication process of numerous buyouts, and with a UK market share of more than 40% in that space, 3i was not spared its share of problems. It failed to find co-investors for £30 million of equity it held in Moores Furniture, for instance.[12] A shaky equity market wasn't only affecting syndication. It was making exits through public listings nigh on impossible.

Yet the market crash did not affect the economy. The latter continued to show healthy signs of growth, encouraging financial innovation. The 1980s had been kind to buyout engineers, seeing 1,720 UK transactions worth a total of £6 billion between early 1980 and mid-1988.[13] The year 1989 alone recorded £6.5 billion worth of buyout transactions in the country.[14]

## Market correction

Given its short history, the LBO sector had not yet operated in a recession. As the economy gradually slowed down, both in the US and the UK, the financial markets reined in their perverse appetite for leverage. Between 1990 and 1992 the buyout market declined steadily – in 1990 alone, transaction values cratered by 60%. By the third quarter of 1992, volumes hit a six-year low.[15]

Britain went through a painful economic crisis in 1991-93, its deepest contraction since the war. Caused by double-digit interest rates, an overvalued exchange rate and falling house prices, the recession was coupled with high inflation: retail prices rose 20% between the start of 1990 and the end of 1992. The country was plunged into further turmoil when, on 16 September 1992, the government had to devalue, thereby withdrawing the pound sterling from the European Exchange Rate Mechanism, a structure it had joined only two years earlier to try to bring inflation under control. The boom in consumer borrowing and spending experienced under the Thatcher era had come to a brutal end.

The consequences for the venture capital and buyout sectors were not just a marked decrease in transactions. Fund managers had to enforce operational improvements, both at the portfolio level and within their own investment teams. The tough economic conditions led several high-profile buyouts to default on their debt commitments.

One such example was the £2.2 billion buyout of Gateway, the UK's third largest chain of supermarkets. Bought in the summer of 1989 by two PE-sponsored investment vehicles, including holding company Isosceles backed by American deal-wrangler Bruce Wasserstein, it was, at the time, the largest buyout ever orchestrated in Europe. The 75% leverage proved too much to handle and impaired the business, forcing it into hurried disposals to source badly needed cash to meet over £1.4 billion of bank loan commitments. Several CEOs and refinancings later, Gateway was taken over by its lenders in April 1993, wiping out the equity holders in the process. As the largest LBO fund manager in Britain, 3i was, quite appropriately, among the losing PE backers; it also had to write down its mezzanine debt position in Gateway. It was an expensive lesson. The investment firm went through a painful restructuring to refocus around its best performing activity: SME financing. To facilitate a fresh start, in 1994 it shed its headcount by 45%, down to 570 employees.[16]

Historically, under the ICFC brand, the firm had taken a very hands-off approach to portfolio management. For its bank-shareholders not to have to carry portfolio companies on their books, all participations were aggressively syndicated. The economic recession of the early 1990s proved that this loose portfolio management approach was not optimal. From then on, the firm began taking majority ownership positions.

## Seeing eye to eye with business

Understandably, the very visible collapse of investments like Gateway led public markets to adjust their expectations about asset managers. For most of 1993, the latter traded at a significant discount to their net asset value, the underlying book value of an investment firm's portfolio. This was far from ideal for 3i's shareholders, the commercial banks that had held onto their stakes since 1945 and were keen to dispose of them. But the tide soon turned in their favour.

In early 1994, as the UK came out of the recession, management buyouts once again proved popular. In February, 3i announced the launch of a £225 million fund, raised from external investors, including UK pension funds and international institutions. The firm admitted that the market opportunities were so large that its sole balance sheet was no longer sufficient to take advantage of them.[17] Managing third-party money would also reduce the exposure of the syndicate banks and supply a healthy stream of fees.

The investment group had grown tremendously since its inception, in part thanks to constant advertising in the financial press to attract entrepreneurs looking for external funding. Throughout, the banks had remained sole shareholders; that was all about to change. In July 1994, after much delay due to depressed valuations during the recession, 3i listed on the London Stock Exchange, with the commercial banks selling 40% of their shares to the public and City institutions. The firm dropped the Investors in Industry label and officially became 3i Group plc, with an initial market capitalisation of £1.5 billion. About 390,000 private investors had registered interest in the venture capital specialist.[18] But only 75,000 of them subscribed for shares in a business that represented a very risky investment proposition – the firm's returns had lagged the FTSE All-Share index in the ten years preceding the float.

Yet 3i benefited from its status as an investment trust – meaning that it would not pay corporation tax on realised capital gains. In addition, the fact that all the major banks in the country still held a significant proportion of the group's stock would make it easier and cheaper to raise funds in the wholesale money markets. By October, 3i joined the FTSE 100 index, its stock having risen by a fifth in the three months post-IPO.[19]

After more than four decades of unchallenged leadership in the financing of private businesses, 3i had unique access to the secret corridors of ministerial power and banking. But working on behalf of Her Majesty's Government had its limitations, particularly in terms of strategy and accountability. What was the point of market domination if 3i was not able to dictate its own commercial terms and set the rules of engagement? Claiming independence from overbearing shareholders and gaining access to public capital markets gave 3i's management seemingly limitless powers, a fantastic weapon in the deregulated environment spearheaded by successive Conservative governments since 1979. The question, for shareholders, was whether management would be able to make the most of its newly earned freedom without messing it up.

The firm was gaining its independence at a critical time. Its market supremacy was no longer unchallenged. That year of 1994 had seen the 100 or so members of the British Venture Capital Association raise more than £2 billion.[20] In the 1950s ICFC had a virtual lock on SME financing. In the mid-1990s 3i still accounted for half of the country's venture capital investments and over a quarter of amounts invested. But while 3i's position was solid at the small end of the deal spectrum, larger transactions were a lot more competitive. Making the future even more difficult to predict, in early-stage financing a technological revolution was about to introduce significant opportunity and uncertainty in equal measure.

## Everything ventured, nothing gained

The faster pace of growth, both at home and abroad, exposed management to a multitude of fresh and unpredictable issues. Having opened an office in Singapore in 1997, 3i was then confronted by the Asian crisis of 1998. The British firm had no prior experience with financial crises, let alone those in emerging markets. The international bent was creating new headaches. Still, expansion had its upside. As it grew third-party funds under management, 3i saw fee income jump 38.2% in 1998.[21]

In the margins of market activity, new initiatives surfaced somewhat unexpectedly. With the dotcom epidemic of 1997 to 2000, 3i's executives could not help themselves and followed the herd by investing massively in unproven tech start-ups. The technology mania and strong demand for management buyouts created a unique climate where euphoria and utopia uncomfortably mingled.

The firm started the year 1999 by making an audacious £1.2 billion offer for its publicly listed rival Electra Investment Trust plc.[22] Although the bid ultimately failed, it proved that 3i had lofty goals. It had become the first truly global private equity group. Before any of the American giants spread across the world in the mid-2000s, 3i was the leading investor in the UK and in continental Europe. With 32 offices in Europe, Asia and America, it was extremely influential. It was also cash rich. In the fiscal year ended 31 March 2000, the firm deployed £1.4 billion in almost 600 companies – in just a 12-month period! In the UK alone, it injected £900 million in over 350 businesses.[23]

**Figure 5.1 – 3i Group plc stock performance between July 1994 and December 1999**

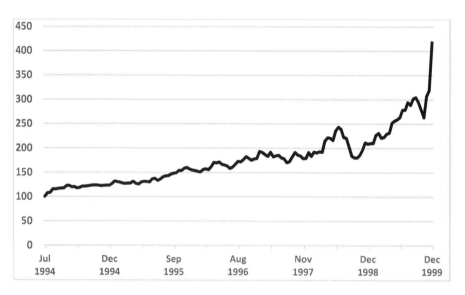

*Note: rebased to 100 on IPO day*

Lending a loose edge to the firm's stiff corporate culture, tech deals also added a patina of ferocity and vigour to an otherwise civil history. As can be appraised from Figure 5-1, it had taken 3i's stock almost four years after its IPO to double in value. But it took only 12 months for it to double again between late 1998 and December 1999. The dotcom bubble was in full swing.

## Crash course

At the end of March 2000 – when the tech-heavy Nasdaq index was at its all-time high – 3i Group plc was in rude health. Its total assets under management were close to £6 billion, twice what they were five years earlier. Two-fifths of these assets were invested in buyouts and start-ups, but the group also had a major presence in listed equity, fixed income, and private debt.[24] In full efflorescence, management was so excited about the numerous investment opportunities that presented themselves in the technology space that it acquired sector specialist Technologieholding, its closest rival in Germany.

Yet the group had grown far too quickly. Its corporate structure had failed to adapt. Irrespective of 3i's global presence, the entire senior executive team and all board directors were British. Corporate governance was not the only issue. The firm did not seem to master the most basic of risk management principles. Technology assets now represented 40% of the firm's portfolio. Management had forgotten one of the core rules of investment strategy: diversification.

By the same token, 3i had relentlessly pursued its international expansion, closing its first investments in the Benelux in 1999, in Austria, Denmark, Sweden and Switzerland in 2000, and in Finland in 2001, shortly after acquiring local firm SFK Oy.[25] At least management had diversified the business geographically. But if anything, the firm had overdone it. Overstretched, the group had become difficult to steer. The firm had aggressively ridden the Internet bubble of the late 1990s; it would duly get front row seat during the dotcom crash of 2000-03, a period during which the Nasdaq index shed more than three-quarters of its value.

As always happens in these situations, in the face of a violent market correction, the firm needed to regroup. First, it went through a management reshuffle. In December 2001 Sir George Russell, the chairman who had overseen the 1994 IPO, resigned. The company was about to report its worst performance ever. During the fiscal year to 31

March 2002, 3i recorded a total loss of £1 billion, adding to the £142 million loss recorded the previous year.[26] As the tech markets fell off a precipice, the firm's results went into reverse.

That same fiscal year, fee income dropped 22% – lower investment levels resulted in lower arrangement and management commissions. In October 2001 the company axed 185 employees in order to match its resources to new anticipated business levels. The group incurred £18 million of reorganisation costs and wrote off £73 million worth of goodwill.[27] By now, 3i was managing three quoted funds: the 3i Smaller Quoted Companies Trust plc, focused on smaller UK companies; 3i Bioscience Investment Trust plc, which invested internationally in healthcare; and 3i European Technology Trust plc, exposed to quoted tech companies across Europe. It also handled €7 billion in six separate third-party private equity funds and was in the process of raising a seventh, Eurofund IV, with a €3 billion target, half of it originating from 3i's balance sheet. In short, even though management had tried to simplify the group, it still exhibited a high level of complexity. A telltale sign was the firm's heavily centralised matrix chart, with reporting lines divided between geographic regions and product divisions, comprised of 174 separate legal entities. And it continued to invest at a fast pace, in too many companies and countries. In 2002 its annual investment run-rate totalled £1 billion in 550 companies across 36 offices.

This complexity did not enthuse public shareholders. Tagging itself to all major stock market indexes, the firm's share price went from 1,376 pence on 31 March 2000 to 417 pence three years later, a fall of 70%.[28] Its market capitalisation tanked from almost £11 billion to less than £3.5 billion. The company's stock had seen its value triple between the start of 1999 and September 2000. But the dotcom-flavoured hangover led to an equally impressive disintegration of value. By the end of 2003 the firm's stock was on par with its January 1999 value, as displayed in Figure 5.2.

Total return for the year to March 2003 was a negative 23.7% on shareholders' funds, a loss of almost £1 billion, 70% of which related to early-stage technology assets. Three years into the dotcom crash, 3i was still restructuring, closing its Tokyo, Berlin, Hamburg and Dublin offices and incurring £10 million in reorganisation costs in the 2003 fiscal year.

**Figure 5.2 – 3i Group plc stock performance between January 1999 and December 2003**

Note: *rebased to 100 on 4 January 1999*

## Welcome to yo-yo land

The year to March 2004 finally registered a positive performance, with 3i recording an 18% return on equity, even if the various divisions did not fare equally: returns for buyouts and growth capital were up significantly, but venture capital suffered a negative return of 6%. The group continued to shut offices, bringing its number to 30 worldwide, down from 39 four years earlier. The main reorganisation occurred at home, with the UK presence shrinking to ten locations. After seven years at the top, including four years of painful reorganisation, 50-year old CEO Brian Larcombe bowed out, realising that his legacy would forever be tarnished by the ill-fated strategy he had spearheaded in tech ventures.[29] He was replaced in the summer of 2004 by Philip Yea, a former managing director at rival Investcorp.

As the investment community was putting the Internet revolution behind it, it was time to take stock. Unfortunately for management, 3i's performance did not compare positively to that of the FTSE All-Share index. Over the previous 5 years, 3i's annualised return lagged that of the index, with the investment firm showing a negative 4.7% compound annual return compared to the FTSE All-Share's negative 1.4%.[30]

This persistent weakness led to rumours that several American competitors, including Blackstone and KKR, were circling the firm, seeing it as a great candidate for a rationalisation strategy. While bids failed to materialise, under Yea 3i pursued its interminable restructuring. In 2005 the group reduced its number of employees by 70, closed two offices, and discontinued the underperforming quoted fund management activities to focus exclusively on unquoted assets: buyouts, growth capital and venture capital. Since 2000 the number of portfolio companies had almost halved from 2,874 to 1,502.[31] The operational reorganisation was run in parallel with the group's balance sheet restructuring. From 35% in March 2003, 3i had managed to bring its net debt to shareholders' equity ratio below 15% two years later.

After such a harrowing experience, one could expect management to be down in the mouth, but 2005 signalled a fresh beginning. The new chief executive was assigned two critical missions. He had to indicate to the market that 3i was still a force to reckon with. Yet his main challenge was internal. In the months preceding his arrival, concerned that the troubles in the venture capital division would bring the rest of the firm down, the buyout team had threatened to walk and spin itself out. Yea wanted LBOs to be very much part of 3i's future. In fact, during his reign they were expected to become the firm's paramount activity.

Finally forgotten was the dotcom craze. It was time to chase the next investment mania head down. As the saying goes, what's bred in the bone will come out in the flesh. Just as it had done with tech investing in the 1990s, by the mid-noughties 3i's senior management was leading the rest of the pack by building a huge buyout practice in one of these fitful spurts of economic activity. In the previous four years, the amount of capital invested in LBOs globally had risen from $70 billion to $250 billion. For seasoned veterans, that offered an abundance of riches. Predictably, 3i succumbed to temptation.

Although the firm aimed swiftly to shift its business model towards more mature companies, the tech era was hard to erase. The reorganisation continued apace. The number of portfolio companies shrivelled. By the end of March 2006, the 1,087 investees represented only one-third the number of companies held in 2000. While certainly eager to erase his predecessor's mistakes, the new chief exec needed to eradicate any remaining trace of the dotcom epidemic that infected the portfolio under the previous regime, while launching the firm onto a more optimistic path. Trying to stop the rot, the group expanded its presence in Asia by entering mainland China and India to gain an early foothold in these promising emerging markets. The new game plan also implied making fewer but bigger-ticket investments. In the 2006 fiscal year, 3i only completed 58 transactions, a fraction of the 700 closed in the year to March 2001. Completing larger transactions meant targeting industrial projects. As the credit hysteria reached fever pitch, 3i launched an infrastructure division. Through its buyout unit, the group invested in European mid-market transactions with a value of up to €1 billion, aiming to close around 15 investments per year. Now discontinued, the quoted assets accounted for only 6% of 3i's portfolio value while unquoted equity represented 61% and corporate loans 31%.[32]

Helped by the booming markets, the firm recorded a considerable fall in net borrowings thanks to £2.2 billion in realisation proceeds. At 1.4%, 3i's gearing ratio in 2006 was a fraction of the 35% reported three years earlier. The inflation in asset values fuelled by the free flow of credit was providing a welcome respite for an investment group that was frantically trying to redeem itself. But what seemed like great news for any prudent asset manager was seen as a missed opportunity for chief executive Yea. The latter had built a corporate career, notably as a finance director for consumer brands Guinness and Diageo, before getting into private equity in 1999. Yea was therefore fairly new to the world of high finance, but he thought that was his strength. In his opinion, the way the City valued 3i was inadequate.

Instead of being assessed at a discount or premium to its net asset value, the venerable investment group should be gauged on its return on equity. That would more appropriately reflect management's skilled handling of the firm's capital structure. Since, unlike most PE firms out there, 3i invested from its own balance sheet, its capital had an intrinsic cost. For instance, holding cash on its books was far from optimal since it yielded very low returns. According to Yea's thinking, 3i was seriously, unjustifiably under-leveraged. To bring its weighted cost of capital down, it needed to demonstrate that it could play on both sides of the capital equation: debt as well as equity. He took the necessary steps to remedy the situation. A key decision, in mid-2005, was to return £500 million to shareholders: half of it in a special dividend, the rest through share buybacks. Then, he worked on ways to raise 3i's leverage.

Thanks to debt-fuelled M&A activity, LBOs became routine affairs. Globally, almost $700 billion worth of transactions were completed in 2006, a number that would be matched the following year. In this trigger-happy milieu, 3i displayed a reassuring resurgence. The total shareholders' return for the years to March 2005, 2006 and 2007 was 15.2%, 22.5% and 26.8% respectively. Public stock markets had followed a similar trend even if more subdued. The setbacks registered during the tech crash were evidently forgotten.

This bull run encouraged 3i to pursue a relentless international expansion. Private equity was becoming a truly global trade. Almost 60% of 3i's assets were located outside the UK; and just 9% of them in Asia, which offered great growth expectations.[33] Long gone were the days of ICFC's exclusively regional investment policy across the UK. With the growing focus on sizeable deals, the number of portfolio assets dwindled further, totalling 762 investee companies as at 31 March 2007. But the amounts invested increased, up 37% in the year to March 2006 and 41% the following fiscal year. Unsurprisingly, the chunk of that growth came from more sizeable debt-gorged buyouts and infrastructure projects.

As management confidently stated in its analyst presentation for the 2007 annual results, the group's buyout model was 'market-tested'. With its Eurofund V, the firm managed one of the largest LBO funds in Europe. Closed in late 2006 with €5 billion of commitments, it offered 3i significant firepower to deliver on its international plan of action. In addition, the firm raised €700 million for its new division, 3i Infrastructure. The latter's portfolio was valued at £469 million by the end of March 2007, compared to just £92 million when the activity was launched the year before. With the LBO bubble simmering with excess, 3i realised £2.4 billion in sale proceeds.[34] Thanks to this astonishing performance, the group's gearing was brought down to zero. The investment team was so active that 70% of the portfolio was less than three years old – 3i had finally turned a corner.

When reporting these 2007 results, 3i stated that the market opportunity was significant. In particular, management saw potential to apply its PE model to public markets, where there was "limited liquidity, increased regulation, and reduced analyst coverage." Confident that the economic environment could only head in one direction (upward), management had not limited itself to establishing infrastructure activities. Like an addict seeking the next narcotic tingle, 3i launched the Quoted Private Equity division, destined to take the agenda to listed companies in some form of hybrid alternative investment product (think: hedge fund). Only £14 million of investments had been done in that area, but the goal was to expand this activity big time. Two years after discontinuing its quoted asset management unit due to serious underperformance – admitting in the process that its team did not have any competitive advantage in public equity – the firm was getting back into the space.

For the first time since 2001, the group reported a positive net increase in staff numbers. The negative effects of the dotcom crash had been replaced by the positive impact of intense buyout activity. Yet, just like the firm had benefited from the frenzied markets to exit portfolio assets at high multiples, the valuation of 3i shares was getting unreasonable – they traded at a 27% premium to book value in the first half of 2007. The credit squeeze that emerged in the summer would soon bring market expectations back down to earth.

## Basic instincts

It took a while for 3i to adjust to the Credit Crunch. In its fiscal year to March 2008, Yea achieved his goal of bringing 3i's leverage to 40%. The timing would prove most unfortunate. For now, the troubles in the debt markets were still seen as temporary. That same year the group pursued its expansion and innovation blueprint. It launched an India Infrastructure Fund, which exceeded its target size by raising $1.2 billion. Management listed Quoted Private Equity Limited. To give you an idea of what that meant, think that 3i Group plc, itself a publicly listed fund manager, floated an active-investment vehicle whose purpose was to invest in other listed companies – try to follow, will you! In short, 3i was turning into an activist fund of hedge fund manager, without any relevant track record in that field.

Pursuing its endless reorganisation, in an attempt to deal once and for all with its underperforming venture assets, 3i merged that unit with its growth capital team.[35] But as it was firmly putting this matter behind it, more problems piled up. With the debt markets frozen, in early 2008 opportunities were scarce for large buyouts. Markets were on edge, bringing 3i's realisation proceeds down 29% over the 12 months to March 2008. But the firm's deal team refused to adapt to the new reality and increased investments by 37% on the prior year.[36] By mid-2008 the prevailing wisdom was that the softer credit conditions would bring in a welcome reduction in valuations, enabling active acquirers like 3i to boost investments. In fact, management was proud to mention during its analyst presentation in May 2008 that the group had closed its first buyout in Asia a month earlier. They did not know then that the Credit Crunch was about to mutate into a full-blown financial crisis.

All hell broke loose when Lehman Brothers filed for bankruptcy in mid-September. In a giant game of dominoes, the banking sector went into meltdown, forcing one government after another to bail out any bank that represented a systemic risk for national economies. In late 2008, 3i shares fell below their 1994 IPO price. In the frenzy of activity that marked the top of the deal cycle, the firm's expansion had followed a scattergun approach. After so much extravagance, it was time to refocus.

On the heels of the tightening credit markets, 3i faced its own existential threat. As the economy slowed appreciably and debt and equity markets crumbled, the fiscal year to 31 March 2009 showed a scary picture: 3i's total return on equity was a remarkable negative 53%, or a loss of about £2 billion. Management appraised the LBO portfolio, 60% of which carried debt in excess of 4 times EBITDA. Almost a quarter was leveraged at more than 6 times earnings.[37] In the context of the enduring Credit Crunch, refinancing these assets was likely to prove laborious even if two-thirds of that debt was due six years out and beyond, according the portfolio team enough runway to manage the debt wall.

Financing buyouts had been challenging ever since the distribution channels of credit had clogged up in the summer of 2007. Between 2007 and 2009, PE investments in Europe tumbled from €72 billion to €24 billion.[38] Understandably, 3i's number of new investments fell by 20% in the fiscal year of 2009, even if management knew that the restive credit market conditions were likely to create opportunities. With infrastructure assets typically more resilient than other assets, the group could be confident that this part of the business would see through the economic cycle. The $1.2 billion infrastructure fund in India, raised in March 2008, was already two-fifths deployed.[39] In late 2007 the group had also set up a €550 million debt warehouse facility to capitalise on the opportunity to buy, at a discount, high-quality debt in non-3i investments. By March 2009, €445 million of that facility had already been put to good use.

The tenuous state of the firm in the wake of the financial crisis was also symbolised by the dip in valuations across all asset classes. This reassessment did not spare 3i's portfolio. On a fully diluted basis, the firm's net asset value per share shrank 54%. The reduction in portfolio value pushed the firm's gearing from 40% in March 2008 to 103% a year later. The firm's troubles were clearly not only macro-driven. Thanks to Yea's recent initiatives to push 3i's leverage up, the accounts showed that it carried debt of £1.1 billion. Yea's all-important return on equity was a negative 53%, showing the flaws in the former Diageo CFO's thinking. While financial risk is manageable in the fast-consumer goods sector, it can be lethal in the highly volatile world of fund management. With such a bloated capital structure, 3i was constrained in its traditional strategy of making investments from its own balance sheet – it had, for instance, committed €165 million of its own capital to the private debt division.

# 3i

## All pain, no gain

Cheap access to credit in recent years had abetted 3i and many of its peers to pile up debt on their books. Not a great situation to be in for a fund manager also using significant third-party loans to acquire and refinance investee companies.* This double layer of debt compelled management to launch a £730 million rights issue in May 2009 in a bid to recapitalise its decrepit balance sheet.[40] After returning half a billion pounds to shareholders in 2005 with the goal to ramp up its own indebtedness, management was forced to go cap in hand to those same shareholders, begging them to rescue the investment firm by forking out 50% more than what they had been handed four years earlier.

Yea's erroneous obsession with 'return on equity' threatened 3i's survival, or at the very least its independence. The firm needed to degear urgently. The fresh equity injection aimed to reduce leverage, strengthen the books to protect against further falls in value, and support the firm's credit rating. It also provided capital for new investments at a time when asset valuations were at a low point.

Anxious to improve the group's liquidity, in its confused, unsettled state, management executed a fire sale of core and non-core assets in the first quarter of 2009, generating £366 million in cash. But the total realisation proceeds for the year to March were still down 25% on prior year. It was difficult to find buyers, at least those willing to offer a decent price. Even though equity markets were deflated, in a bid to produce badly needed cash a small stake in 3i Infrastructure plc was also disposed of.

While market pundits wondered about the group's likely demise, management accepted that no strategic move could be considered taboo. In February 2009, less than two years after its IPO, 3i Quoted

---

* For another example of the effect leveraging can have on a PE firm, read the Candover story in *Private Equity's Public Distress* (2011)

Private Equity plc, which traded at a significant discount to net asset value, was wound up. Its assets were pooled with 3i Group plc's growth capital portfolio.[41] After the closure of the Quoted Funds division four years earlier, it was the second time that 3i admitted its inability to manage publicly listed investment funds.

The firm was in a renewed fight for survival, only seven years after going through a painful post-dotcom era restructuring. Management sacked close to 150 employees, bringing its headcount down to 600. An investment group that operated across 39 offices in March 2000 was left with only 15 of them nine years later. As a sign that 3i had faced punishing competition at home, over the same period UK offices had gone from 18 to just three.[42] It seemed inconceivable that 3i's decades-long dominance could end so disgracefully. Like all its peers, the firm was mired in the economic malaise. Keen to show that it was serious about corporate governance 3i, a global investment firm with over £8 billion of assets under management, finally created a Chief Investment Officer role. Two financial crises within a nine-year stretch had convinced the downcast management team that someone should have sole responsibility for watching over all that capital.

By early 2009, as Figure 5.3 demonstrates, 3i's stock was almost 90% down on the price recorded in mid-2007, when the debt bubble reached its apex. Tellingly, the stock also sat at a fraction of the value warranted in early 2003, when the dotcom crash had hit its nadir. The LBO boom, sustained by cheap debt, had had an even more devastating impact on the firm. As 3i's stock remained stuck below the introductory price of July 1994, Yea stepped down in January 2009, having spent less than five years at the helm. Under his rule, instead of following a prudent growth strategy after the dotcom debacle, the firm had jumped head first into another investment fad. It was now taking a giant backward step.

Figure 5.3 – 3i Group plc stock performance between January 2003 and December 2009

Note: *rebased to 100 on 2 January 2003*

Fifteen years of tireless investment policy under Larcombe and Yea had been all for nothing. Hard work had not been equally matched by discipline and diligence. As Warren Buffett once professed: "It takes 20 years to build a reputation and five minutes to ruin it. If you think about that, you'll do things differently." Perhaps, from now on, 3i would behave differently, but it was little consolation for the shareholders who, for 15 years, trusted senior management's investment acumen.

## Headless chicken

During the fiscal year to March 2010, under the leadership of Michael Queen, promoted from the CFO position after Yea's departure, the firm slowed down its activity further. That year it only put £386 million to work, 80% less than in 2007-08. It intentionally elected to back existing investees, making only one new investment.[43] The financial crisis and the Great Recession had already resulted in a spate of embarrassing bankruptcies for several PE-backed businesses. The goal for 3i was to avoid losing its equity on too many of its overleveraged portfolio companies.

In parallel, the group pursued a programme of disposals by selling off £1.4 billion worth of distressed assets. Together with the equity injection from the rights issue of the previous year, cash proceeds contributed to significant improvement in the firm's net debt position, bringing gearing down to 8.4%. It also reduced the value of assets under management by 11%. The remnants of the Yea era were being erased at speed.

With the LBO sector still facing a challenging credit environment – investment levels in 2009 were the lowest for a decade – 3i paid attention to smaller transactions (less dependent on the appetite of lenders) and closed its first growth capital fund at €1.2 billion. It was a somewhat surprising decision since growth capital was 3i's worst performing business line: in the fiscal years 2009 and 2010 respectively, buyouts had lost 34% of their value before recovering 38% the following year, infrastructure assets had yielded -10% and +27%, but growth capital had delivered -44% and +11%.[44] Still, until then 3i had mostly invested growth capital from its own balance sheet. Raising third-party funds enabled the investment firm to produce management fees irrespective of performance. Recurring fees would at least cover staff salaries and bonuses.

Tight cash management was coupled with savage cutbacks, with a further 148 employees leaving in the year to March 2010.[45] The firm was shrinking fast. In view of the firm's performance, that was essential. But the eagerness to drive growth remained too much of a temptation. Though 3i's stock continued to lag the broader market, the group launched 3i Debt Management, following its relatively successful foray into debt investing four years earlier. In February 2011, the newly formed entity housed the assets of Mizuho Investment Management (MIM), a unit acquired from the eponymous Japanese bank.

The fallout of the dotcom crash and the Credit Crunch, all within a ten-year stretch, would have deterred less earnest individuals. Instead, 3i's management declared its intention to look actively at the Latin American market by recruiting a team with experience in Brazil.[46] And the international strategy also included raising a follow-up infrastructure fund for India. Whereas Yea had championed expansion in China and South-East Asia, Queen sought to make his mark in India and Latin America. Although a new Chairman had joined in July 2010, senior management still seemed as unfocused as ever.

Instead of spreading its wings into so many directions, the firm should certainly have paid attention to its core business. In the year to March 2012, the firm reported another set of poor results. For the fourth year in a row, 3i's returns lagged that of all major public indexes. With a negative return on shareholders' funds of 19.5%, the investment firm underperformed the FTSE All-Share. After the humbling disposals of the quoted and venture capital activities, the core LBO business, where 3i had made its name in the past twenty years, was no longer yielding the kinds of results investors expected. To ensure that the headcount was appropriately sized for the level of business generated post-financial crisis, management went through another round of cost cuts. Oddly, the Italian office was closed and the group announced its decision to withdraw from new investments in Spain just as the group was launching its Brazil activities. A group that had built its brand around the strength of its Europe-wide network was entering markets where it had no track record.

After such an abysmal year, in October a new CEO – the fourth in nine years – was named in an attempt to rekindle 3i's long-extinguished fire. Simon Borrows, a stoic, career investment banker, bethought himself to deliver a more methodical strategy. Originally appointed Chief Investment Officer in early 2012, within months Borrows had been elevated to the top executive role.

## Changing everything so that nothing changes

The Credit Crunch left 3i in a financially subservient state. With its clout enfeebled, as was to be expected the new chief executive came up with fresh and draconian downsizing initiatives. After conducting a portfolio review, he nuked a big part of the legacy operations. To be sure, a dramatic overhaul was overdue. In the last five years, 3i had accumulated £1.25 billion in losses. For most of 2012 its stock traded at or below 200 pence a share, almost 90% off the peaks registered in the spring of 2007, to say nothing of the record valuation logged in March 2000.

On the restructuring front, in a direct and swift manner almost two-fifths of staff were let go. The toughest measures were applied to North America, Southern Europe and Asia. While 49 investment professionals were fired, the brunt of the cuts was felt by 119 back-office and support staff.[47] By year end, the company was left with 267 staff – less than a quarter of the headcount carried in 2000. In the process, management had once more reshaped the office network with the closure of outposts in Barcelona, Birmingham, Copenhagen, Hong Kong, Milan and Shanghai, reducing the number of offices to 13.

Between the 2008 and 2013 fiscal years, operating expenses were halved.[48] But the private equity strategy didn't seem much more coherent than in the past. The new management team chose to prioritise core geographies, limiting its new investment activity on northern Europe, North America and Brazil. For performance reasons, Asia and southern Europe were put into the same non-core bucket, to be ignored from now on even though they represented almost £1 billion in assets.[49] What had partly influenced management's decision to pull out of these regions were macro considerations. Private equity activity in Asia had fallen 38% in 2012 as economic concerns, political uncertainty and regulatory obstacles made investors nervous. Trouble in the eurozone had gone on unabated, with Greece, Italy, Spain and Portugal fast becoming basket-case economies.

The goal of the new high command was to improve consistency and discipline of investment processes. In parallel, 3i showed its resolve to keep growing. During the fiscal year of 2013, it built its assets under management by 23% to £12.9 billion, including a 45% increase in third-party funds. All that growth came from the debt management division, which doubled in size. The other two activities, private equity and infrastructure, actually shrunk.[50] Private equity in particular had reduced its funds under management by 38% in the past three years, as the firm exited non-core geographies and focused exclusively on mid-market LBO transactions.

Restructuring and cost-cutting exceeded expectations. Strong realisations during the year also contributed to a dramatic reduction in gearing. On the back of improved trading, after an absence of five years the firm was reinstated in the FTSE 100 index in mid-2014.[51]

Between 2012 and 2015 the new management team achieved significant savings, turned its net debt position into net cash, closed eight offices, decreased its headcount by more than a third, refocused its activities on core geographies, and shrank its private equity portfolio from 90 to 65 investees, representing a £1.6 billion drop in assets. Though it had not raised a new LBO fund since 2010, management put further fundraising on hold, choosing to manage its existing portfolio rather than add complexity to an already stretched organisation. The firm added £4 billion of assets in its debt management division, and increased its infrastructure asset base by £700 million.

By March 2015 third-party funds represented three-quarters of total assets, up from 60% three years earlier.[52] The goal was to turn the business into a more traditional asset manager, a fee-earning engine dabbling with external funds rather than with its own capital. When, in the 12 months to 31 March 2016, 3i saw its share price tank 6% as financial markets around the globe experienced a correction, the new CEO pursued its relentless strategic redesign, selling off part of 3i's stake in the infrastructure division before disposing of the debt management activities in October 2016. The group's private equity activities were scaled down further, to be left with about 50 portfolio companies, down from 336 ten years earlier and over 2,870 in the year 2000, as exhibited in Table 5.1.

**Table 5.1 – 3i Group's key performance indicators in 2000 and 2017**

| Year ended 31 March | 2000 | 2017 |
| --- | --- | --- |
| Portfolio value (incl. third-party funds) | £8.16 billion | £5.68 billion |
| Net asset value | £5.17 billion | £5.84 billion |
| Net asset value per share | 847 pence | 604 pence |
| Number of portfolio companies | 2,874 | Around 50 |
| New invested amounts in the year | £1.07 billion | £0.5 billion |
| Average monthly number of employees | 838 | 281 |
| Number of offices (UK + international) | 39 | 8 |
| Number of UK offices | 18 | 1 |

*Source: Company filings*

Impaired by a stupefying sequence of broken portfolio assets, failing international offices and slovenly strategic plans, the firm had the dubious honour of overcoming two life-threatening events within a decade. The Credit Crunch had finished the work started by the dotcom implosion. Having jumped at every opportunity like a headless chicken, during both the tech bubble of the late 1990s and the buyout mania of the mid-noughties, the firm had little to show for it. Table 5.1

demonstrates that its performance parameters in 2017 were no longer comparable to their 2000 levels.

## Everything for everyone

In 2009, the British firm had wound up its quoted activities and sold its venture capital arm. In 2016 it had sold off its debt management unit, bought from Mizuho only six years earlier, supposedly to capitalise on areas in which it had investment expertise. It was left with only two divisions: private equity and infrastructure. Management had tried to do it all, attempting to create a one-stop shop in alternative asset management – in line with the model adopted by its American peers Blackstone and Carlyle – without developing or acquiring the necessary expertise.

Its international expansion had been a disappointment. In the UK, the group was left with only its London office. Its European network had gone from 18 outposts in 2000 to five by 2017, while the US presence had shrunk from three offices to just one. In Asia, 3i had shut its Chinese operations, keeping only Singapore and Mumbai open in a footprint that lacked any sense of strategic intent. The ill-timed attempt in 2011 to start a Latin American operation had been short-lived.

The headcount had gone from more than 1,000 in the early noughties to approximately 240 employees in late 2017. The strategy to grow assets under management at all costs had failed to account for one key variable: asset management is subject to fierce cyclicality, as displayed by the firm's swings in net asset value (see Figure 5.4). Two market crashes had defeated the management's ambition. Across Europe, snarky commentators often referred to the '3i mafia' to emphasize the scope of the alumni network. The group had hired and fired so many investment executives over the years that it had built the largest roster of private equity professionals, not that quantity necessarily equates quality.

**Figure 5.4 – 3i Group's net asset value and headcount from March 1994 to March 2017**

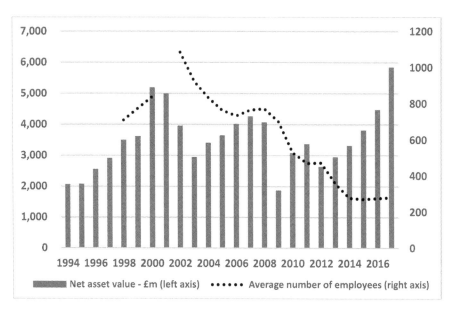

*Source: Company filings*

With only eight offices still open in early 2017, two-thirds of 3i's employees were based in the London office,[53] making the group less geographically diversified than at any point since the early 1980s. Long the foremost PE fund manager across Europe, 3i had become inconsequential in an industry dominated by far more aggressive American players.

But Simon Borrows and his team needn't despair, for public investors are a forgiving (and forgetting) bunch. In June 2017, as 3i's stock valuation gingerly passed the mark of 900 pence a share, a 40% premium to its net asset value, it was worth keeping in mind that, in 1993, investment managers like 3i traded at a 30% discount.[54] Back then, the rueful situation had forced 3i's owners to delay the firm's IPO. Conversely, in 2007 the firm's stock was quoted 30% above its book asset value, before crashing down ferociously. All this to explain that the huge premium at which 3i's stock traded in 2017 would eventually revert to the mean, as it had done repeatedly in the past. To reiterate: investing is cyclical.

## Not as easy as 1, 2, 3

While throughout the 1960s and 1970s ICFC had held undisputed leadership in the UK, its quasi-monopoly in SME financing was eventually corroded via the emergence of new entrants and product innovation. From traditional commercial lending, enterprise financing gradually morphed into early-stage equity funding, then into leveraged buyouts. In 1986 the Tory government of Margaret Thatcher initiated sweeping deregulation, as an ideological attempt to modernise and energise the City of London. From that point onward, the humming financial hub witnessed the invasion of foreign buyout groups, most of them emanating from the more sophisticated American market. In the 1990s, 3i gradually saw its domestic market share eaten away, and chose aggressively to expand into new territories where its brand had no influence, and into product categories where its skill set was irrelevant, such as quoted equity.

Central to the rise of 3i was its claim to be a superior moneymaking machine. By the time a new chairman and a new CEO took the reins in the early 2010s, that claim lay in tatters. In the previous 20 years, 3i's stock had gone through a repeated yo-yo cycle that made it clear to outside observers and public shareholders that its investment methodology was not fit for purpose. The stock climbed and crashed in line with the economic cycle and market gyrations, as seen in Figure 5.5. Between January 1999 and December 2017, the FTSE 100 index had risen 30%, or 1.4% annualised (excluding dividends reinvested). Although far from stellar, it was much better than 3i's compound 8%, or 0.4% per annum.

The appeal of investment management is that risk is spread over an entire portfolio. But what 3i's leadership found out the hard way is that when a portfolio comprises almost 4,000 investments, as it did in 1992, complexity outweighs the benefits of diversification. At the time, one 3i executive might be responsible for 30 or 40 portfolio companies, which prevented close involvement and proper monitoring. Performance greatly suffered. The firm began taking majority ownership positions and board seats on a systematic basis around the time of its 1994 market listing, but it soon reverted to its passive investment methods when it financed the speculative growth plans of hundreds of tech start-ups in the late 1990s. This loose approach backfired. Again, diversification has its limits, a point clearly made in Chapter 3. For all that, investing in thousands of companies yielded few benefits because, during the dotcom days, 3i concentrated too much of its funding into one sector: by 1999 as much as 40% of its portfolio was in high-tech.

**Figure 5.5 – FTSE 100 index and 3i Group plc stock performance between January 1999 and December 2017**

Note: *rebased to 100 on 4 January 1999*

The firm's style was to chase new trends on an opportunistic basis with suicidal frequency; without much care for the required degree of expertise or strategic fit. In the mid-1980s, one of its ads often placed in financial pages saw the firm boast about its "creative use of money."[55] But creativity was not matched with proficiency. After seeing its buyout assets suffer in the early 1990s recession, the firm jumped into the late-1990s tech VC frenzy with both feet. The group never completely recovered from this excess. Maybe it had pushed its creative use of money too far. The resonant dregs of the tech portfolio were eventually sold off, never to be mentioned again.

The firm's geographic enlargement accelerated in the 1990s as market deregulation and European political and economic integration gained momentum. But 3i's obsessive focus on size and growth gave no evidence that it paid particular attention to developing homegrown managerial talent. In fact, by expanding and shrinking its headcount and activities so rapidly between 1995 and 2015, the group demonstrated none of the methodical processes deemed vital to the long-term health of an organisation. Investment styles had evolved away from ICFC's genteel approach. The firm's founding fathers had been cosseted in the City's fashionable private clubs; a new breed of much more adaptable and effective financial engineers had emerged in the 1990s from the bottomless fount of Wall Street buccaneers.

Management muffed the chance to redeem itself when it chose to participate in the credit pandemic of 2004-07. Seemingly afflicted with attention deficit disorder, management probably expected the cross-pollination of ideas to give its various divisions a unique competitive advantage. The inchoate strategy failed because instead of running leading activities, 3i ended up building also-rans. A company that was the undisputed leader in UK venture capital in the 1950s and 1960s, and the clear pioneer in LBOs across Europe during the late 1970s and early 1980s, never adapted to the financial deregulation and its corollary, unbridled competition.

One of the issues at the core of this story is that risk management was inadequate. Repeatedly, management genially ignored various warnings, wending its way confidently, if at times haphazardly. As the markets billowed, 3i's entry into new investment sectors, asset classes and geographies miscarried with a biblical magnitude. Following the second law of thermodynamics, which posits that disorder increases over time, 3i's corporate apparatus evolved into a real mess, damaging the brand in the process.

Restructurings took place, in fits and starts, throughout the firm's history: in the early 1990s ahead of the public listing, in part due to the first LBO crash; then in the early noughties to recover from the dotcom days; again in 2009-10 to correct Yea's intemperate focus on leverage; in 2012-14 to scale down to a core mid-market buyout unit and a small infrastructure activity. Twenty-five years after its IPO, the firm no longer carries the cachet it once held.

## The Rowlands gap

The 3i story has a fascinating if slightly mystifying coda. Recall that the firm had seen the light as a quasi-governmental institution – post-war Britain needed a big push from the state to resurrect a moribund economy. Three decades later Thatcher converted the country to a government-free religion, which gained ground until the financial crisis of 2008. The idea of state interventionism lay dormant during the interval, but it did not die. A violent economic meltdown was all it took for it to resurface.

As the Great Recession lingered, with its market approach in limbo, 3i acted in the confined financial banding of €25 million-to-€150 million funding. Management had forsaken the very large and very small transactions orchestrated in previous decades. Transactions worth hundreds of millions of euros and above were left in the clutches of global specialists, many of them American. But the lower bound of deal-doing seemed up for grabs. The British Government decided to investigate. It appointed former 3i executive committee member Chris Rowlands to look into the matter. Rowlands, a managing partner in charge of growth capital and small and medium investments before leaving 3i in early 2009, set up the customary panel and got to work.

In November 2009 the Rowlands Report duly identified a gap in the market, in the £2 million-£10 million band. There was an apparent need for a new operator at the smaller end of enterprise financing. Fittingly, that was the view held by government officials.

The general elections of 2010 threw Prime Minister Gordon Brown out of office, but the new team in charge, led by the Conservative David Cameron, took the view – inaccurate, according to many observers – that the UK small and medium-sized business segment continued to be underserved by the financial services industry. After the financial crisis, British banks had chosen to cut back significantly their lending practices in order to rebuild their balance sheets.

In a free market worthy of the name, recessions are meant to act as cleansing mechanisms. But Cameron's team considered that the lack of bank lending represented a threat to the wider economy. A reduction in SME financing could accentuate the economic slump. A new investment initiative to provide funding to small businesses was needed. But the British state was more or less broke by that stage, what with the fortune it had already spent bailing out the entire banking sector. Once dubbed a worthy competitor to New York's financial centre, the City of London was in deep shock.

Thus, amid the fog of desperate state interventionism, the decision was taken to force the largest British banks (Barclays, HSBC, Lloyds, Royal Bank of Scotland and Standard Chartered) to provide the funds that a government-backed investment vehicle would lend or invest on very preferential terms to struggling British businesses. The banks ended up making a combined commitment of £2.5 billion. No details were provided about how that number was arrived at. But to leave no room for misunderstanding, this vehicle was named the British Growth Fund, or BGF.

## BGF: 3i's avatar

The most surprising about the corporate world is how little it seems to learn from the past. You would think that the British business community gathered pertinent warnings from the 3i saga. But let me finish this chapter on a foreboding tale.

The capstone of 3i's history was to be the creation of the Business Growth Fund. As the recession settled, few institutions or individuals had either the time or the confidence to raise capital. There was not a great deal of interest in growth capital, considered a relatively risky type of investment given the prevailing environment. Which is why BGF raised funds from the same clearing banks that had backed the Industrial and Commercial Finance Corporation in the 1940s.

If this is oddly reminiscent of 3i's early days, it is because the government embraced the same master plan. The BGF executive team is following a well-trodden path. Like its predecessor, the government initiative was launched in 2011 to provide both debt and equity to small companies. Just like 3i ended up straying away from its original purpose of taking minority stakes in established SMEs, the Business Growth Fund started dabbling in venture capital within 5 years of being set up. Shortly thereafter, in 2016, it launched a Quoted division to invest in publicly listed companies. It is only a matter of time before the group enters the leveraged buyout arena. Once BGF's financial empire has widened to encompass the whole gamut of investment products, from mundane corporate loans to more complex equity-flavoured instruments (including infrastructure and property, who knows), 3i's story will have come full circle, its resurrection complete.

BGF was 3i's reincarnation. In the face of the worst economic crisis since World War II, the government was ready to go through the whole rigmarole again. In view of 3i's eventful history, it is not necessarily a good thing. As we saw, the reason why 3i kept failing was due to the management team's desire to chase the next investment trend, without properly adapting the firm's business design. Senior executives naively believed that the skills they had developed in the 1950s by backing British companies during the country's post-war reconstruction efforts would be seamlessly replicable in international markets, in LBOs, in public stock markets, and in early-stage high-tech ventures. It turns out that these separate segments of the asset management industry require different skill sets and investment strategies. The financial acumen needed to complete buyouts is useless when investing in new technologies. For the latter, product, technical and engineering expertise as well as a well-honed gut instinct to identify successful entrepreneurs are more relevant. In an LBO, corporate executives running the portfolio company are very much expendable. By contrast, in start-ups a visionary founding team is often priceless and irreplaceable.

One of the reasons for BGF's expansion beyond its original remit was the fact that it could not find sufficient growth opportunities to put its £2.5 billion of capital commitments to work. Despite the impact of the Credit Crunch, the market had soon become bloated with excess capital thanks to the Bank of England's programme of quantitative easing. Not to mention that compared to other Western economies, the UK has a plethora of fund managers.

The most striking about the BGF story is that, even though it is sponsored by the government, the firm is not accountable to the public. It would seem appropriate for the group to reveal its annual rate of return, so that taxpayers can judge its achievements. If performance is not deemed a priority, is the group not at risk of distorting the SME financing sector? After all, if returns do not matter, BGF is likely to be the most generous bidder in all the transactions it backs, which would be greatly anticompetitive. Ensconced in the highest political and business circles, the group holds an 'unfair advantage', code for a free rein to distort market rules. Given the circumstances behind its creation, it would be too much to hope that BGF can avoid the sort of slapdash, almost primitive approach to investing that 3i was guilty of throughout a history dramatically patterned according to the economic cycle, the way vegetation matches the seasons.

## PRIVATE EQUITY AND THE HABIT OF REPEATING MISTAKES

This case study introduces points about human psychology. It raises major questions about humans' inability to learn from past mistakes as well as our neurotic tendencies to repeat them. It is a complex matter. Some reasons behind human errors are cognitive, others institutional. Over-confidence, competitive instinct, wrong incentives, inadequate governance, negligence and lack of accountability are part of an extensive list of factors behind underperformance.

To explain why we keep making the same blunders, some experts speak of the 'toddler brain', which is associated with weak impulse control, poor judgment, volatile behaviour and self-obsession.[56] Of course, we cannot rule out bigger psychological or pathological issues, including self-destructive tendencies. As the saying goes: "The definition of insanity is doing the same thing over and over and expecting different results."[57]

# CHAPTER 6

# Toys "R" Us: Leveraging in retail is no child's play

*No one can dispute that fashion retail is cyclical and should therefore be shunned by LBO investors. But other segments of the retail industry offer more resilience in a downturn.*

*On the face of it, toys and baby apparel fit the bill. Although seasonal and clearly not left unaffected by economic recessions, they do not generally experience the whims of the fashion world. That makes a leveraged buyout of the largest toy specialty retailer in the world a decent bet. But things don't always pan out in the real world as they look on paper.*

At the time of its buyout, Toys "R" Us was the leading independent toy and baby products retailer in America. In retail parlance, it is called a category killer. The group was founded in 1948 when 25-year-old Charles Lazarus launched a baby furniture store in Washington D.C. Lazarus gradually added baby toys and toys for older children before changing the company name to Toys "R" Us in 1957. Nine years later, the business was acquired by Interstate Stores, owners of Children's Bargain House. It eventually expanded overseas, starting with Canada in 1984. Three decades later, it operated in 35 countries. Toys "R" Us also developed new store concepts, opening the children's clothing chain Kids "R" Us in 1983 before launching Babies "R" Us in the mid-

1990s to serve the toddler and pre-schooler market. While Kids "R" Us had limited success, the Babies "R" Us concept flourished.

In the early years of the 21st century, independent toy retailers struggled to deal with the constant, brutal price war launched by big-box retailers Wal-Mart and Target, notably during the all-important Christmas holiday shopping season. These discounters used toys to draw shoppers into their outlets, selling them at or below cost. KB Toys and upscale toy retailer FAO Schwarz filed for bankruptcy protection after the 2003 year-end festive season. During the final quarter of 2003, Toys "R" Us had seen its profits halve.[1]

The discounters had caught the specialist toy distributors unawares. In the mid-1990s Toys "R" Us sold one out of five toys in the country, well ahead of non-specialists Wal-Mart (with 11%), Kmart and Sears. Smaller toy retailers like Child World and Kiddie City had perished during the early 1990s recession, unable to match prices and offering at Toys "R" Us's huge superstores. But by the mid-noughties Wal-Mart accounted for about 22% of the $27 billion US toy business, leaving Toys "R" Us trailing behind with a 16% market share.[2] The share of the discount channel represented more than half of the market, and it was growing fast.

Toys "R" Us's woes were not all to be blamed on its rivals' deeds; some were of its own making. Management had tried to segmentalise its offering by creating specific lines of clothing and toys for babies and for kids, leaving the mainstream stores for a general audience. Management was forced into retrenchment. In the year ended 31 January 2004, Toys "R" Us shuttered seven out of ten Kids 'R' Us stores and all 36 of its Imaginarium educational toy stores. That fiscal year, earnings fell to $119 million, down from $275 million two years earlier.[3]

In the summer of 2004, with the stock price sitting 61% below its 1993 peak, management confirmed that a strategic review was in progress. It cut head office costs, halved capital spending, and took heavy markdowns to liquidate stock. Press reports spoke of the real possibility of Toys "R" Us being driven out of business in the face of Wal-Mart's success in selling classic toys like Barbie dolls, Cabbage Patch Kids and Hot Wheels cars as loss leaders.

## Boys and their toys

Management considered various strategic alternatives, including spinning off the hugely successful Babies "R" Us, which operated 216 stores and accounted for three-quarters of group operating income. Another option was to split the depressed toy business – for which same-store sales were 7.7% lower in the May-to-July 2004 quarter – and the thriving baby activities into separate units.[4] But management's preference went for an outright delisting that would give the group time to enact a proper restructuring.

In early March 2005, four private equity parties submitted offers. All the bidders were large investors: KKR, the quintessential expert in mega buyouts; a duo assembling Apollo and Permira, both global in their ambition; an alliance between Bain Capital and real estate specialist Vornado Realty Trust; and a consortium comprised of turnaround artist Cerberus Capital, property investor Kimco Realty, and Goldman Sachs, the bank that needs no introduction.[5]

With the debt markets reaching fever pitch, management was keen to maximise value. It was instructed by its advisers Credit Suisse that the best way to do that would be to sell the group in chunks, with Babies "R" Us, the US toy unit and the international division expected to attract separate bidders. While the traditional domestic toy business was facing intense competition, European and baby apparel activities were doing great. The idea was to auction the group piecemeal.

But interested parties took a different approach by bidding for the entire group. The task of restructuring a global company with as many

THE GOOD, THE BAD AND THE UGLY OF PRIVATE EQUITY

moving parts as a Rubik's Cube did not deter PE firms behind some of the largest M&A transactions in history, including many complex corporate turnarounds. Toys "R" Us promised to be equally challenging; to KKR, Cerberus or Apollo, that was part of the dealmaking fun. The PE firms' unique take on the transaction prompted Toys "R" Us to ask all bidders to submit their offers for the whole group rather than individual units.[6]

The credit bull market was picking up speed, having replaced the dotcom fad and already making the latter look decidedly tame. In 2004 LBO funds had raised $55 billion, up 42% on the prior year. All that money was turning PE fund managers into shopaholics, but they also knew that they ran the risk of overpaying. Analysts had observed that the bids submitted for Toys "R" Us were high, given that the target was not in the best of shapes. Any new owner would need to work hard to address the retailer's operating deficiencies and commercial vulnerability.

To take some of the heat out of the process, two of the bidding parties decided to partner up (we will revisit this sort of practice in Chapter 9, in the context of regulatory investigations into clubbing). KKR found enough common ground with Bain and Vornado; the three of them were prepared to share the spoil that the transaction was bound to yield. On 17 March 2005, after a seven-month-long auction, Toys "R" Us announced that this PE trio had agreed to buy the NYSE-listed company for $5.9 billion, or $26.75 a share, plus the assumption of $800 million of existing debt and $766 million in warrants, restricted stocks and various expenses. The headline price of $7.5 billion sat at 10 times prior-year EBITDA.[7] The financial sponsors agreed to put a minimal cash contribution: the $1.3 billion equity pot represented individual portions of $420 million to $450 million.[8]

By beating Cerberus, Goldman and Kimco, the KKR consortium had factored in a 63% premium to the stock price on 9 August 2004 (the day before Toys "R" Us announced its intention to sell one or several of its divisions). The bid also valued the business at a 123% premium to the price the stock was on at the beginning of 2004 when management had first revealed a strategic review. These were generous terms, thanks in no small part to the credit markets. The LBO loans were adding $4.3 billion to the existing debt, instantly tripling leverage to more than 7 times EBITDA.[9] Moody's and Standard & Poor's ran the numbers into their formula and came up with the usual speculative grade.

## Playtime

Perhaps the re-rating explains why, in June 2005, the company announced that the incumbent CEO, John Eyler, would retire upon completion of the transaction,[10] making room for the type of chief exec with whom PE firms are more accustomed to work. Eyler, who had been president of the retailer for five years and, before that, chairman and CEO of toy store FAO Schwarz for eight years, had unmatched industry knowledge. But he had never run a company under PE-ownership. And that's a completely different ball game. For the same reason, after only five years at the retailer, COO and former general counsel Christopher Kay vacated the premises. His legal background was unlikely to be what was needed to profoundly restructure the group.

Bain Capital was well acquainted with the mores of the retail world. Its origination track record in the retail consumer segment was second to none. Its deal log included Domino's Pizza in 1998, fast-food specialist Burger King four years later, and the chain of dollar stores Dollarama in 2004. Emanated from global consultancy Bain & Company, over time the firm had demonstrated a singular ability to tackle complex corporate turnarounds by re-engineering business models. Perhaps the most relevant transaction in Bain Capital's recent history was its $305 million acquisition of KB Toys in 2000. The PE firm had recouped some of its investment via a dividend recap in 2003, just in time before seeing the toy retailer file for Chapter 11 protection. Clearly not put off by the experience, Bain Capital was intent on proving that it had learned something valuable from it. Toys "R" Us would call for the full contribution of the firm's in-depth industry knowledge.

KKR was the ultimate deal-doing machine. Although in its early days it had built a reputation as an asset-stripper and an aggressive financial engineer, in the second half of the 1990s KKR had demonstrated that it could also take the time necessary to build value. Although its investment style could hardly be labelled 'patient capital', it had enough fire power to fund grandiose turnarounds if necessary. Given the market dynamic, Toys "R" Us fit the bill perfectly.

As for the third party of this triumvirate, Vornado, it was not a seasoned LBO investor. Its exclusive focus was on maximising yield from property-intensive assets. With hundreds of stores across the world, the target was likely to need Vornado's input in optimising value extraction from its real estate portfolio.

To be sure, the bona fide operative Bain, the debt junkie KKR and the property connoisseur Vornado formed an odd threesome. Maybe by combining their respective sets of skills, they could work wonders. Toys "R" Us could source great expertise from these transformers. Under PE ownership, the hope was that the specialist retailer would become leaner and successfully adapt to the fast-changing competitive landscape.

The transaction was consummated on 21 July 2005. The company issued a $2 billion asset-backed loan to help finance the buyout.[11] With the capital structure split 80/20 in favour of debt, the level of leverage left no room for error. But these were exciting times for the world of buyouts. The strong cash-flow generation enjoyed by Toys "R" Us and the booming credit markets were clamouring for a much bigger debt package. Observers were reporting a healthy appetite for more debt to be piled onto the retailer's books. Global Toys Acquisition, the PE consortium's bidding vehicle, had in fact received debt commitments for up to $6.2 billion,[12] or 94% of the enterprise value. Though it was unlikely that the financial sponsors would be allowed by the lenders to stretch the capital structure that much, it gave an idea of possible refinancings they could engineer after taking ownership.

## Deal rationale

The target was the largest toy retailer not just in America but worldwide. For the PE consortium, it offered several interesting routes to riches.

### Real estate play

With asset-rich companies, the obvious way to produce cash expeditiously is to do sale and leaseback deals. To kick-start the typical 100-day plan KKR is famous for, a vast sale and leaseback programme was in the offing. The trick was to retain a solid asset base to use as collateral for some of the LBO loan tranches.

For this to take place, the property market needed to be buoyant. By the time the deal was completed in mid-2005, the Federal Reserve had continued its policy of rate hikes started in June 2004 – from 1.25% that month, the Fed funds rate had steadily risen, reaching 3.25% in June 2005 and 4.25% in December of the same year. The policy had the effect of cooling off real estate prices. Yet, the financial sponsors had other strings to their bow.

### Driving the top line

An attractive idea was to keep expanding the Babies "R" Us chain, which was the fastest growing division at the retailer; it was also the most profitable. In the year to January 2006 that division had reported sales growth of 5.7% and EBITDA margins in excess of 14%. With over $2 billion in revenues, it still accounted for just one-sixth of the group's top line.

Another growth plan was to develop the retailer-branded business. Although the group had closed its Imaginarium stores, it kept the brand and planned to use it to offer private label toys, as an alternative to premium-branded products from the likes of Mattel, LEGO and Hasbro. The approach had been espoused by Wal-Mart and Target with notable success.

Internationally, the business was also doing great. Like-for-like sales growth in the year of the LBO was 3.1%, but given the number of new store openings, future growth potential was in double digit. With EBITDA margin of 11%, this division promised to be a great cash generator, in part because in international markets discounters did not exert as much pressure as they did in America.

Finally, no genuine top-line growth strategy could be taken seriously without focusing on e-commerce. While the toy retailer had launched its own website in 1998, two years later it had signed a 10-year agreement with Amazon to be the latter's exclusive seller of toys and baby products. The companies also agreed at the time that Toys "R" Us would give up its online autonomy, with ToysRUs.com redirecting back to Amazon. Toys "R" Us paid Amazon $50 million a year plus a percentage of its sales through the Amazon site. By 2004 the deal had dissolved into acrimony when Amazon breached the exclusivity agreement. As it was embarking on its LBO journey, the toy retailer was also relaunching its online activities in-house.[13] With online sales only accounting for 6% of the total market, the potential was there. It needed to be reaped.

*Pursue operating efficiency*

Under the scrutiny of the public markets, management had launched a programme to close the weakest stores. In the three years to January 2006, stores across America (other than the Babies "R" Us outlets) had registered negative sales growth of close to 3% annually. The restructuring strategy had started to deliver decent results. Under the watchful eyes of PE owners, the new CEO was expected to redouble the team's efforts to drive efficiency across the network.

Underperforming locations required immediate attention. Tens of domestic stores were ear-marked for closure, while a dozen of others were to be converted in the better performing Babies "R" Us format.[14] As Figure 6.1 demonstrates, erratic revenues had hampered concrete improvements in profitability. Operating gains were meant to remedy this situation.

**Figure 6.1 – Toys "R" Us's sales and EBITDA margin from 2000 to 2006**

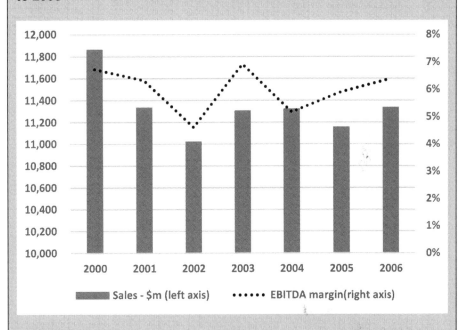

*Source: Company filings – Notes: numbers for 52 or 53 weeks ended in January or February of years shown*

## Not all fun and games

In February 2006 Gerald Storch was hired to replace Eyler as chief executive. After 13 years at discounter Target, Storch was bringing in the management tools to run Toys "R" Us with the required attention to cost and cash management, micro-marketing and merchandising for which Target is known. As one sector analyst rightfully commented: "Pound for pound, Target does the best job in toys. If you were going to take an executive from a rival, you would take from Target."[15]

To infuse a bit more liquidity into the business, a £356 million sale and leaseback of 29 stores and one distribution centre of the retailer's independent UK division was organised. Although the parent company had a very speculative rating due to the LBO loans sitting on its books, most tranches of the sale-and-leaseback package earned solid investment grades given their relatively low loan-to-value ratios.[16] In plain English, the mortgages were amply backed by the value of the assets used as collateral.

In June 2006 the toy retailer issued a $1 billion debt facility, comprising an $800 million long-term loan and a short-dated $200 million asset-sale facility. The aim was to refinance the outstanding portion of the $1.9 billion bridge loan used to acquire the business. Appetite wasn't strong, many potential investors considering that the yield on the term loan wasn't generous enough.[17] What didn't help was the issuer's trading results.

By mid-2006 Toys "R" Us's share of the domestic toy market had fallen further to 14%; Wal-Mart continued to dominate with a 22% share.[18] Perhaps more worryingly, Amazon announced its decision to invest in its toy business now that its exclusive agreement with Toys "R" Us had been terminated.[19] Nevertheless, the booming economy offered enough opportunities for all market participants to grow. Sales at the freshly PE-backed group jumped 15% in the fiscal year to 2 February 2007, thanks to significant store openings overseas and at Babies "R" Us. The retailer also pursued the programme of closures started in 2004 by shutting 87 underperforming outlets. In the following two years, it upped the ante by converting over 100 stores, putting traditional toy stores and Babies "R" Us formats in the same locations.

## Shop till you drop

A product of frothy markets, the Toys "R" Us buyout was structured using a paraphernalia of fancy innovation and newfangled debt instruments. The company controlled a variety of domestic as well as international operating subsidiaries whose assets could be employed as security for the various LBO loans. The real estate (i.e., the stores) naturally offered the opportunity to structure part of the debt as high-yielding commercial mortgage-backed securities, a popular product of the days. In essence, that was the main reason behind the involvement of property expert Vornado. In the end, the complexity of the capital structure was only reined in by the Credit Crunch that emerged in the summer of 2007.

Despite the distress witnessed by the debt markets, in late July 2008 one of Toys "R" Us's backers, KKR, announced its intention to float on the NYSE at a valuation of $10 billion. The PE group had filed its registration document a year earlier – one month after its key rival Blackstone had successfully listed, but the Credit Crunch had forced a reassessment. The delayed IPO would automatically grant KKR a new access route to fundraising. Although the firm had listed a private equity vehicle on the Amsterdam Stock Exchange two years earlier,[20] the lacklustre performance of that vehicle's stock had convinced KKR's executive team that a listing in America would offer a more reliable flow of capital. Unfortunately, the collapse of Lehman Brothers in mid-September 2008 forced governments to bail out the entire global banking sector. When stock markets crashed, KKR had to postpone its listing indefinitely.

The PE firm's troubles were shared by Toys "R" Us. Thanks to aggressive cost cuts, the group's EBITDA margin had shot up from 5% in the year to 31 January 2004 to 8% four years later.[21] But the second half of 2008 outweighed these efforts when trading started to flag. In March 2009 Moody's put loans of the retailer's UK division under review due to significant decrease in the value of the assets used as collateral. Refinancing and default risks were on the rise; the Great Recession was starting to bite.[22] By the summer, the group's unsecured bonds traded two-thirds below par.[23]

The PE-owned retailer was not the only one hurt by the savagery of the recession. That created unique opportunities. In May 2009 Toys "R" Us acquired New York and Las Vegas toy store group FAO Schwarz. Management put temporary FAO Schwarz boutiques in its domestic stores for the year-end holidays. A year later, the concept was expanded into permanent boutiques. Yet, there was no question that the group's heavily stretched balance sheet represented a major risk. Toys "R" Us spent the second half of 2009 refining its capital structure. In the summer it issued $950 million in high-yield notes partly to refinance a $1.3 billion unsecured facility maturing the following year. The new loans were repayable in 2017; surely the PE owners would be out by that time!

At any rate, it granted the retailer some well needed breathing space. Its bonds started trading up, above 80 cents on the dollar. In parallel, the company extended by two years the maturity of secured loans coming due in July 2010, a deadline that was uncomfortably getting closer. In exchange, Toys "R" Us accepted to grant creditors a higher interest on the instrument.[24] Then, in October, the group refinanced a revolving loan, gaining access to $200 million for its European and Australian operations. Over in the US, the group also issued a $725 million secured high-yield note to repay $600 million of existing loans. It was getting rather complicated, but that allowed rating agency S&P to revise its outlook on the business to stable.[25] The group had been forced into a sizeable refinancing, raising new debt with longer maturity, and amending and extending the existing loans that it could not refinance. Toys "R" Us was facing its first real test under LBO.

The Great Recession was not kind to consumer-facing retailers, leading them into a mad rush to the bottom: ever greater price reductions. Partly for that reason, Toys "R" Us reported year-on-year revenue drops in 2008 and 2009. Still, there was no question that it remained a highly admired brand: in 2009 70% of US households with children had shopped at Toys "R" Us while 84% of first-time mothers had shopped at Babies "R" Us.[26]

## Batteries not included

For a while the financial sponsors had been toying with the idea of getting out of their investment. Due to the recession, potential buyers were not showing much interest. Yet, reintroducing the toy retailer to the vagaries of the public markets seemed like a sensible option. Maybe the paucity of IPOs in the past two years would encourage avid institutional investors to sate their appetite by taking a bite at a chunk of fresh equity.

About to celebrate its fifth anniversary under LBO, in late May 2010 Toys "R" Us filed registration for a relisting, aiming to raise $800 million to partially shrink its debt load.[27] In anticipation, it announced a series of refinancing initiatives to extend $2 billion of existing debt tranches. It would give the business room to breathe in the first few years post-IPO, a period often prone to reassessment for PE-backed companies that get exposed to the uncomfortable scrutiny of equity analysts.

Although sales continued to wane, the corporate restructuring introduced by management was paying dividends: at 8.5% of sales, EBITDA margin in the year to January 2010 was at its highest point since the buyout. Equally, net debt was at its lowest, at 3.3 times

# THE GOOD, THE BAD AND THE UGLY OF PRIVATE EQUITY

EBITDA, having halved in the past five years. The number of international stores was up a fifth over the same period while the closures of sickly domestic stores and the openings of profitable Babies "R" Us formats had produced strong gains.

Regardless of whether the toy retailer looked hale and hearty to convince the punters, KKR was getting ready to attempt its own market listing for the third time. Three years after the initial filing, the PE group renewed its intention to float. It had increased the value of its portfolio by 10% in the first quarter of 2010, so things were looking up. The Great Recession had lingered and threatened on more than one occasion to turn into another Great Depression, but the path was now clear for big corporate projects to resume. The credit and equity markets had commenced a comeback. Yet no one knew how long that would last; it was best for KKR to get its listing out of the way in case the markets' revival was short-lived. At a $9 billion valuation, marginally down on the price tag hoped for initially, the firm was prepared to make some sacrifice to provide liquidity to its founders and senior executive team. On the day of the IPO in mid-September, the stock traded 3% down.[28]

No doubt Toys "R" Us would have agreed to make sacrifices just to engineer its relisting. Management kept working its way through the balance sheet, tackling each tranche of debt one at a time. In August 2010 it extended the maturity of the working capital facility and increased the group's borrowing capacity. The same month it issued a new $350 million bond and $700 million in term loans to repay existing facilities.[29] That gave the retailer the luxury to wait until the IPO window opened with more conviction.

Early the following year, all parties – lenders, underwriters, investors – waited to see how the year-end trading figures would look. They needed to be robust to win over the markets. Especially because the IPO plan faced a major challenge. Comparable valuations had tanked since the time of the toy retailer's delisting. Bain, KKR and Vornado had bought the business at a rich valuation exceeding 9 times trailing EBITDA, or 10 times prior-year earnings. With comparable companies trading below 8 times in 2010, down from 10 times five years earlier,[30] the PE owners were looking at a negative-multiple arbitrage upon exit. That is, if they could exit.

EBITDA was up two-fifths since the LBO, but it had been hovering at around $1 billion for the past four years. The lifeless state is not a healthy one in a leveraged buyout situation. Debt payments accrue according to the all-powerful and universal law of compound interest, the eighth wonder of the world according to no less an authority than Albert Einstein. If debt commitments go up, so must EBITDA as a cash proxy and safeguard against the threat of loan covenants. Logically, the company's financial sponsors were eager to get on the IPO bandwagon. Proceeds raised from the markets would be more than welcome. They would help pay down some of the loans; bonds worth $500 million were falling due in the summer of 2011.

Alas, the retailer's new-found prosperity proved evanescent. The year-end holiday season of 2010 saw sales fall on the prior year, both domestically and internationally. American consumers were bargain-hunting while the UK and Spanish economies were still reeling from the financial crisis. Sales were only up 2% despite the company's extensive use of pop-up stores.[31] With fourth-quarter trading accounting for two-fifths of group revenues, only a great festive season could have provided the perfect background to an IPO. Instead, poor results hurt the group's financial position. In the year to 29 January 2011 cash flows from operations crashed 80% due to aggressive marketing and discounting. Net debt shot up 10%, while the interest cover reverted to 2, meaning that earnings were only twice as large as interest payments, an uncomfortably tight level even for a covenant-lite LBO. The relisting had to be parked away for now. The NYSE would have to wait.

To secure more runway, the company actively tried to refinance a quarter of its debt, if only to benefit from the all-time low interest rates. But all the market would let management do is amend and extend part of its existing loans.[32] Ongoing trading difficulties prevented a more favourable negotiation. In the year to January 2012 competition intensified, affecting profitability and cash flows. Over the previous two years, EBITDA margin had fallen from 8.5% to 7%. For the second year in a row, operating cash flows failed to cover either capital expenditure or interest expense.[33]

With $1.4 billion in near-term maturities, the company was soon forced into another round of re-engineering. In March 2012 management launched a $300 million issuance to refinance domestic loans.[34] In April, it was the turn of the British operations to be restructured ahead of a deadline to repay more than £400 million of loans.[35] Then, in July, the group launched a high-yield note worth $350 million.[36] In the face of competitive pressure, throughout 2012 Toys "R" Us continued to experience poor trading, to such degree that revenues from new store openings no longer compensated for the ferocious slump in like-for-like sales. Full-year revenues and EBITDA to 2 February 2013 were both down more than 2%.

The frustrating situation was made even more untenable by the successful portfolio exits that private equity firms achieved in these early stages of the economic recovery. In March 2011 Bain Capital and KKR themselves scored America's biggest ever PE-backed IPO by listing hospital operator HCA,[37] finally heading for the door five years after buying the target at the peak of the cycle. KKR also made over 2.2 times its equity on the partial realisation of British wholesaler Alliance Boots when, in June 2012, it sold 45% of the business to US giant pharmacy store chain Walgreens. Because of its weakened market position, Toys "R" Us was proving a more problematic exit candidate.

## All work, no play makes a dull deal

A new year brought more debt restructuring. Playing a fast game of financial engineering, in the first half of 2013 the retailer's UK unit partially refinanced a total of £400 million of the securitised loan raised at the outset of the LBO. The French and Spanish securitised debt was also rejigged.[38] While management was busy rearranging the balance sheet, the picture presented by the income statement got worse. In the first quarter of 2013, sales crashed more than 5%. Down 8.5% domestically, they also dropped in the usually strong overseas territories. Although leverage was falling, EBITDA was wearing away faster.

Inescapably, the game was up for Storch. Brought in by the PE sponsors to champion their vigorous rejuvenation plans, the CEO left in May 2013. It was unfinished business, but the serial recapitalisations, the relentless market shifts and competitive disruption had got in the way of success. Three years after registration, the company officially pulled the plug on its relisting plans.[39] Which did not take away the need to pursue the interminable refinancing. That summer, the group issued a six-year covenant-lite $985 million loan.[40]

It is against this background that, in a move that it would soon come to regret, management applied a price-match policy, not just for brick-and-mortar rivals (something it had already done the previous year), but also for online competitors, essentially Amazon.[41] It was a case of force majeure, a desperate attempt to retain market share. In its home market, almost two out of every five toys were purchased online, while the proportion in foreign markets was equally concerning: in Britain and Germany respectively, about a third and a quarter of toys were bought via the Web.[42] The market shift was unmistakable; Toys "R" Us needed to adapt. With its "Buy Online, Pick Up In Store" programme available in the US and the UK, the retailer was fighting back. By originating only 5% of its sales online in France, for instance, where the

Internet accounted for 14% of total toy sales nationwide,[43] it was evident that Toys "R" Us had some catching-up to do.

Price matching was initiated by Antonio Urcelay, the interim chief after Storch's defenestration, and a 17-year veteran at the company. He had been president of the European operations before inheriting the top job. Everyone hoped that his deep market knowledge would help the group turn this difficult corner. Just in time for the holiday season, in October Urcelay was handed the CEO role on a permanent basis.[44] His first annual results presentation proved that his task would not be easy.

In the year to January 2014, mostly due to the price-match policy and persistent online migration, group sales fell 7.4%. EBITDA almost halved. That was before exceptional items. Post-restructuring costs, cash earnings were practically non-existent. The scale of the business had never been more imposing: Toys "R" Us employed 70,000 employees worldwide, approximately 45,000 domestically; its stores numbered 1,762 in 35 countries, half of them in the US;[45] yet the LBO had reached its nadir.

With the business reporting its worst EBITDA in 12 years, it was time for more management changes. In June 2014 CFO Clay Creasey resigned, 16 months after the departure of Storch, the CEO who had hired him. Creasey had tried to thread his way through the company's financial mine field; to no avail. Maybe a new number cruncher would help present the financials in a better light. But it wouldn't change the weak fundamentals of a stagnant retail story.

The rest of 2014 delivered the same predictable mediocrity. Despite the weak comparables of the previous year, the group only returned to modest sales growth in the first half before experiencing another disappointing holiday season. Like-for-like international growth of 1.2% could not compensate for a 5% decline in the retailer's home market in November and December.[46] Despite the new finance chief, in the year to January 2015 sales were down 1.5% and EBITDA margin, though much improved on the prior year, was still below 5%.

Earnings barely covered interest expense. The real problem was leverage: due to weaker profitability, net debt now exceeded 7.2 times EBITDA. If this transaction had not been completed on a covenant-lite package, the lenders would already have called in the bailiffs.

With an exit still unlikely for its PE owners, in the final quarter of 2014 the retailer had launched another refinancing, this one worth $1.4 billion, to redeem loans coming due the following year. But the new loans came under pricing pressure soon after their launch, indicating that investors were getting nervous about the issuer's creditworthiness. Within days they traded at a 15% discount to par.[47]

## All play, no work makes a mere toy

Still very much in charge, the PE firms were losing patience. When it comes to performance improvements, fund managers do not assign much value to corporate loyalty or industry knowledge. The sorts of skills that help corporate executives earn the favours of their financial sponsors are earnings and cash maximisation, capital structure optimisation, and surgical attention to debt commitments. On this set of criteria, chief executive Antonio Urcelay did not win many points. The fact that his recent experience was international had justified his promotion given that sales growth in recent years had come from abroad. But Toys "R" Us still sourced 60% of revenues from its domestic market, and that is where the heavy lifting needed to take place.

In June 2015 Urcelay was replaced by David Brandon. Brandon had already worked with Bain Capital when the latter appointed him in 1999 to lead Domino's Pizza. Sixteen years later, he was still chairman of the restaurant chain. He was not intimately acquainted with the toy industry, but in view of recent trading the incoming CEO had to concoct a turnaround similar to the one orchestrated at Domino's.

Also relevant was that, in 2004, he had led the successful listing of Domino's in the largest PE-backed IPO of a restaurant group globally.

In the past decade, Toys "R" Us had been on a roller coaster, yet Brandon optimistically observed: "I believe our best days are ahead of us and I'm eager to get started."[48] One of the first decisions taken by the retailer's third chief executive since the LBO was the closure of the eminent retailer FAO Schwarz. The acquisition hadn't panned out as expected. In July 2015 FAO Schwarz's 145-year-old flagship New York store was closed, in a clear sign that drastic decisions were on the cards.

But closing stores of international repute was not a way to rebuild the top line. In the year ended January 2016 the new CEO reported further revenue deterioration, even if comparable-store sales had risen during the holiday season for the first time in many years. Although EBITDA margin edged up above 6%, the group was unable to grow into its bloated debt structure. It had no alternative but to keep refinancing. Mid-year, the unsecured bonds totalling $850 million and due over the coming two years became eligible for a swap against higher-coupon instruments, with maturity pushed back to 2021.[49]

With a debt-to-EBITDA multiple exceeding 5.5 times, the company was in no position to invest in its future. Yet macroeconomic conditions were improving, paving the way for a reintroduction to the stock market. In October 2016 the IPO idea resurfaced. After two strong quarters – and 11 years under PE ownership – the toy retailer was keen to face the public markets. A relisting would depend entirely on how strong trading would be during the year-end holiday season. Anything other than sales growth would confirm that the negative trend recently observed was a fundamental shift, not just an unfortunate blip.

In the past four years, the retailer's top line had shrunk 15%. Sadly, the full-year numbers to January 2017 did not turn the tide. Down 2.2%, sales were off both domestically and in foreign markets. Though Toys "R" Us was benefiting from consumers' online migration, recording an

11% jump in Internet sales in the year-end holiday quarter,[50] competition from discounters and electronic retailers remained implacable. With prices as the main differentiating factor of increasingly standardised products, the group's EBITDA margin remained below or on par with pre-buyout levels (fiscal years 2005 and 2006 in Figure 6.2 below).

**Figure 6.2 – Toys "R" Us's sales and EBITDA margin from 2005 to 2017**

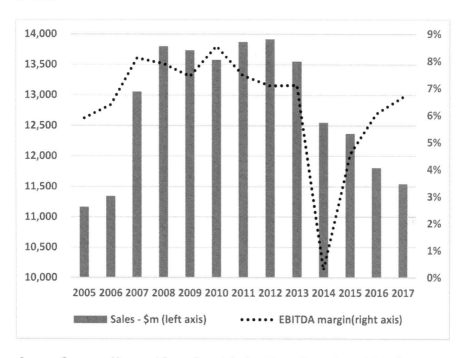

*Source: Company filings – Notes: financials for 52 or 53 weeks ended in January or February of years shown*

With operating performance falling behind plan, the company pursued a series of refinancings. In October 2016 management again came to market with a $500 million commercial mortgage bond backed by several of the company's stores. But when a company keeps disappointing and its management fails to deliver on its projections – not just on the base case but on any of the downside scenarios – issuing new debt becomes a hard sell. While part of the proposed bond was triple A rated, with the company still on a speculative grade, raising fresh capital was getting expensive: potential lenders were asking for a higher yield or more security, sometimes both.

## Toys "R" bust

In the year to January 2017, the toy retailer generated sales in line with those recorded at the time of the buyout 11 years earlier, a poor showing since the number of stores had increased by a quarter globally. EBITDA was down 30% on its 2010 level, stuck in the $700-to-$800 million range for the past three years. But the picture was actually bleaker than it appears. EBITDA is an accounting measure that can easily be manipulated. To assess the true underlying performance of a leveraged business, it is best to look at operating cash flows. Those had gone from more than $750 million per annum in the two years preceding the LBO to $240 million in the year to 30 January 2016. They plummeted to zero the following fiscal year. A business sapped by over $4 billion of LBO loans and at least $450 million in annual interest payments was no longer producing any cash from its operations.[51] That made the next chapter in its corporate history all but inevitable.

Crushed by the burden of its capital structure, on 18 September 2017 the retailer filed for bankruptcy protection for its American and Canadian operating entities. On the day, the retailer's bonds traded below 20 cents on the dollar as the market digested the news.[52] As a dense pall of uncertainty settled over the business, the real estate entity and the activities outside North America continued to trade as usual. It was fortunate that the debt package had been sliced and diced across so many operating entities; the US business did not have to drag the entire group with it. Somewhat spared the bankruptcy embarrassment, overseas employees cannot have felt very safe. For proof, within six months the UK operations were also placed into administration, and the French subsidiary fell into receivership in July 2018.

Of course, the decision by Toys "R" Us to file did not only affect the company's lenders and employees. Its suppliers, including toy manufacturers Mattel and Hasbro, both deriving 10% of their annual sales from the retailer, were likely to experience further pressure on sales and cash flows, even if Toys "R" Us was expected to keep trading as normal while in Chapter 11. Mattel, in particular, had its own debt requirements and trading issues to look after.[53] The digitalisation of toys had deeply affected traditional toy makers; the bankruptcy of one of their main distributors was the last thing they needed. Within months, plans for Mattel and Hasbro's merger were in motion.

As Figure 6.3 demonstrates, from 2010 onward Toys "R" Us made no progress in improving its capital structure despite repeated attempts to wean itself off an enslaving debt habit. Its PE sponsors, usually eager to exhibit majesty in finding solutions, had failed to deliver. Not only was the leverage ratio still too high for comfort, but interest expense was not adequately covered by earnings. After so many years under LBO, in 2014-17 cash earnings were stubbornly stuck below 2 times annual interest payments.

Between 2006 and 2017, annual interest charges related to the LBO loans ranged from $400 million in 2009 to a peak of $517 million in 2014. Accruing debt commitments eventually made earnings and cash flows positively lacking. Over the full period of PE ownership, $5.5 billion was spent on interest payments, representing 107% of the company's annual operating cash flows. That's billions of dollars that didn't go into R&D, or into store refurbishment, or into business remodelling. A fortune that could have, if well invested, enabled a digital transformation.

**Figure 6.3 – Toys "R" Us's leverage ratio (Net debt/EBITDA) and interest cover (EBITDA/interest) from 2003 to 2017**

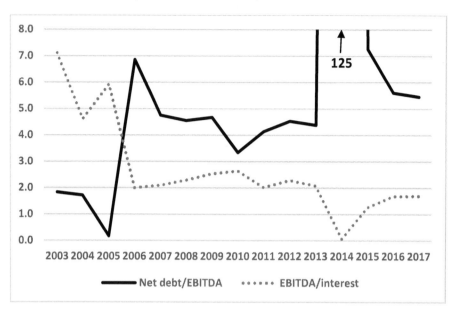

*Source: Company filings and author's analysis – Notes: In 2014, EBITDA was non-existent, leading to a leverage ratio of 125 times earnings. Financials for 52 or 53 weeks ended in January or February of years shown*

Chapter 11 protection gave the group a chance to restructure. Yet, with years wasted away in zombie mode trying to protect the equity interests of fatally imprudent financial sponsors, the toy retailer had lost all hope of survival. In March 2018, both the North American and UK operations were liquidated, putting 33,000 jobs at risk after the administrators failed to find any party willing to purchase the business as a going concern. As a sign that the toy industry had unremittingly moved on, one of the corporate vultures eager to feed off the retailer's carcass by picking up some of its auctioned stores was its main online rival: Amazon.

## Toys in the attic

Preaching like a prophet in search of disciples, upon filing for bankruptcy in September 2017 CEO Brandon declared: "Today marks the dawn of a new era at Toys "R" Us, where we expect that the financial constraints that have held us back will be addressed in a lasting and effective way,"[54] adding "we are confident that we are taking the right steps to ensure that the iconic Toys "R" Us and Babies "R" Us brands live on for many generations."

Toys "R" Us had not managed to re-establish a connection with the public equity markets. Its performance had never shown sufficient consistency to offer prospective investors the stability they demand before participating in a fresh IPO. The reasons behind the toy retailer's permanent impairment are manifold.

*Downward pricing trend*

Toys are a very competitive consumer segment. There are several factors behind this. They can be mass-produced, offering economies of scale. They are ideal products for automated assembly-line manufacturing. Globalisation led developed countries to offshore production to south east Asia and China. Global scaling-up of toy manufacturing heaps pressure on pricing and margins. In the five years leading up to the buyout, Toys "R" Us's revenues were flat and EBITDA margin hovered around 7%.

*Seasonality*

The main specificity of the toy industry is its seasonality. In the US and the UK, up to half of toys are sold in the last two months of a calendar year, reflecting the importance of the Halloween, Thanksgiving, Hanukkah and Christmas festivities.

Toys "R" Us reported: "more than 40% of the sales from our worldwide toy store business and a substantial portion of the operating earnings and cash flows from operations were generated in the fourth quarter."[55] There was very little management could do to smooth the seasonal cash flow patterns, other than lobbying governments to enact changes to the holiday calendar.

*Competition from discounters*

For years Wal-Mart and Target were Toys "R" Us's fiercest competitors. Between 2004 and 2006, both discounters increased their share of sales from the two leading toy makers Mattel and Hasbro, taking business away from Toys "R" Us in the process.[56]

Hiring Storch away from Target in 2006 made sense. But consumers became ever more cost-conscious during the Great Recession. All the money Toys "R" Us and even traditional discounters poured into marketing and promotions added to the cost of selling toys. That gave an edge to retailers like Costco that took a no-frills approach and did not advertise. In 2015, thanks to ever expanding legions of bargain-hunters, Costco grew revenues twice as fast as Wal-Mart and four times as fast as Target.[57] The traditional marketing style that Storch brought with him from Target when joining Toys "R" Us in 2006 was made obsolete by the cataclysmic economic environment. By the time it filed for bankruptcy protection in what was the third largest Chapter 11 filing in US retail history, Toys "R" Us was experiencing a similar hyper-promotional context in the UK and other international markets, where discounters were gaining market share.

*Online distribution*

Another impact of the Great Recession was the acceleration of online migration, both at home and in foreign geographies. No-frills were a specialty for many online retailers; none was better at that game than Amazon.

When it completed its buyout, Toys "R" Us originated about 3% of revenues through its own website.[58] Its online strategy was nascent.

That should have been an opportunity. The toy trade was mature and ultra-competitive. Moving to a leaner online model was a way to alleviate some of the pressure experienced on margins. Yet, between 2005 and 2009 online sales at Toys "R" Us only grew 5.5% per annum.[59] These results look weak when compared to those of other physical store chains like Macy's, which recorded double-digit annual growth. They were also paltry relative to pure e-commerce plays. In 2016 alone, Amazon experienced a 24% jump in toy sales in the American market, booking $4 billion or one-fifth the total value of toy sales in the country that year.[60]

Amazon's market share gains over the years greatly affected pricing across the various product categories: toys as much as learning and video games. In turn, sales growth and margins went south at Toys "R" Us and all major retailers. That led to a sector re-rating. From 14 times in 2001, the average enterprise value-to-EBITDA multiple for physical store chains had depreciated to 8 times nine years later.[61] By contrast, in 2010 Amazon's valuation exceeded 25 times cash earnings.

## Digitalisation of 'toys'

Video games were already a major part of sales by the time the PE consortium invited itself to the retailer's playroom. In any given year, video games represented 10% to one fifth of the group's revenues in the US.[62] This space was even more competitive and unpredictable than traditional toys, a segment in which Toys "R" Us had moulded its brand name around reliability and excellence for almost sixty years.

Video games are subject to unusual market rules. Differentiation derives from the 'cool' factor and the latest craze rather than trust and conformity. Another major feature of video games is that they are often one-hit wonders, subject to the law of blockbusters where the game might generate fantastic sales for a year or two before disappearing in the annals of mass-consumption history. Of course, some video games, like Call of Duty or Super Mario, can become franchises and go through regular upgrades, but they are unlikely to become cross-generational products like Barbie dolls or LEGO building bricks. For retailers like Toys "R" Us, video games require to closely monitor the market for latest trends. Failing to discover the latest 'it' game can mean missed sales without a chance to make up for it the next year.

One of the main effects of digitalisation is what marketeers call 'age compression'. In short, children are getting older younger; they adopt mature tastes and lose interest in traditional toys at an earlier age than children of previous generations. The digitalisation of games and Web-based entertainment are behind this trend, and it accelerated throughout Toys "R" Us's period of PE ownership. This explains why Babies "R" Us proved more resilient – toddlers are not susceptible to age compression…yet.

As a result, many retailers with a strong expertise in technology or with a video game specialty, such as Gamestop and Best Buy in America and the Game Group in the UK, provided better service to consumers who were becoming more tech savvy. Of course, the most threatening digital toy of all is the smartphone, taking ever more kids away from traditional toys and games and diverting their pocket money on the latest mobile app rather than board games or action figures. And the smartphone didn't really exist until Apple launched the new product category in 2007. By then, Toys "R" Us was knee-deep in expensive LBO debt.

*Sector cyclicality*

Before closing its doors for good in 2015, FAO Schwarz had already experienced failure. After an aggressive period of growth in the 1990s under Eyler's leadership, the group operated over 40 stores by the time the 2001-02 recession hit trading. FAO filed for bankruptcy in January 2003, emerging from it three months later in a rushed restructuring that proved ambitious, forcing the business back into bankruptcy by the end of that year. The New York and Las Vegas stores were reopened the next year and remained independent until their acquisition by Toys

"R" Us during the recession five years later. Cyclical sectors are not great hunting grounds for leveraged buyouts. Toys "R" Us and its PE backers found out at their expense, although as mentioned Bain Capital had already damaged its reputation when losing control of KB Toys shortly before investing in its largest competitor.

*Real estate value erosion at home*

The poor financial and operating fundamentals of the world of retail had a marked impact on the value of real estate, in particular for property dedicated to retail. The migration of consumers to online alternatives was felt all the more intensely that, in the decade leading up to the financial crisis, significant footage of retail space had been added in shopping malls across the US. With fewer consumers shopping in store, that excess square footage devalued the real estate holdings of all retailers.

The need to maximise property value was a reason behind KKR and Bain Capital's decision to partner with Vornado, a real estate investment trust with strong expertise in street retail. But the structural decline of the US real estate market that started soon after the LBO did not help produce as much upside from the property portfolio as originally intended. While in the first five years of ownership, the PE firms completed the redevelopment of the US stores, between 2011 and 2017 the number of retail units managed by Toys "R" Us in its domestic market remained the same. Perhaps the question is why, even as late as June 2017, three months before filing for Chapter 11, management was still adamant that it did not intend to shut many more stores.[63]

Thankfully the retailer had an international presence where it could partly offset the negative trend at home – the international expansion saw the number of stores jump by two-thirds. Alas, by 2017 Europe seemed to experience the same neglect from consumers for physical stores. Property value destruction was spreading in tandem with online

> consumption and was partly to blame for the UK division's bankruptcy filing in early 2018.

## Losses "R" Us

Like candies, toys are primarily targeted at children. Perhaps for that reason, they are equally subject to impulse buying. Children are notorious for falling prey to most of a marketer's ploys to encourage spending. About 45% of toys belong to the 'pocket money sector' – priced under a fiver – where impulse purchase is prevalent, with parents often giving in to pester power from their offspring.[64] The Great Recession had not been kind to this pocket-money segment, the prime victim of squeezed consumer spending.

In view of the pricing pressure derived from product standardisation, competition from discounters and etailers, as well as the sector's cyclicality and seasonality, Toys "R" Us turned out to be a poor candidate for an LBO. The bankruptcies of KB Toys and FAO Schwarz in 2003 following a slow holiday season were good enough clues.

The fact that the credit markets were going through one of their sporadic bubbles contributed to the decision by Bain Capital et al to complete their 2005 buyout. Back then, the rationale behind the move was to give the toy specialist a chance to restructure. Yet, despite the migration of demand to the Internet, despite the re-rating of retail stocks, and despite the digitalisation of toys, it is odd that management and its PE backers stubbornly pursued an expansion of their store portfolio. Between January 2006 and January 2018 Toys "R" Us increased its number of stores by 400 to 1,948. It is as if all parties involved had failed to pay attention to the transformation the industry was going through.

By 2017 the main threat was no longer the discounters but an even bigger foe, Toys "R" Us's previous online partner: Amazon. A decade is a very long time in retail. In the mid-noughties, Wal-Mart was criticised for destroying local businesses, ripping the heart out of town centres and driving wages down. Ten years later, Amazon was tagged with the same nefarious nature. The fact that it took it so long to go bankrupt shows that Toys "R" Us was resilient, but there is no denying that the category killer had been slain by margin killers.

If only the PE community had shown a bit more impulse control and left Toys "R" Us well alone. Perhaps the retailer would have orchestrated a successful digital transition. Buried deep in a debt mineshaft, it was forced to save on capex and to go through a series of cathartic restructurings, disheartening the foot soldiers and instigating the substitution of top-drawer executives. As a result, Toys "R" Us's name is forever engraved onto the PE industry's Hall of Shame.

---

## LEVERAGED BUYOUTS AND MARKET DISRUPTION

*If fully priced – as is usually the case with delistings – a leveraged buyout cannot afford to see its business plan derailed. In the case of Toys "R" Us, turmoil came in the form of a fierce financial crisis, a deep economic recession and intense competition from online, digital games and mobile apps distributors. Few companies can escape unscathed when disruption throws a spanner in the works of the LBO machinery.*

*In the last decade, the impact of technology on many business models has been nothing short of revolutionary. Which implies that, in most cases, leverage ratios in excess of 70% are not recommended. On that point, Toys "R" Us provides a costly but valuable lesson.*

# PART THREE

# The Ugly: Greedy or wicked?

*"The grabbing hands grab all they can*
*All for themselves*
*After all, it's a competitive world*
*Everything counts in large amounts"*[1]

**Depeche Mode, 1980s English electronic-music band**

*Sharp practices in dealmaking are nothing new. Ever since the advent of capitalism, in their obsessive search for wealth and power, financiers have rarely stopped to consider moral principles. In that respect, the next three chapters cover nothing out of the ordinary, just modern versions of ancestral practices.*

# CHAPTER 7

# Bhs: A roadmap to bankruptcy

> *To most readers, a leveraged buyout is an acquisition carried out by a fund manager with the contribution of corporate lenders.*
>
> *Occasionally, entrepreneurs can lead leveraged transactions, with or without the involvement of financial sponsors. These kinds of deals are called owner buyouts, or OBOs.*

At first sight, owner buyouts do not seem all that common. I suspect that few readers will have heard the expression and be able to come up with names of companies or individuals that went through such a transaction. Yet many memorable buyouts are owner-led. Probably the most visible OBOs in the United States are the ones carried out by President Donald Trump in his former capacity as chairman of the Trump Organization. Trump completed a vast number of leveraged transactions for his real estate activities.

As is common with any deal, owner buyouts can attract controversy when they fail. Trump has had his fair share of bad publicity following the serial bankruptcies of his casino and hotel operations. Similarly, for all the wrong reasons, in Britain the transaction portrayed in this chapter received a lot of press coverage.

## Once upon a time

Before inflation brought the dollar and pound stores that Americans and Britons are today familiar with, discount shops had set prices at a more reasonable level. In the US, in 1879, Woolworth Bros. launched the five-and-dime format, where everything was priced at 5 or 10 cents. Because Woolworth's stores (and subsequent copycats) offered a wide range of products, without much focus on one category or the other, they also came to be known as variety stores.

Thirty years later, Frank Woolworth introduced the same format to the UK, opening in Liverpool what was immediately baptised a penny-and-sixpence store. For readers curious to know what a sixpence coin was worth, it was equivalent to one-fortieth of a pound – the British were late comers to the concept of decimalisation!

Two decades after Woolworth's UK launch, British Home Stores was founded in 1928 by another group of American entrepreneurs.[1] To avoid going head-to-head with Woolworth, the newcomer priced its goods at one shilling, the equivalent of one-twentieth of a pound. Within a year of opening its first store in Brixton, in south London, British Home Stores introduced products priced at up to five shillings in order to broaden its offering.

Listed on the stock exchange in 1931, gradually the business opened branches across the country and proposed cafeterias and grocery departments. By 1970 British Home Stores had 12,000 workers and 94 stores.[2] Twelve years later, the company went through a major transformation by moving away from the supermarket model in favour of a department store concept.[3] In 1986 it merged with home-design specialist Habitat and mother-to-childrenswear retailer Mothercare to form Storehouse plc. At that time, it also executed a marketing revamp with the new BhS logo (later to become Bhs). The merger did not work out as planned. Habitat and other smaller divisions were sold off in 1992.

By the late 1990s Storehouse was still strategically challenged, with Mothercare and the chain of Bhs department stores offering little synergistic benefits. In May 1999 the conglomerate jettisoned its CEO following six years of underperformance. To help both Mothercare and Bhs regain their erstwhile glory, a strategic review was implemented. After a series of M&A discussions between Storehouse and various retail groups, in May 2000 Bhs was sold to retail entrepreneur Philip Green.

## Green's story

Aged 48 at the time, Green had more than thirty years of experience in the fashion retail sector. His dad Simon had been a mildly successful electrical retailer until his death, when Green was just 12. Raised in Hampstead Garden Suburb, a well-off middle-class enclave in north London, Green helped his mother run the family self-service petrol station and property companies before leaving school and striking out on his own at the age of 16. He started by importing shoes but later pursued a series of deals, buying weak businesses on the cheap and turning them around.[4] He made his first fortune after buying the Jean Jeanie chain for £65,000 in 1985 and selling it a year later for £3 million.[5]

Given the intrinsic level of risk associated with the cyclically challenged retail industry, not all his ventures proved successful. His spell as chairman and chief executive of Amber Day in the late 1980s, following his acquisition of a minority stake in the struggling textile and clothing retail group, ended with his resignation in September 1992 – the economic recession had hit the business, leading to a 75% drop in the group's share price in a matter of months.[6]

By the mid-1990s Green had recovered from his disheartening Amber Day experience. After the 1994 purchase of Owen Owen, the fifth largest group of department stores in Britain, he combined that business with his 50 Xceptions discount shops. He then acquired two divisions from retail conglomerate Sears – sports specialist Olympus, bought in partnership with Scottish entrepreneur Tom Hunter, and the chain Shoe Express – offloading both shortly thereafter at huge profits. But Green was in a rush, and acquiring Sears's divisions one at a time was clearly going to take too long. At the end of January 1999, he successfully bid £530 million for the whole group, cooperating once more with a bunch of Scottish entrepreneurs: Hunter alongside brothers and property experts David and Frederick Barclay. They spent the rest of the year dismantling Sears piecemeal, flipping the Wallis, Warehouse, Richards and Miss Selfridge brands to retailer Arcadia.[7]

Green's ultimate goal was to find vulnerable and unfocused targets in the very fragmented British fashion retail sector. With a keen eye for property, he imposed himself as one of the most aggressive predators in the industry. Among others, in 1999 fashion-clothing groups Marks & Spencer and New Look were considered worthy targets. Both managed to escape Green's grasp. With Bhs the enthusiastic entrepreneur had cornered a hopeless prey.

## Bhs's buyout

Although on the small side for Green, who had tabled an £11 billion takeover bid for Marks & Spencer a few months earlier,[8] Bhs was a typical candidate for revitalisation. The chain had reported a profit of £13 million in the year ended 1 April 2000, down 85% on the prior year. With revenues of £822 million, like-for-like sales had fallen 6.5%.[9] For a total consideration just north of £200 million, partly financed with £125 million of debt from German bank WestLB,[10] Green and his minority deal partners Tom Hunter and WestLB financier Robin Saunders were buying a deflated business that offered significant restructuring opportunities. Storehouse's management had already enforced staff cuts, but with operations spread across more than 150 stores and a headcount in excess of 14,000,[11] much more could be achieved.

In a bid to slash costs while maintaining Bhs as a middle-market retailer, one of Green's first moves was to ask suppliers to drop prices if they wanted to keep working with the chain.[12] Green wanted to initiate radically different business methods to improve performance and product quality. He planned to acquire stock on a more regular basis than Bhs's habit of seasonal buying. That policy had the twin advantages of maintaining the stock fresh and ensuring suppliers were kept on their toes.

The intention was also to raise sales per square foot, stock new ranges and modernise shopping sites. To deliver on his middle-market strategy, within six months he hired Terry Green (no relation) as chief executive, away from the same position at rival Debenhams, and Allan Leighton, previously chair of Wal-Mart Europe, as chairman.[13] After intensely focusing on selling basic apparel to the traditional core market of 40-to-55-year-old women, in the year ended March 2002 Bhs tripled operating margin to 11.8%. At £100 million, earnings were up eight times since the acquisition, and the highest in the group's history.[14]

A couple of months after celebrating his 50th birthday in style by spending £5 million flying 200 'close friends' to Cyprus, in May 2002 Green paid himself a £165 million dividend.[15] Not a bad return on the £70 million he had invested in exchange for 95% of Bhs.[16] With a valuation for the High Street chain in excess of £1 billion, Green's OBO had paid off handsomely.

Ranked 16th in the *Mail on Sunday*'s list of the richest Brits that year, the freshly minted billionaire admitted that his job at Bhs was not done yet. The turnaround had worked out, but the retailer was still seen by younger shoppers as old-fashioned and 'uncool' despite recent efforts to shake up its image.[17] Ideally suited for homeowners and families, Bhs needed to broaden its appeal. Green wanted to turn it into a destination for the fashion-conscious.

That kind of transformation was likely to take a while. Partly for that reason, in June 2002 Terry Green quit. In November of the previous year, the CEO had failed to lead an £800 million management buyout of Bhs with the backing of private equity firm PPM Ventures.[18] He was also disappointed that, as an alternative, the group was not being IPO'd despite a very successful turnaround. But Philip Green had been stung by his experience at Amber Day – during his tenure there he had gone through no fewer than five different stockbroking advisers – and was not keen to get back on the stock exchange.[19] Instead, he chose to pursue a formidable growth plan, first by unsuccessfully pursuing a £2 billion merger with Woolworth,[20] then by launching a hostile takeover of retail conglomerate Arcadia.

For this purpose, he originally planned to partner with Baugur, an Icelandic investment group specialised in retail and the holder of 20% of the target's shares. Unexpectedly, as the bid for Arcadia was announced, Baugur found itself the subject of a fraud investigation, leaving Green stranded. Proving that he had not unjustly built a reputation as a relentless deal-doer, he managed to put the financing together thanks to the support of Bank of Scotland. Not for the first time, the Scottish community backed his designs for High Street domination.

With a pushy £866 million offer, he bagged Arcadia in October 2002, adding women's fashion brand Dorothy Perkins and men's specialist Burton as well as Topshop, Topman and Miss Selfridge – the latter sold to Arcadia by Green himself as part of his dismantling of Sears three years earlier – to family-focused Bhs. Funded via the issuance of more than £800 million of bank loans secured on freehold and leasehold property,[21] the Arcadia delisting promoted Green to the premier league of retail, granting him a 10% market share of the UK clothing market. In a short three-year span, he had combined a UK retail empire ranking second only to Marks & Spencer.

With Bhs he had become the richest man in UK fashion after making the fastest billion pounds in the history of British commerce.[22] Arcadia was an entirely different ball game. He had originally planned to break it up. But he quickly changed his mind, deciding instead to offload an 8% stake to the company's lender, Bank of Scotland, and to seek more assets for his trophy cabinet.[23]

## Portfolio management

Green quickly put his stamp on the business. In November 2002, he hired Lord Grabiner away from rival fashion retailer Next to become chairman of Arcadia. Grabiner was a top commercial lawyer who had, among other distinguished assignments, advised Green on the Arcadia deal.[24] To bring more focus to his retail conglomerate, Green also made a handful of fire sales. In late 2002 he sold Arcadia's 45% stake in Rubicon – the holding of poorly performing brands Principles, Warehouse, and Hawkshead. And in July 2003 he sold discount clothing chain Mark One to its management for £50 million.[25] These efforts at scaling down were meant to make the implementation of the group-wide strategy easier. He had already put significant pressure on suppliers across the whole range of goods provided to its various brands. Just before Christmas 2002, he changed the terms of suppliers' agreements, marking invoices down by more than 10%.[26]

The Arcadia OBO was going smoothly, making its flamboyant backer confident enough to enter the £3 billion bidding war for food supermarket chain Safeway.[27] Although his attempt did not succeed, the fact that Green was seen as a serious contender against mighty strategic buyers like Tesco, Morrisons and Asda, as well as PE firms KKR and Texas Pacific Group, shows how much respect he had earned from the City following his Bhs and Arcadia transactions. That same year, he was even rumoured to be a possible bidder for upmarket London-based retailer Harrods.

Internally, his goal was to make each brand of Arcadia's portfolio individually accountable. By running separate profit and loss accounts, they would be easier to develop into unique identities and to remodel if needed. It soon became evident that Green was far more involved in Arcadia than in Bhs. The latter was run by a separate management team. And this two-pronged strategy certainly seemed to produce plenty of cash: by the summer of 2003, Arcadia had already repaid more than £400 million of the £800 million borrowed at the time of the buyout.[28]

Despite a meagre 2.5% rate of sales growth, Arcadia announced that its operating profits had risen 96% to £228 million in the year ended 30 August 2003, the first time it reported under Green's ownership.[29] This stellar performance was driven by lower buying costs, improvements in the speed of stock deliveries, the introduction of new fashions, clearance of out-of-date stock, better property management, and increased efficiency in the purchasing of general supplies. The jump in operating margin, from 6.6% to 12.7%, led many to observe that the institutional investors who had sold their stakes in Arcadia a year earlier had sold out to Green at too low a price. It was felt by many that they had left 20% value on the table.[30] Easy to say once Green had delivered on his efficiency programme! Anyway, after financing the Arcadia buyout with more than 90% debt and put in only £39 million for his 92% stake,[31] Green had made another quick billion pounds, at least on paper, in just ten months.

At his other retail business, Bhs, he did not get a chance to repeat the margin improvements engendered the previous year, but the 5.5% growth in operating profits in the year to 29 March 2003 still helped the company declare another hefty payout. Green took home a cool £201 million dividend as part of "normal, prudent financial planning", as he put it.[32] What was less prudent, at least from Bhs's standpoint, was that the company had to take on a £200 million bank loan to finance the dividend distribution.[33]

## Retail therapy

Because sales growth at Bhs had stagnated, critics matter-of-factly observed that Green's miraculous machine had run out of steam. The businessman again argued that it was still work in progress. He was planning to make ranges more fashionable, to improve the products and the supply chain.

Indeed, difficult trading conditions warranted caution. In late 2003, Bhs and Arcadia did not enjoy the best Christmas period, even if Green did not acknowledge it, refusing to issue sales figures for either group. On the personal front, however, Green knew what to do with the dividend he had paid himself. Heading out for a spot of shopping, he added a multi-million-pound private jet to his superyacht and Monaco penthouse.[34] His special kind of retail therapy was not restricted to purchasing personal luxury goods. The question everyone wanted answered was how long it would be until his next deal. So, in the spring of 2004, armed with the irrepressible drive and uncompromising obduracy of the entrepreneur, he launched 'Operation Socrates', a plucky bid for his main rival on the High Street: Marks & Spencer.

It was the third time Green was going after Britain's leading but dozing fashion retailer, having tried his luck while at Amber Day, and again shortly before acquiring Bhs. Considered the jewel of the British retail crown, Marks & Spencer had just seen its stock hit a year-low after announcing disappointing results. The group had lost some of its lustre in recent years following the fragmentation of consumer segments, but also due to its brand positioning, primarily serving the 40-year-old-plus consumer. Incidentally, M&S's pre-tax profits had declined from £1.2 billion in 1998 to less than £800 million six years later while sales had remained flat. Would it be third time lucky for Green?

His main issue, despite unmatched credentials in turning around faded retailers, was the sheer size of the deal. At £10 billion, the enterprise value towered over Green's own empire. Could it even be financed with the usual blend of hefty leverage and puny equity injection? He was prepared to fork out £600 million to £1 billion, not an inconsequential chunk of his £3.5 billion fortune, but he needed to find £9 billion of external financing.[35] He called in the help of Bank of Scotland, the lender behind his Arcadia buyout.

Everyone agreed that M&S, Britain's most famous High Street brand whose stores offered grocery as well as clothing, had failed to react to the fast-fashion methods recently enforced by a new breed of retailers. M&S would buy 50,000 items for an entire season where Zara would bring in 5,000 items one week and then another 5,000 the next, but the range and style would be slightly different each time. That approach required a different supply chain.

To win over the crowds, Green made a proposal for Lord Stevenson, the chairman of Bank of Scotland, to become senior non-executive director of the company once the acquisition had taken place. But the ailing target was not willing to remain idle in the face of the onslaught. In June 2004 it appointed as new CEO Stuart Rose, the chief exec of Arcadia until its acquisition by Green two years earlier. Armed with a £1.25 million 'golden hello' and a potential £2.1 million 'golden parachute' should M&S be sold,[36] Rose's explicit brief was to torpedo Green's proposal. His appointment coincided with the elevation of non-executive director Paul Myners as interim chairman. Both had a proper battle on their hands.

Another obstacle for Green's bid was that the stock of the target had risen 40% since rumours of his interest had first emerged. In early June 2004, in what would have been Europe's largest LBO and take-private to date, the earnest entrepreneur submitted a cheeky offer: a blend of £7 billion in cash and equity worth £2 billion in Revival Acquisitions, the investment vehicle set up for the occasion and to be floated on the timidly regulated Alternative Investment Market.[37] Given the City's lukewarm reception, a fortnight later he raised his offer to £11.9

billion, or 370 pence a share. To fund the bid, he secured about £9.4 billion in LBO loans, plus equity contributions from Goldman Sachs and Bank of Scotland, diluting his stake to 44%.[38] For M&S shareholders, the dilemma was whether to retain their shares in a focused, even if dated, national institution that was part of the FTSE 100 index, or to hold a minority stake in a highly leveraged entity controlled by Green and listed on a second-tier stock exchange. There was also the small matter of valuation: shareholders felt that the target was worth 400 pence a share, not a penny less.

Aligning himself with the market's expectations, in July Green upped his final proposal to 400 pence, with £1.6 billion of his own money, for an enterprise value in excess of £12 billion and an operating profit multiple of 14.6 times. It was swiftly spurned by the company's board as significantly undervaluing the group.[39] The board believed that shareholders would be better off if they gave new chief executive Rose a stab at a proper turnaround. To make the pill easier to swallow, they were offered a share buyback plan and dividend payouts worth more than £2 billion, partly financed through the disposal of Marks & Spencer's financial services arm.

Green's third approach ended the way the previous two had. He was considered too much of an uncouth, disreputable chancer for the City to let him take ownership of such a cherished, if troubled, High Street name. M&S's management, shareholders and advisers had conspired to stiffly rebuke his advances. Perhaps some City professionals found it hard to stomach that their backing of Green's Sears, Bhs and Arcadia acquisitions had helped turn the bombastic dealmaker into Britain's fourth-richest man. Not prepared to overpay for what most observers considered damaged goods, Green slowly grappled with the unfamiliar feeling of not getting his way. Despite the strong backing of Goldman Sachs, Operation Socrates failed in the face of fierce opposition from the City establishment. Almost 2,000 articles had appeared in the press during the seven weeks of the bidding process, so giddy was the reaction toward, often against, the retail entrepreneur.

For now, Bhs and Arcadia would have to sate his appetite for glory. Yet there was no question that his ambition could not be satisfied by the existing portfolio of assets. During the M&S bidding process, there were reports – denied by Green – that he was considering selling Bhs to allay regulatory concerns. A combination of Bhs, Arcadia and M&S would have given him a 20% share of the British clothing market and a 26% share in womenswear.[40] Was Bhs truly considered core to his long-term strategy, or was it worth sacrificing to his ultimate plans for fashion retail domination?

## High Street war

Following his failed bottom-fishing bid for M&S, Green pledged to fight his rival on the High Street. In July 2004, with an audience to play to, he announced in a Churchillian style:

> *"They are going to have us breathing down their neck in every street in every shopping centre in the UK. And that's where I am going to be fired up. It is going to get my best shot. And we will see who is the best retailer."*[41]

Within months, he unveiled an expansion and revamp plan, including dozens of new store openings, in particular for the Topshop brand. In the year to March 2004 Bhs had recorded flat sales and single-digit growth in operating profits. It was in sharp contrast to M&S's 7.7% fall in non-food sales for the 12 weeks to 2 October 2004. To increase the pressure on his main rival, Green launched the chain's first television advertising campaign for a decade.[42]

By mid-October he announced that he had already repaid the £800 million borrowed two years earlier to acquire Arcadia. Green's recipe of store refurbishment, supply chain optimisation and stock control was paying dividends, literally: over the same two years, Arcadia had distributed £200 million to shareholders, and it announced another huge dividend that same month.[43] Operating margins had shot up by 300 basis points, the result of efficiency enhancements, bringing the group's valuation to £2.3 billion, up 167% since Green's buyout.[44] The feel-good factor was reinforced by Marks & Spencer's disastrous trading performance in the second half of 2004, including over Christmas, forcing its management to issue a profit warning.[45] Things looked so bad that, with M&S's share price sitting more than 15% below Green's 400 pence bid, rumours emerged that the entrepreneur was preparing a fresh proposal. But it wasn't to be.

His retail empire faced its own challenges. In the year to 2 April 2005, Bhs reported weak trading. Instead of paying himself a dividend as he had done in previous years, Green spent the money on smartening up the chain. Under attack from value players like Primark, Bhs was trying to move upmarket, spending £20 million in the previous year on refurbishments, and acquiring or opening 12 new stores.[46] On 7 April, Green acquired the loss-making Etam, a clothing retailer of 200 stores,[47] to extend Arcadia's footprint and gain economies of scale. A few months later, Bhs absorbed ten ex-Allders and six ex-Littlewoods stores, and opened four new stores, bringing the total trading Bhs stores to 180 by April 2006.[48]

Everything looked promising in Britain's most diverse retail group. Revenue growth was flattish to low single-digit at both Bhs and Arcadia, but operating margins consistently crept up year on year, which enabled dividends to keep flowing. But, then, gradually and unremittingly, the magic faded away.

In 2005 cut-price outlets, such as Peacocks, New Look and Matalan, forced department store groups Debenhams, M&S and Bhs to reduce prices across the board.[49] Cut-throat competition led many participants to report grim sales figures that year, in what was described as the toughest retail climate for 20 years.[50]

Following the gargantuan dividends he had paid himself in the past two years, Green was widely expected to go on the hunt for new targets.

But he had his hands full with his own stable of assets. The years leading to the financial crisis registered low revenue growth at Arcadia and negative growth at Bhs. The most troubling effects of the High Street war were felt at the profitability level. Bhs's operating margin sank from 15% in 2004-05 to less than 5% in the year to March 2008, in part because the group failed to adapt its product offer, leaving it with excess stock on several occasions. Arcadia fared better, yet it recorded margin erosion from 17% to 13% over the same period.[51] Both groups were still very cash generative, but the times of dividend recaps were well and truly on hold.

## Fashion combination

The economic recession provoked by the Credit Crunch of 2007 and the ensuing financial meltdown had devastating effects on the retail sector. In the year ended March 2008, Bhs recorded a 40% drop in operating profits.[52] In the 17 months to August 2009, it reported an operating loss for the first time since the buyout nine years earlier. Arcadia was doing marginally better thanks to its three leading fashion brands: Topshop, Topman and Miss Selfridge.[53] The only option for all participants was to battle through the downturn, by opening new stores for the best performing brands and by trimming debt.

The biggest casualty of the crisis was undoubtedly Baugur, the overleveraged Icelandic group with stakes in a host of British retailers including Debenhams, House of Fraser, French Connection, Goldsmiths, Nine West, Principles, Coast, Oasis, Karen Millen, Whistles, toy store Hamleys and frozen food chain Iceland. Talks with its lenders broke down in February 2009, forcing it into administration and a fire sale of all its investment holdings.[54] But the troubles at Baugur did not make life on the UK High Street any easier. The Great Recession kept consumers away, and a 5% rise in business rates – a UK tax on business properties – in early 2009 made it harder for retailers to maintain prices low enough to attract bargain hunters.[55]

Under pressure, in the spring Green decided to simplify his group structure by consolidating Arcadia and Bhs under the same umbrella company, Taveta Investments, an entity controlled by his Monaco-domiciled wife Cristina. The consideration paid by Taveta to acquire Bhs was funded via subordinated loan notes of £200 million, a practice widely used in private equity transactions. As part of this process, the group merged back-office functions, including logistics, property and finance, and harmonised supplier discount rates, raising them from 11.25% to 14.25%.[56] Another refreshing idea was to relocate brands into Bhs's over-spaced store estate, especially in cities where space had become expensive.[57] At the same time, Bhs went through a profound reorganisation, incurring over £32 million in exceptional expenses, redundancies and asset impairment. Even pre-exceptionals, the group incurred an operating loss of £34 million in the 17 months to August 2009.[58] Taveta Investments carried over £1.1 billion of debt on its books, or approximately 3.2 times its net cash inflows,[59] so weak trading was potentially life-threatening.

As a kind of consolation, Green's nemesis Marks & Spencer did not fare much better. Although between 2004 and 2007 its management had done a good turnaround job, to preserve market share it had invested massively. Capex exceeded £1 billion in the fiscal year 2008 alone. By March of that year, net debt sat at £3.1 billion, up 80% over the previous two years. The M&S stock had once briefly traded above 400 pence a share – the price at which Green had bid – but by the spring of 2008 it had sunk to about half that level on the back of poor trading. In the year to March 2009, the group incurred £135 million of property write-offs and other restructuring costs. Operating profit was down 28%. Aiming to cope with the recession, in the year to March 2010 the group cut down capex by two-fifths to preserve cash; it refinanced under duress by issuing a new long-term bond to give itself more headroom; and it was forced to cut its dividend.[60]

Thanks to past investments, M&S still held the largest share of the UK clothing market, with 13% for the 12 weeks to 31 January 2010, whereas Bhs's market share eroded further, down to a lowly 1.9%.[61] Nevertheless, ten years after failing to acquire M&S, Green could be satisfied that his biggest rival had not performed as its board of directors expected when, in 2004, it had turned down his £12 billion offer.

Table 7.1 underscores that the High Street war of attrition prevented M&S from creating shareholder value, though other reasons behind the operating margin squeeze included changes in consumer habits to the benefit of cheaper and leaner fast-fashion retailers, clothing discounters and online distributors.

In fact, Table 7.1 offers a flattering picture. If M&S reported its clothing unit separately from the food division, the results for clothing would show a much greater deterioration in profitability.

**Table 7.1 – Financial indicators for Marks & Spencer in 2004 and 2014**

|  | **Marks & Spencer** |
|---|---|
| **Year ended March 2004** | |
| Sales | £8.3 billion |
| Operating profit/EBIT | £866 million |
| Operating margin | 10.4% |
| Market cap | £8 billion |
| Enterprise value | £10.7 billion |
| **Year ended March 2014** | |
| Sales | £10.3 billion |
| Operating profit/EBIT | £695 million |
| Operating margin | 6.7% |
| Market cap | £7 billion |
| Enterprise value | £9 billion |

*Source: Company filings*

## Topflop

In the year to August 2010, Bhs delivered less than £800 million in revenue for the first time under Green's ownership. The business recorded another operating loss, though smaller than the previous year's. Arcadia, on the other hand, recorded double-digit growth in operating profits thanks to the stellar performance of leading brands Topshop and Topman.[62] Despite the still challenging economic situation in the UK and the rest of Europe, between August 2009 and August 2010 the group's holding company Taveta managed to make a dent on its financial gearing, bringing net debt from £1.1 billion to £935 million. Leverage subsided from 4.4 times to 3.6 times operating profit.[63] Desperate to turn Bhs around, Green reorganised store space by consolidating more of Arcadia's niche brands – such as Dorothy Perkins, Burton, Evans and Wallis – into Bhs stores.

The retail slump, caused by high unemployment and limited wage growth, hurt the High Street severely throughout 2011. In May of that year, Green tried to sell Bhs stores to cut loose some of the group's spare capacity. Over the next few months, 300 leases were reviewed to renegotiate or close shop.[64] Following this corporate purge, in the year to August 2011 Taveta recorded £253 million in restructuring costs, reflecting asset impairment and goodwill write-off. Bhs alone recognised £88 million of exceptional charges. Operating margin was at all all-time low of 3.6%, down from 17% in 2005. Proving that the sluggish economic recovery was taking its toll, Green announced plans to close 260 stores over the next three years, a bit less than 10% of the group's estate.[65] The following year, Taveta recorded flat sales, though the 3.2% drop in like-for-like UK sales contrasted with the 22% rise in Internet sales and an even brisker 33% jump overseas.[66] With 2,500 UK stores and 600 abroad, the group was a mixed bag of lively fast-fashion brands like Topshop and an invariably depressed department store chain like Bhs.

Post-financial crisis, the UK economy stubbornly remained in the doldrums. After registering negative GDP growth of 4.3% in 2009, the country registered anaemic growth of 1.9% in 2010, and averaged 1.6% per annum over the subsequent three years. The jobless recovery had one main victim: the retail sector, as consumers hunted for bargains, finding many of them online. Green tried everything to adapt Bhs's timeworn department store model, including adding a homeware offering and considering the acquisition of national bed retailer Dreams in early 2013. A year later, he spoke of introducing a food section in almost half of the chain's outlets. But his relentless fight with M&S did not deliver the expected results. Table 7.2 provides an overview of performance ten years apart.

## Table 7.2 – Financial indicators for Bhs in 2004 and 2014

| Fiscal year ended 27 March 2004 | |
|---|---|
| Sales | £882 million |
| Operating profit/EBIT | £104 million |
| Operating margin | 11.8% |
| Enterprise value | £800 million |
| **Fiscal year ended 30 August 2014** | |
| Sales | £673 million |
| Operating profit/(loss) | (£55 million) |
| Operating margin | - 8.3% |
| Enterprise value | £256 million * |

*Source: Company filings. *Net liabilities as at 30 August 2014*

For years Bhs's woes had been widely reported in the press. Green argued that he would engineer its revival, most likely because he could not imagine being a forced seller at a rock-bottom valuation. In late 2013, rumours emerged that foreign investors, including turnaround specialists, were taking a look at the troubled business.[67] Weighed down by expensive leases, an undifferentiated product offering and a pension fund deficit, Bhs was not easy to assess. In the four years to August 2014, it had incurred £165 million in restructuring costs.[68] Its business model was broken, with sales falling 16% over the same period. Although it was debt-free, it had accumulated huge trading losses, turning its balance sheet into a £256 million net liability position.

Throwing in the towel, Green put the heavily loss-making business on the market in January 2015. He had received several approaches, but expressions of interest had been rejected on price grounds.[69] The parlous state the chain was in was unlikely to attract anything other than low-ball offers. A long list of suitors included supermarket chains, other department stores from the UK or abroad, as well as fast-fashion retailers and discounters.

Two months later Bhs, recently rebranded BHS, was sold for a nominal sum. As a sign that the chain was far from a stellar asset, Taveta agreed to waive £217 million of intercompany loans to entice the buyer, Retail Acquisitions.[70] The immediate question one could ask was: would the acquirer succeed where Green had failed?

## How Green made his fortune

Clearly, from a personal standpoint, Green's dealmaking over the previous 15 years could hardly be termed a failure. He had paid himself up to £2 billion in dividends between 2003 and 2005. While he had bought Bhs during a performance dip, which eventually turned into structural deficiency, the way he had made money was by applying the standard techniques of modern-day financial engineering.

1- Bhs was temporarily deflated when Storehouse sold it – the vendor took a £300 million hit on the disposal.[71] Storehouse's decision to sell Bhs two months after recording a terrible profit drop could be described as poorly timed, or even irresponsible – at least from Storehouse's shareholders' point of view.[72]

2- At Bhs and Arcadia, Green cut fat, including central costs by practically eliminating the head office. By watching the pennies at all levels of the organisation, he instilled a culture of waste reduction and cost discipline.

3- His ability to squeeze suppliers was made easier by increasing the amount of goods sourced from cheaper contractors in the Far East and Central Europe. He studiously applied fast-fashion stock-management techniques by buying smaller amounts of stock and increasing the frequency of purchases. A typical example of the sort of pressure he put suppliers under came in July 2006, when he unilaterally decided to double payment terms to 60 days with immediate effect and demanded a 1% discount on goods. To be clear, the approach was an industry-wide practice. That same year M&S asked for a 5.5% discount and Debenhams went for 2%, while New Look extended payment terms to 75 days.[73]

4- Property-heavy companies, as many retailers are, can generate cash by completing sale and leaseback transactions. Green used that trick on 20 December 2001, for instance, when Bhs sold its interest in certain properties to Carmen Properties, an entity also controlled by Green, in exchange for £106 million.[74] It was a great way for Bhs to produce cash, and for Green to retain exclusive control of the real estate while adding cash to his war chest.

5- With his wife domiciled in tax haven Monaco, Green was able to avoid paying tax on dividends by registering holding company Taveta Investments under his wife's name. Until 2003 Taveta was Jersey-based, making it liable to UK tax. The following year, Green saved a reported £150 million on his share of a £460 million dividend by switching Taveta's controlling party to his wife.[75]

6- Green took a leaf straight out of the PE playbook. As he stated in March 2004:

*"I believe you're only worth what you have in your pocket. In other words, your assets aren't worth anything until they have been converted to cash. That's something we saw in the dot.com boom, which had some people worth a fortune on the Thursday morning but by Friday night they were skint."*[76]

He was keen to carry out dividend recaps to cash in his winnings before the tide turned – including a generous £1.2 billion dividend in 2005, distributed to his wife. This is the typical approach of private equity fund managers – get your money out while you still can, and do so at regular intervals, because no one knows when the good times will end.

He was a fervent user of debt, occasionally in the same contentious manner as many PE firms. The approach used for Bhs was aptly reproduced with Arcadia. Green was prudent enough not to stretch his group's balance sheet permanently. Within 18 months of closing the Arcadia buyout, he had repaid three-fifths of the bank loans; within two years, they were fully repaid, leaving only property mortgages on the books. While he refinanced Taveta aggressively in 2005, through £1.7 billion of bank loans, to pay the aforementioned dividend, he painstakingly brought down Taveta's leverage ratio from 4.7 times operating profit in 2006 to less than 1 times ten years later (see Figure 7.1).[77]

Note that factoring in the long-term impact that such overleveraging has on portfolio companies is not part of the PE equation. In addition to the strain they exercised on cash flows, the debt-financed dividend payouts led to a dip in staff morale and to a brain drain with the departure of disillusioned senior and middle managers.

7- He made sure to keep lenders happy. With Bank of Scotland – the provider of £775 million of loans for Arcadia's buyout – also an 8% shareholder in Arcadia, Green secured his main lender's cooperation by helping the bank earn dividends during the various recapitalisations he engineered. Since Bank of Scotland was the main provider of these refinancing rounds, it was playing on both sides of the LBO scales. The bank had every incentive to make sure the group was given sufficient headroom to manage the vast sums borrowed over the years.

8- Green's use of financial dexterity was not limited to dividend recaps. It included clever corporate structuring, via the creation of separate entities, to manage properties leased by Bhs and Arcadia and to earn operating and management commissions. Over the years, Green earned millions of pounds in lease payments and fees. Although, post-2005, Taveta did not pay Green or members of his family any dividend, high interest was still paid on the subordinated loan notes registered under his wife's name. Thanks to a legal loophole, the UK allowed tax-free interest payments to investors based overseas. Under the scheme, an offshore company lends money to its British sister company, which pays interest on the loan. The interest payments would normally attract a 20% withholding tax in the UK. As part of its merger with Arcadia in May 2009, Bhs was bought by an offshoot of Taveta for £200 million. Taveta did not pay cash. Instead, it issued loan notes bearing 8% annual interest, subscribed by Green's wife and redeemable in ten annual instalments. These were estimated to total £88 million, representing a tax shield of £18 million.[78]

9- Lastly, as we are about to see, Green managed to exit his Bhs investment by finding a gullible buyer, a failed entrepreneur desperate to prove himself (and the outside world) that he could turn around the burned-out department store chain.

## Fast failure

Retail Acquisitions was backed by a group of eight to 10 business personalities with different industry backgrounds who had "decided to do something in the retail sector."[79] What was intriguing was the identity of the main individual behind the bidding vehicle. Dominic Chappell was a former racing car driver with a history of bankruptcies and virtually no retail experience. His business partners were as inexperienced when it came to fashion or department stores. As the *Financial Times* stated, bargain fashion group Bhs was itself "in the bargain bin — sold for just £1 to a little-known group of financiers, lawyers and accountants."[80] Despite the chagrin he must have felt after repeatedly failing to turn the group's fortunes around, Sir Philip opined that it was "an honest deal", adding for no particular reason that there were "no skeletons in the cupboard."[81]

The deal led sector observers to question how these inexperienced investors could do a better job of running the business than Sir Philip, a veteran of the industry. This motley crew had apparently outbid turnaround investors like retail specialist Alteri, a firm partly backed by US special-situations expert Apollo.

Brimming with confidence, one of Chappell's associates, former City small-cap broker Keith Smith insisted:

> *This is a fantastic opportunity to breathe new life into this iconic British High Street brand. We are convinced that with strategic and focused support we will return BHS to profitability, and safeguard the workforce.*[82]

Yet, sustaining the brand would be hard. Stores would need to be shut; staff would be let go. Everyone agreed that most of the value was in the real estate. Some prime locations would be of interest to other retailers; ailing sites could be sold, downsized or sublet. Over the years, Bhs had lost most of its competitive power. While Green had spent a decade obsessing about M&S, the market had been transformed by two categories of new participants: fast-fashion outlets and online retailers. Between the early noughties and the mid-2010s, department stores had lost their leadership and been supplanted by standalone, fast-fashion discounters like Zara, H&M and Primark.

The latter, founded in Ireland in 1969, was a case in point. After opening its first continental European store in Madrid in 2006, the value retailer had expanded its business model across Europe before entering the American market nine years later. By comparison, Bhs's foray into Lithuania and Russia in 2004 had not led to a successful international roll-out. Department stores were no longer what consumers wanted. Instead of fighting a helpless war against an equally dated M&S, Green should have acknowledged that fashion trends had moved on. While he managed to adapt the Topshop brand to a model somewhat similar to Primark's, he left Bhs trailing behind.

A review of Primark's performance during the period when Green was busy running both Arcadia and Bhs illustrates that the flamboyant entrepreneur from North London had missed a trick. Between 2002 and 2014 Bhs recorded a 25% drop in revenue and turned a positive 11.5% operating margin into a negative 11.5%. By contrast, Primark multiplied revenue fourteenfold between 2000 and 2016; its number of stores more than tripled and operating margin hovered around 12% during the same period. Between 1998 and 2008 the market share of value retailing in the UK grew from 11% to 25%.[83] Mid-priced groups, like Bhs and M&S, gradually lost the High Street war to low-priced alternatives, offering a fast-fashion product to a young target audience.

Not only did the High Street experience a market shift towards value and quick stock turnover, but the number of out-of-town shopping malls exploded in the 1990s and noughties, attracting customers to a uniquely large-scale retail environment and adding to the vast footprint of open-air retail parks that had seen the light in the 1970s and 1980s.

Then, as if these trends were not powerful enough to unsettle the British town centres where Bhs stores were traditionally located, a more fundamental shift gradually took hold. Ideal for disintermediation, supply-chain optimisation and low-cost delivery, the Internet also targeted the fashion-conscious and price-sensitive under-35s. In 2017 online sales accounted for 24% of total spending on clothing and footwear in the UK, up from 17% four years earlier and less than 5% in the early noughties.[84] To make the brick-and-mortar model work and cover the rent, property taxes and other charges that online fashion groups did not have to pay, stores needed a unique value proposition. Bhs was stuck in the middle, neither cheap fast fashion, nor chic high fashion.

Green, who had turned down an £800 million offer by Bhs's chief exec Terry Green back in 2001 – asserting at the time that the business was worth more than £1 billion – as well as a £700 million bid by the company's chairman Allan Leighton six years later,[85] sold it to Chappell for just £1, in one of the most unorthodox deals ever witnessed. The catch of such a low valuation, for there is a catch, is that the business was carrying hundreds of millions of pounds in liabilities sitting on and off the balance sheet.

For Chappell and his posse of City professionals, taking on the task of restructuring Bhs was a huge gamble. One that would have required the well-honed skills of turnaround specialists, deep retail expertise and oodles of nous. The team leading Retail Acquisitions had none of those. Consequently, they never stood a chance to make it work. Judiciously, not many of Green's team members decided to hang around after the disposal. As soon as Bhs was sold, both its finance director and CEO departed. The day after their purchase, the new owners were desperately looking for a chairman to run the loss-making 171-store chain.[86]

The upshot of it all was that on 24 April 2016, a year after Green's exit, Bhs was put into administration, the UK equivalent of Chapter 11. Philip Green was apparently one of the lenders to Bhs who had vetoed a crucial £60 million refinancing. He would not relax the terms of a charge he held over the assets, meaning the retail chain was unable to secure a lifeline from specialist lender Gordon Brothers.[87] The process threatened to throw many of the group's 11,000 employees out of work and leave many suppliers out of pocket – the amount of unsecured creditors stood at £1.3 billion, including pension liabilities and rent charges on loss-making stores.[88] It was the biggest retail bankruptcy since that of Woolworths in December 2008. Bhs's original rival had gone belly up eight years earlier due to a combination of factors, ranging from the obsolescence of its variety store concept, fierce competition from supermarkets and Internet alternatives, consumer recession, as well as the clichéd corporate ailment of our times: inordinate debt levels rendered unmanageable by the financial crisis.

Perhaps the massive loss of value at Bhs confirmed what many of his critics had stated for years; that the 'miracle' Green had worked at the store chain owed a lot to financial trickery and less to retailing genius.[89] Fashion being the cyclical and fickle industry that it is, only people who sell at the top of the cycle can hope to keep their reputation intact. About the only subterfuge in his arsenal of wheeler-dealer that Green had not applied was to strip and flip the business the way he had offloaded Olympus and other Sears brands in the 1990s. After buying the company off Storehouse for £200 million in 2000 and building it into a business worth four to five times that amount in less than two years, he had been too greedy by refusing to exit. Instead, he witnessed the group's value crash back down to earth. The turnaround miracle of the early noughties had failed to translate into a meaningful and enduring competitive advantage. In fashion, nothing lasts forever.

There was also the small matter of the pensions of 20,000 current and former employees. Bhs's pension deficit had gone from approximately £70 million in April 2006 to twice that amount in late August 2014.[90] Although it was assessed at £200 million at the time of the company's disposal to Retail Acquisitions, after careful consideration a year later it was estimated to be closer to £500 million.[91] Suddenly, it seemed clearer to outsiders why Green had been so eager to flog the chain into the arms of any buyer, even one as unsuitable as twice-bankrupt Dominic Chappell.[92] A month before Bhs was put into administration, the Pensions Regulator and the Pension Protection Fund revealed that they were putting pressure on Sir Philip to fill the hole in Bhs's pension scheme. At the time, Green's suggested additional contribution was reported to be £80 million, comprising £40 million of cash and £40 million in loans.[93] But negotiations with the regulatory authorities were only just starting.

## Shop-soiled

Green was widely disliked by the City and vilified by the press for his brash style – some opprobrium he reinforced when he splashed £5 million on his gaudy 50th birthday party in 2002 and £4 million on his son's bar mitzvah on the French Riviera three years later. Traditionally, the British preferred to honour the dignified opulence of the sedate gentility. They acknowledged self-made men with stifled condescension. They considered it a rightful return to the natural order of things that after, in his own words, saving Bhs from neglect by buying it off troubled conglomerate Storehouse, Green be held responsible for its demise.

What seems to have happened is that Green fell in love with Arcadia, a blooming collection of fashion-focused brands with distinct personalities spread across hundreds of stores. Topshop, in particular, unashamedly copied high-end clothes worn by celebrities by offering affordable replicas, investing in young designers and growing an own in-house design team. To give the womenswear retail chain more cachet, in 2006 Green even hired the services of British fashion poster girl Kate Moss. Between 2007 and 2017, in an attempt to turn the chain into a global brand, the number of Topshop stores and franchises doubled to 620, located in over 40 countries.[94] In December 2012 Green even sold a 25% stake in Topshop and Topman to American PE firm Leonard Green & Partners (no relation), a retail expert and the owner of apparel retailer J.Crew. The move, granting the two brands a £2 billion valuation,[95] helped him hit two birds with one stone: repay the bank loans still sitting on Taveta's books and gain local expertise in his attempt to conquer the US, a market notoriously difficult to crack for British retailers. Similarly, Green signed an agreement with US department store chain Nordstrom to bring the Topshop brand to its branches. Perhaps the unequivocal sign that the retail entrepreneur had lofty aspirations for Topshop was his decision to move upmarket, opening a flagship store in London's very posh Knightsbridge area in a site opposite Harrods in the spring of 2010, and one on Fifth Avenue in New York four years later.

By comparison, Bhs was a chain of bland department stores with no real differentiator other than price.[96] Its expansion in Eastern Europe and India had not delivered the expected results. The half-hearted attempts to market Arcadia brands inside Bhs and to convert some of the chain's stores into food outlets did not improve performance. From 188 stores in 2013, the group managed fewer than 170 at the time of its collapse three years later.

It is easy to understand why any owner would rather spend time on the former than on the latter, but it meant that the tycoon's assemblage of businesses was decidedly lop-sided. As early as November 2005, Green admitted to having taken his eye off the ball at Bhs; an excuse that he would use on numerous occasions.[97] Record trading at Topshop and Topman was matched by a persistent downturn at Bhs, which had become a high-maintenance liability. Over an entire decade when the clothing retail industry was tackling the fast-fashion trend, Bhs was involved in a slow-motion car crash.

In an interview with the *Sunday Telegraph* on 20 January 2002, Green had confidently reflected on the fantastic turnaround he had engineered at the department store in the first two years of ownership:

> *'I love this business and working in it. It's now on its way back and making proper profits because it's being run properly. It has been around*

*on the High Street for 80 years and there's no reason why it shouldn't be around for another 80.'*[98]

Instead, ravaged by the compound of industry meltdown and financial distress, it fell apart within 15 years. A large proportion of the efficiency improvements and cost-cutting plans imposed at both Bhs and Arcadia delivered signal benefits in the short term, but they soon ran out of steam as the stores proved unable to pass on rent increases and rising production costs to the consumer.[99] Once the low-hanging fruit of quick fixes has been gathered, it is harder to lift profits by slashing fixed costs from rents and salaries. That probably explains why Green was rumoured to have touted Bhs for sale in early 2006, in mid-2007, and again the following year.[100] After no party showed much interest at the right valuation and Bhs reported a 54% drop in operating profits in the year to March 2006, he elucidated: "We have got the time and the money to fix it."[101] Yet he didn't.

By 2014 Green was managing over 3,060 outlets across nine separate brands – Bhs, mid-market menswear specialist Burton, mid-market womenswear specialist Dorothy Perkins, plus-sizes womenswear retailer Evans, young fashion brand Miss Selfridge, out-of-town multi-brand fashion retailer Outfit, Topman and Topshop (for women) serving the fashion conscious, and Wallis, another womenswear retailer. To these must be added 44 brand specific websites.[102] It is apparent that it was too much for one single individual to handle, even one with Green's commercial flair, energy and drive.

With so many separate brands, the group was in constant reorganisation. In the fiscal year to August 2015, for instance, Taveta had closed almost 300 stores but also opened 335 of them.[103] Although the group had remained cash generative (see Figure 7.1), its prosperity depended on perpetual reinvention and upgrades. While the amounts reinvested in Topshop and Topman worked wonders, Bhs only just managed to stay alive – its flagship store on Britain's most famous commercial district, Oxford Street, was reportedly losing £1 million a year when Green decided to exit.[104]

**Figure 7.1 – Taveta's net debt, operating profit and leverage ratio from 2006 to 2016**

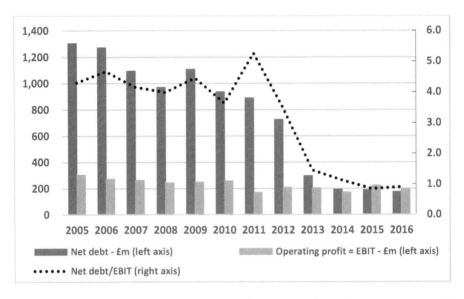

*Notes: Net debt includes property mortgages; Operating profit is shown pre-exceptional items; Bhs numbers not included from 2005 to 2008, in 2015 and 2016 – Source: Company filings and author's analysis*

To implement their rescue and regeneration plan, the new owners went looking for cash. Their desperation was demonstrated by various announcements in the months that followed their buyout, including the disclosure that they were considering a big push abroad with a proposed store opening in war-torn Iraq the following year![105] But their lack of credibility scared third parties. Within a month of Green's disposal, several of Bhs's suppliers saw their credit insurance slashed or withheld,[106] a sign that, without Green's backing, Bhs was at higher risk of defaulting on its trade liabilities. Before selling Bhs to Retail

Acquisitions, Green had been approached by other, more sector-savvy, parties. One of the conditions formulated by these bidders was for Green to provide a 'dowry' of several hundreds of millions of pounds to plug the pension deficit. The dowry was also needed to cover dilapidations, that is the cost of returning stores to a decent state. It seems that under Green's ownership, Bhs stores had not received much tender loving care.[107] Chappell and his entourage had been more accommodating, naively so it turns out.

## Policy of retaliation

Two weeks prior to the 2010 general election, Green had come out in support of the Conservative Party, stating that the Tories understood "what needs to be done. They get it." A few months later, to return the favour, freshly elected Prime Minister David Cameron asked Green to carry out a review of the government's spending and procurement. The irony was not lost on many that one of the most noteworthy tax-avoiders in the country was put in charge of an initiative to identify cutbacks for a cash-strapped government. [108] The summary report, *Efficiency Review by Sir Philip Green*, published in October 2010, alleged significant failings in financial controls, the use of public property, and procurement processes, though it fell short of recommending that civil servants move offshore in the pursuit of fiscal austerity. As RMT union boss Bob Crow suggested despondently: "The idea that public sector workers in the UK, struggling on low pay and under constant attack, should start taking lectures in cuts from a billionaire taxdodger is outrageous."[109]

But despite his political connections, Green would not be spared the political onslaught that was to follow Bhs's downfall six years later. In the days following the chain's bankruptcy filing, several officials, on both sides of the political spectrum, referred to Green's conduct in very acerbic, unflattering terms. Richard Fuller, a Conservative Member of Parliament, described him as the "unacceptable face of capitalism."

# THE GOOD, THE BAD AND THE UGLY OF PRIVATE EQUITY

His colleague David Davis took exception to the fact that Green had decided to splash money on his third yacht and invidiously declared:

> *"Sir Philip, with his billions, his yachts and his willingness to walk away from a failing business, pension liabilities and job losses, is just the sort of capitalist to give capitalism a bad name."*[110]

Not to be outdone, the Labour party's Angela Eagle, shadow business secretary, stressed:

> *"In this situation it appears this owner extracted hundreds of millions of pounds from the business and walked away to his favourite tax haven, leaving the Pension Protection Fund to pick up the bill."*[111]

Even preeminent business figures chipped in. Simon Walker, the plainspoken Director General of the Institute of Directors, gratingly noted that Green was guilty of a "lamentable failure of behaviour", which would likely accentuate the loss of trust in the business community.[112]

Green complained that he was the victim of a witch-hunt. In truth, the interest he had received was of his own making. His desire for his business prowess to be in the news had earned him the opprobrium of the City and of a few businessmen. As far back as the year 2002, fellow Londoner and garrulous Jewish entrepreneur Alan Sugar had drily remarked that there wasn't a week when he wouldn't see an "article about Philip Green in *The Sunday Times* or *Daily Mail*", adding "Green's love of money has gone to his head." [113] Now that the Bhs collapse was putting Green once again in the spotlight, the media and politicians asked for the relevant protagonists to be called before parliament. But the committee running the hearings did not get much respect from the City. The senior partners at law firm Olswang and accountants Grant Thornton, both advisers to Retail Acquisitions on the deal, had to be virtually dragged to appear. Goldman Sachs's bigwigs downplayed the importance of their advisory role in the Bhs disposal, insisting that they had not been paid for their trouble, a sure sign if there was one that their involvement cannot have been that serious.

While politicians and eminent business representatives competed to make the most out of this remarkable event – leading Green to accuse some Members of Parliaments of conducting a "trial by media" – the administrators Duff & Phelps never found a buyer for Bhs. After racking up £415 million in losses in its past seven years of operation,[114] the chain was to be disposed of piecemeal. Nevertheless, the process delivered a surreal anecdote. In the weeks that followed the group's collapse, Dominic Chappell considered buying back Bhs out of administration and tried to gather the necessary funding. The fact that the media, the public, politicians, the pensions regulator, several of his former business acolytes and some Bhs directors and employees questioned whether Chappell had been a fit and proper person to acquire the business the first time around had seemingly failed to register with the individual.

Green's wife, who the media thought should be summoned as being the main Bhs shareholder, was never called to testify before parliament, but Sir Philip rose to the challenge. On 15 June 2016, twelve days after Bhs was put into liquidation, he explained to the investigative committee that there had been "poor communications on both sides" between him and the pensions regulator; that he had invested £600 million into Bhs during his 15 years of ownership so could not be accused of misappropriating all the cash in dividend payouts; and that his and his family's move to tax haven Monaco in 1998 had occurred for health reasons.[115] Still, he pledged to resolve the pension problem.

When, in July, the House of Commons' Work and Pensions Committee published the posthumous findings of its inquiry into the bankruptcy of Bhs, the report revealed, among other things, that "BHS declined to make the employer contributions necessary to maintain the sustainability of the pension schemes over the duration of Sir Philip Green's period in charge." What the parliamentary committee underlined is that a long list of parties, from Green to Chappell and their respective advisers, had failed to properly assess the consequences of the transaction that had taken place in March 2015. Of course, we could also take the opposite view and agree with Chappell, who affirmed in an elegiac tone on the day administrators were appointed:

> *"No one is to blame. It was a combination of bad trading and not being able to raise enough money from the property portfolio."*[116]

## What's a knighthood worth?

In June 2006, Labour Prime Minister Tony Blair awarded Green a knighthood. The funny thing about it was not so much that a Labour government, supposedly serving the poor and underprivileged, was acknowledging the social and economic contributions of a billionaire retail tycoon. The irony about Green's knighthood was in the timing of this honour for 'services to the retail industry.' Only ten months earlier, Sir Philip had granted himself, or more accurately his Monaco-based wife, a £1.2 billion dividend, entirely free of tax. This tax-avoidance scheme had helped the entrepreneur and his family save a reported £285 million.

Because it was entirely debt-financed, the dividend brought another huge benefit. The £1.5 billion loans raised in the refinancing exercise cut Arcadia's corporation tax liabilities: interest charges on the loan were offset against taxable profits. Between 2006 and 2016, £450 million worth of net interest payable was expensed through Taveta's income statement, enabling the holding company to save a bundle on taxes.[117]

Ten years later, Green was in the British Government's black books. Yet, what had got the best of Bhs was not Green's tax shenanigans; it was the good old law of competitive pressure. Similarly, supercilious reports by the press and regulators indicated that the new owners, in

224

particular the freshly labelled "Premier League liar" and "Sunday pub league retailer" Dominic Chappell,[118] had behaved unscrupulously. But the fact remains that the retail chain's business model was broken. Which is the reason why the attention soon switched to Green and his decision to sell Bhs in early 2015, leaving the business with a massive pension deficit and a collection of under-invested stores. Too little time had elapsed to insulate the former owner.

Pension issues were not new at Green's retail empire. Arcadia and Bhs had remarkably onerous pension schemes. For over a decade, both groups had introduced changes related to contributions and retirement benefits.[119] All this was public knowledge. Various facts leaked to the press seemed to indicate that, in the years preceding the group's disposal, Green was unwilling to put more than £10 million a year in the Bhs pension plan and even put a restructuring on hold only months before the sale.[120]

Following a vicious campaign by the British media, which some of Green's cronies characterised as thinly veiled anti-Semitic bigotry, on 20 October 2016 the House of Commons approved a motion to ask for the Honours Forfeiture Committee to recommend Green's knighthood be annulled. One hundred Members of Parliament voted in favour of the motion. Ever since his appearance before the parliamentary committee, Green had been under pressure to fill the pension hole. MPs wanted him to pay £600 million as a quid pro quo for keeping his knighthood, providing further evidence that the 'cash for honours' scandal that had plagued Tony Blair's government a decade earlier might not have consigned to history the purchase of political influence in Britain.

On 28 February 2017, in part to appease his detractors, and after heated negotiations with the Pensions Regulator as well as a visit to the Work and Pensions Committee, Sir Philip agreed to increase his contribution to plug the pension hole from the original £80 million to a settlement amount of £363 million.[121] In response, the regulator withdrew its claim against the entrepreneur. Four months later, it published a final report on the matter, finding that the 'main purpose' in selling Bhs had been to prevent taking on liability for the scheme.[122]

In August of the same year, the regulator announced that it was taking legal action against Dominic Chappell and the latter's investment vehicle Retail Acquisitions due to their lack of cooperation during the inquiry. For the seller and the buyer, there was nowhere to hide. Neither was there for accountancy firm PricewaterhouseCoopers, which was investigated for its audits of Bhs, after repeatedly giving the company's accounts a clean bill of health despite its pension deficit, huge cumulative losses, and poor liquidity. One of the questions the auditors were expected to answer was how they got comfortable with the £800 million net liability position in Taveta's 2005 annual accounts when, according to the UK's Companies Act, dividends should only be paid out of accumulated realised profits.[*]

Whether his knighthood was worth that much, only Green can determine. But the full cost of his foray into Bhs could now be quantified. To his pension contribution must be added the £217 million of intercompany loans owed by Bhs and waived by Arcadia group at the time of the 2015 disposal. Back then, Green also transferred £24 million in cash to entice Retail Acquisitions to take on the inconvenient parcel. Finally, in August 2017, Arcadia agreed to pay more than £30 million to settle out of court a claim made by unsecured creditors. In summary, in addition to the £70 million of equity invested in 2000 to buy the business from Storehouse, Green contributed an extra £650 million to get rid of it 15 years later. Thankfully, he paid himself £400 million in dividends between 2002 and 2004, but that still left him short of £320 million.[123] When one thinks that Sir Philip

---

[*] In June 2018 PwC was fined £10 million as part of a settlement over the audit of Bhs while its senior partner in charge of the account was banned from audit work for 15 years

turned down an £800 million offer back in 2001, it shows the importance of timing one's exit.

## Green's dressing-down

As if seeing his wealth melt under the heat of the retail crisis was not enough – Green's fortune had reportedly shrunk from £4.2 billion in 2011 to £2.7 billion six years later – he was subjected to a national campaign of shame and blame orchestrated by the mainstream media and given prominence by many politicians.

Britain had had a love affair with Topshop and other fashion brands in Arcadia's empire, but it had not shared the same feeling towards the group's owner. Over the years, the media had portrayed Green in a very unflattering way. In November 2010, for instance, a Channel 4 Dispatches broadcast had revealed that Green's wealth and profitability at Bhs were partly due to the immoderate use of suppliers that paid people half the minimum wage and crammed them into sweatshops.[124] A month later, in the run-up to Christmas, he had earned himself the moniker 'Green the Grinch' for his tax-dodging habits.[125] But the press went to town after the Bhs fiasco. From Sir Philip Gree*d* to 'Sir Shifty',[126] his knighthood provoked a lot of rancour.

While many acknowledged his business acumen, variously crowning him 'king of British buyouts' or 'king of the High Street',[127] his aggressive financial engineering and tax-maximising techniques did not win him much respect. Dubbed the UK's answer to Donald Trump by *Vanity Fair*, a legitimate analogy given his permatan, craving for media attention, volatile temperament, bullying manners and enduring chutzpah, his unrequited love for OBOs could be added to the list of similarities. Adding emphasis to their kinship was the fact that Green had been approached (but declined) on several occasions to front the British version of The Apprentice, the reality TV show presented by Trump in the original US format. With parents involved in the property business, another point he had in common with the President of the United States, Sir Philip closed the loop when Bhs went bankrupt. Trump knew the world of corporate bankruptcies inside out, having gone through the process on six separate occasions.[128] Green had some catching-up to do, though he had himself experienced a series of receiverships in the 1980s.

In May 2017, as it prepared for the general elections taking place in early June, the UK's Conservative Party issued its policy manifesto, highlighting its programme for the upcoming five years. The party included the proposal to punish those caught mismanaging pension schemes. Immediately dubbed the 'Philip Green law', the underlying idea was to give the pensions regulator powers to issue punitive fines for those found to have wilfully left a pension scheme under-resourced and, if necessary, to disqualify relevant company directors. It also suggested new criminal offence for company directors who put at risk the ability of a pension scheme to meet its obligations.[129] Clearly populist, this programme showed to what extent the Bhs saga had affected the debate around how to reform what the right-wing Prime Minister, Theresa May, called 'untrammelled free markets.' In a form of catharsis, British politicians were falling over each other to condemn the ugly facets of an unregulated economic model they had praised to the skies for two generations, failing to comprehend that the Bhs tale was its dazzling apotheosis.

Green thought that he had got away with the disposal of a cumbersome and swelling liability, only to see a treacherous riptide bring it back to his shores with the added embarrassment of public scorn. However, he knew all along that, with the disposal, he was playing a dangerous game of 'business Frisbee'. Back in March 2015, he hadn't quite managed to sell Bhs lock, stock and barrel. To complete the tawdry disposal of the neglected chain, he was forced to provide a secured loan to Retail Acquisitions and to promise partly to fund future pension liabilities. His financial commitments were ongoing, a subtlety that the media and politicians were keen to emphasize.

What this case illustrates is that corporate executives who are independently wealthy do not need PE firms to complete leveraged buyouts. They can lead deals on their own and keep all the upside for themselves. But what the story also shows, beside the usual mudslinging and revelations of impropriety that accompany any business scandal, is that complex financial structuring and tax avoidance expose entrepreneurs to risk factors most fund managers can avoid: the media's irreverent probing and badgering by agenda-driven politicians. This is the main drawback of owner buyouts. Whereas it is difficult for politicians and regulators to humiliate a large financial institution, the entrepreneur guilty of controversial practices can easily be singled out as a villain, portrayed as the typical embodiment of greedy capitalism. Maybe one way for Green to fend off the political and regulatory attacks would be to follow Trump's example and take his country's political machine by storm.

## BUYOUTS AND THE FASHION RETAIL SECTOR

*Bhs is far from being the only fashion retailer that suffered from an overstretched balance sheet. In the US, several groups recently filed for bankruptcy protection following aggressively structured buyouts, including Bain Capital-sponsored Gymboree, a children's clothing chain employing 11,000 people and stuck with $1.4 billion in LBO loans until its Chapter 11 filing in July 2017. Towerbrook's denim designer True Religion went bust that same month with $535 million in debt. Two months earlier, Apax-backed fashion and accessories retailer Rue21 had sought Chapter 11 protection while carrying loans worth over $800 million.[130] The list goes on.*

# CHAPTER 8

# TIM/WIND Hellas: The Trojan horse of leverage[*]

> *In many industries, the liability of the vendor does not end at the point of sale. If a house collapses because of structural failure, the architect or the building contractor can be on the hook. Similarly, a car salesman or manufacturer is accountable if a vehicle inexplicably breaks down. For that reason, liability insurance is common market practice.*
>
> *No multi-year cover is provided by PE fund managers at the time of disposal – even though they are usually controlling shareholders. Corporate executives of PE-owned companies do provide reps and warranties, but those are restricted in scope. The following scenario explains why the caveat emptor principle is very relevant when buying a business from a buyout firm.*

STET Hellas was founded in 1992 as the first mobile operator in Greece. The original shareholders were Telecom Italia Mobile (TIM) with 74%, Verizon of the US with 21%, and insurance company Interamerican with 5%. Six years later STET Hellas listed its shares on

---

[*] Many of the facts behind this story were made public when two whistleblowers previously employed in the Luxembourg office of accountancy firm PricewaterhouseCoopers revealed confidential information about tax rulings and avoidance schemes set up by their firm on behalf of clients between 2002 and 2010. These revelations are better known as Luxembourg Leaks, shortened to LuxLeaks

# THE GOOD, THE BAD AND THE UGLY OF PRIVATE EQUITY

the Nasdaq and the Euronext, with Interamerican selling its shares to the public.

Despite being the first entrant to the market, the mobile operator steadily lost market share, first to Vodafone-Panafon, which launched its services in 1994, then to Cosmote, owned by fixed-line incumbent OTE, which entered the market four years later. By the time TIM had consolidated its ownership by buying Verizon's stake in August 2002, STET Hellas had already lost its leadership and was playing catch-up with its better-funded rivals.

On 8 February 2004 the company's brand changed to TIM Hellas to adopt the well-established name of its majority shareholder. Oddly, shortly after undertaking this 'massive re-branding campaign', to apply the vernacular used in the company's annual report, TIM Hellas was deemed expendable by its parent company. In December, Telecom Italia and Telecom Italia Mobile decided to merge. With total net debt of €44 billion, the combined group needed cash. TIM started selling off non-core operations, including activities in Peru in 2004, and Chile and Venezuela in 2005. The Greek business was next on the block.

Many hurdles related to competition, pricing, regulation and technology had recently taken their toll on the business. In 2004 the company had recorded meagre growth, with revenues of €829 million only up 2.5% year on year. Among other issues, competition for mobile-phone customers had intensified and fixed-to-mobile interconnection tariffs fallen one-third. In response, EBITDA had shrunk 12% to €243 million, although it was partly due to costs associated with the rebranding efforts. Operating margin was down significantly; the company's chief executive duly resigned. Yet, amid bid speculations, TIM Hellas's stock finished the year on a tear: up 44% versus the main stock index's more mundane 8.6% rise that same year.[1]

## Project Troy

Times were propitious for deals. Private equity firms were out on the prowl, pockets bulging with money to deploy. Sensing that there was an opportunity to buy TIM Hellas at a decent valuation, British outfit Apax and its American peer Texas Pacific Group approached Telecom Italia Mobile in late 2004, in a process they dubbed 'Project Troy'.

Recognising that the Italian parent company was in a rush to generate cash to restore its bloated balance sheet, Apax and TPG obtained a six-week period of exclusivity in January 2005. By April, via a new company called Troy GAC Telecommunications, they agreed to acquire TIM's 81% stake, valuing the target at €1.54 billion – Greece's largest leveraged buyout to date.[2] The transaction represented a healthy 18% premium to the target's six-month average price. The deal was sealed by June.

TPG was a relative newbie in the world of buyouts. Founded 12 years earlier by a bunch of corporate executives, the Texas-based firm had only recently landed in Europe. Although TIM Hellas was TPG's first foray into the European telecoms sector, Apax had done several deals in that space. One of the leading LBO investors in Europe, Apax had in fact begun life as a venture capital firm when launched in 1969 by its American founder Alan Patricof. By the time it approached TIM Hellas, Apax was a pure-play buyout shop and Patricof was about to depart and return to his real passion, early-stage investing.

In the mid-1990s Apax had backed pan-European broadband network operator Esprit Telecom and seen growth shoot up as the Internet bubble took a life of its own. Sector deregulation also spurred consolidation. Apax's recent deal log had included the buyouts of Ericsson's $480 million Enterprise Solutions unit, British Telecom's yellow pages for £2.1 billion, and satellite communications groups Inmarsat and Intelsat. While its negotiations with TIM were ongoing, the firm was in the process of closing its sixth European buyout fund

THE GOOD, THE BAD AND THE UGLY OF PRIVATE EQUITY

with commitments of €4.3 billion. It now needed to put that capital to work.

To fund the TIM Hellas acquisition, the PE duo invested €50 million of equity and €161 million of deeply subordinated shareholder loans. The rest was financed through LBO loans. As a testament to TIM Hellas's cash flow predictability, a jumbo high-yield bond of €900 million was expected to be raised and sliced with a fixed-rate component and a floating rate note, to which a €110 million payment-in-kind tranche (for which all interest accrued until maturity) would be added.* But before the syndication process was over, the debt structure mushroomed to a €1.28 billion package, split between a €925 million seven-year secured floating rate note and a €355 million eight-year senior note yielding 8.5%.[3] For the first time, a European leveraged buyout was financed entirely in the bond market, such was the boundless innovative spirit of this exciting era.[4] Notably absent from bond issuances are maintenance covenants that can restrict capex fundraising and impose loan amortisation payments. This flexible financing, vastly oversubscribed, was completed in October 2005 and duly assigned junk status by rating agencies.[5]

That same month New York-based TCS Capital, the largest minority shareholder in TIM Hellas with a 5.4% stake, went to court in a bid to block the merger between the Greek mobile operator and bidding vehicle Troy GAC. Arguing that the valuation of 5 times EBITDA for TIM Hellas was much lower than average comparables of 7.9 times, TCS Capital stated that a fair price for the target was €25, rather than the €16.4 paid by the PE firms.[6]

Part of the rationale behind the lower valuation was the target's weak competitive positioning. With 2.3 million subscribers at the end of 2004,[7] TIM Hellas was ranked a distant third in the country's mobile

---

* A payment-in-kind note is not amortised during the duration of the loan. Both principal and interest are redeemable at maturity

telephony market. But soon after the completion of the debt syndication process, Apax and TPG announced that they were gunning for Q-Telecom, the fourth and smallest Greek mobile operator, with whom they had been in discussions for several months. As of 30 June 2005, only three years after its commercial launch, Q-Telecom had a 7.3% share of the country's mobile market.[8]

First, Project Troy had to be finalised. So on 23 November 2005, despite TCS Capital's objections, the PE duo acquired the remaining 19% of the shares of TIM Hellas for €263.5 million.[9] The company was delisted and fully under private equity control.

The cash-generative nature and steady revenue streams of the mobile telecoms sector made it an ideal target for voracious dealmakers. But even Apax and TPG must have been stunned by the exit opportunity that soon presented itself. Within weeks of the TIM Hellas take-private, Egyptian investor Naguib Sawiris, controlling shareholder of Italy's third mobile operator WIND Telecomunicazioni, publicly expressed an interest to buy TIM Hellas off the private equity consortium, offering 'a couple of hundred million dollars more' than what they had paid for it.[10] It was nice to know that they had a way out, but for now the two PE owners needed to execute the TIM Hellas and Q-Telecom integration. In parallel, critical cost cuts were introduced to improve efficiency. As can be seen from Figure 8.1, in recent years EBITDA margin at TIM Hellas had been on a downward slope despite top line growth.

Operating cash flows had continued to plummet in the months following the buyout. In 2005 they no longer covered capital expenditures, which had themselves been reduced to limit cash leakage away from debt service. In 2005 alone, interest expense totalled €111 million. Despite these poor financial results, which anaemic revenue growth could not mitigate, operationally the company had improved: the number of subscribers was up 4% and average revenue per user had risen €2 to €29.1.[11]

## Figure 8.1 – STET/TIM Hellas's revenue and EBITDA margin from 2000 to 2005

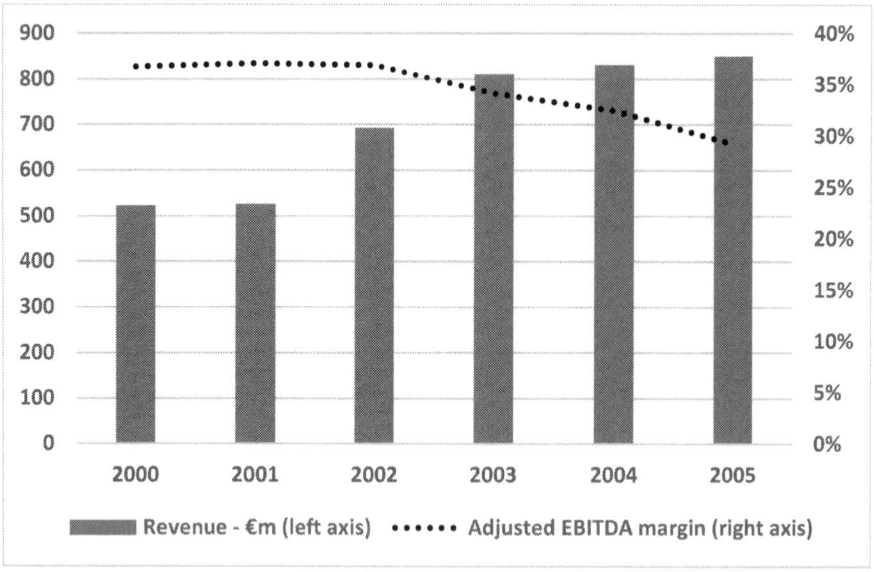

*Source: Company filings and author's analysis*

# Their big fat Greek gearing

In January 2006 the private equity consortium completed the follow-on acquisition of Q-Telecom for €367 million. The target had booked €157 million in revenue and €30 million in EBITDA in the previous 12 months. It was a fairly expensive purchase, but the combination of the third and fourth operators was meant to create a much stronger mobile carrier.[12] The deal was funded partly with cash and partly with debt. To satisfy demand for a top-up and fund the transaction with even more debt, TIM Hellas issued a €200 million tap to its existing €925 million floating rate note.[13]

# TIM/WIND Hellas

Of the €1.98 billion deployed in the two telecoms operators, Apax and TPG volunteered €390 million of their LP investors' capital, of which €311 million was a deep-discount instrument in the form of preferred equity certificates (PECs) and €77 million in convertible PECs – yes, this acronym is relevant to our case discussion. Only €1.6 million of their contribution was issued as share capital.[14]

Strictly speaking, less than 0.5% of the PE firms' financing was in pure equity form. Yet the credit markets were so hot that, in April, TIM Hellas issued a fresh €500 million eight-year note accruing (meaning, non-cash) interest at 8.25% per annum. The proceeds were used to pay a dividend to Apax and TPG, and to redeem existing notes.[15] Because they are not as liquid as senior bonds, non-cash interest-bearing loans are riskier, and thus more expensive. But the cost was to be borne by TIM Hellas, not by its private equity backers. Oversubscribed, the new tranche attracted a large number of risk-seeking and yield-starved hedge funds.

In July, less than a year after taking ownership of the Greek company, in another sign that buyout fund managers are not all long-term investors, Apax and TPG laid the groundwork for an exit. The month before, they had retained the services of KPMG to draw up a vendor due diligence report. By the end of July, they had received proposals from some ten investment banks expressing an interest in arranging the sale. Two months later, they mandated Morgan Stanley and Lehman to run an auction.[16] With a deadline of 30 November for bid submissions, several parties vied for the business. Etilasat from the Emirates, Turkish mobile company Turkcell and US buyout firm Providence Equity were among the bidders.[17]

Alternatively, Apax and TPG were considering a dividend recapitalisation. In such vibrant markets, refinancings were the surer and shorter route to the land of plenty. In December, rumours emerged that the proposed disposal had been parked. Bids had come

THE GOOD, THE BAD AND THE UGLY OF PRIVATE EQUITY

below the target price of €3.4 billion – Turkcell and Providence Equity had tabled final bids of €2.7 billion and €3.2 billion, respectively.[18]

TIM Hellas launched a high-yield issuance instead. With this second recapitalisation in just nine months, the PE duo was in for a neat payday. The debt package had strong innovative streaks, but as one leveraged banker sanguinely put it: "It is a good credit and will be fine."[19] The Greek operator's recap joined a long parade of debt issuances in the sector. Turkcell was in the market for a $3 billion acquisition loan.[20] Another massive telecoms refinancing deal was being marketed; that of the third largest Italian mobile phone operator, WIND. The latter was raising €1.7 billion in payment-in-kind notes (again, non-cash interest-bearing), a record for this sort of instrument in Europe. The aim was to fund the acquisition of Italian utility Enel's 26.5% stake in Weather Investments, the holding vehicle behind WIND controlled by Naguib Sawiris. Weather had bought WIND's majority stake in May 2005 for €12.2 billion, in Europe's largest leveraged buyout.

TIM Hellas's recapitalisation totalled €1.47 billion in a four-part offering, including a €974 million cash dividend plus a bridge to a disposal of the company if one took place shortly thereafter.[21] Things were moving so fast that it was hard to track, let alone anticipate, the mobile operator's next announcement. On 7 February 2007, 20 months after completing the buyout, Apax and TPG sold the business to Weather Investments for €3.4 billion, funded with €500 million of equity plus €2.9 billion of net debt.[22] Despite the short holding period, the Apax press release authoritatively declared:

> *"The company was successfully turned round and set on a growth trajectory leading to a significant improvement in all financial and operating key metrics."[23]*

Thanks to its Q-Telecom add-on, TIM Hellas now had 3.7 million subscribers. It still ranked third behind Cosmote and Panafon, but it was a much more credible market participant. The headline price was almost 80% above the combined €1.9 billion Apax and TPG had paid.

Before moving on to the next phase of TIM Hellas's memorable chronicle, let's briefly review how the two private equity owners made their money.

- First, as argued by TCS Capital, they bought TIM Hellas on the cheap from its overindebted owner Telecom Italia.
- Then, they used significant leverage and twice refinanced aggressively during the period of ownership.
- They strengthened the company's competitive position by acquiring the fourth and smallest participant in Greece's 11 million mobile subscribers market. With 97% penetration,[24] the Greek market was mature, so consolidating the oligopolistic landscape was the surest way to improve margins, even if only temporarily.
- Lastly, and most importantly, the two PE firms got out of their investment as quickly as possible to benefit fully from the impact of the time value of money. Quick flips, that is exiting assets within a two-year time frame, have a tremendously positive impact on the annual rate of return of an investment (the well-known internal rate of return, or IRR, against which all private equity investments are benchmarked).

## Achilles' heel

After Apax and TPG's departure, the Greek mobile carrier entered a brief, misleading period of normality. The new owner was an experienced telecoms investor. Weather not only owned Italy's WIND Telecomunicazioni but it also controlled Orascom Telecom, an operator with 50 million subscribers in high growth markets in the Middle East, Africa and South Asia.

Despite its expensive rebranding exercise three years earlier, TIM Hellas changed its name once more, to be from now on known as WIND Hellas. Leverage remained high at 12.4 times operating profit, while the cash interest coverage declined to 1.2 times.[25] Yet, it didn't matter so much. The Sawirises' intention was for Weather to list by the end of 2007 or early the following year.[26] They wanted to raise capital to finance the group's ambitious expansion plans.

It might be the reason why, in February 2008, Apax entered into discussions with the Sawirises to take a 5% stake into Weather.[27] In June the British buyout firm paid €550 million for the stake while its peers TA Associates and Madison Dearborn jointly paid the same amount for a similar 5% stake.[28] Weather's Egyptian owners had pushed through the sale to repay €1 billion in vendor loans owed to Enel. Incidentally, the stake disposals ascribed a valuation of €11 billion to WIND Hellas's equity.

Weather's float was parked for the time being. In this inflating credit market, no one could yet beat financial sponsors at the overvaluation game. The Lehman Brothers bankruptcy was still three months away.

But immediately after the American bank's collapse in September 2008, in a brutal reversal of fortune, Weather's adventure in Greece turned into an odyssey. With a share of about one-quarter of Greece's mobile users, WIND Hellas remained the weakest of the country's operators – Cosmote's share was 39% while Panafon served over a third of the market. This competitive positioning proved a liability. By the end of 2008, the financial crisis morphed into an economic bust. Mobile telephony entered an all-out price war. Pressure on margins was the last thing that the overindebted WIND Hellas needed. In its 2008 fiscal year, the company reported €243 million in interest expense, still well covered by an EBITDA of €430 million.[29] But operating performance quickly deteriorated.

## Jurisdiction shopping

The first half of 2009 saw sales and operating cash flows at the company register a double-digit fall. With debt of €3 billion, Luxembourg-registered Hellas II, the parent company of WIND Hellas, saw leverage exceed 7.5 times EBITDA. With no surcease from suffering, the business was heading for a debt restructuring. In early September Standard & Poor's lowered its rating of the company's senior secured notes deeper into the speculative category, citing a possible default in the near future. That same month WIND Hellas restructured €500 million of its subordinated debt.[30]

The telecoms operator desperately needed a €50 million cash equity infusion to meet a coupon repayment due in mid-October. Management obtained a waiver and amendment undertaking from lenders for part of the credit facility, but the key challenge was to find a party willing to fund the €50 million shortfall. WIND Hellas had no cash at hand, and the Sawirises did not seem keen to step in. Management had conversations with Weather's minority PE owners. Apax duly ruled itself out. The problem was that earnings were in freefall – EBITDA had sunk 25% in the previous quarter.[31] No one was willing to catch this falling knife.

In November WIND Hellas finally defaulted. Interest expense in 2009 had totalled €222 million. Even before the impairment of goodwill, operating income was only €37 million, a fall of almost 80% on the prior year. It was time for the company to have a serious conversation with its lenders.

Weather Investments proposed to wipe out nearly €1.5 billion of subordinated debt and to keep the most secured loans in place. But some lenders were not in a chatty mood. When Hellas II applied to be put into administration, holders of subordinated bonds considered making a bid to buy the company. Yet they never managed to table their offer in time. Weather won a court battle to keep control of the

Greek mobile operator despite a superior offer from the company's lenders.[32]

Headquartered in the UK after Weather had moved its jurisdiction from Luxembourg four months earlier, on 13 November 2009 WIND Hellas became the biggest pre-pack administration in British history. After days of heated negotiations, the Sawirises' vehicle retained control, costing bondholders a reported €1.5 billion in exchange for a tiny minority equity position in the company.[33]

Although what precedes must have left many readers baffled, it is important to understand why the Greek company bothered to move its head office from Luxembourg to London. The UK has one of the most relaxed corporate insolvency schemes in Europe – debt issuers and investors find the rigidity of the workout regimes in other European countries frustrating. The UK's pre-pack administration process allows a troubled company unable to meet its debt obligations to file for court protection, giving it time to develop a proper restructuring plan before engaging with creditors. That enables shareholders to shop a business around while keeping the creditors at bay. The Greek company's move to London had therefore been engineered by Italian parent Weather Investments, itself controlled by the Sawirises, in anticipation of defaulting on the LBO debt commitments.

This controversial rescue, which would earn London the dubious title 'bankruptcy capital of Europe',[34] did not go down well with some of WIND Hellas's bondholders. It was the beginning of a drawn-out legal battle between the company and its shareholders on one side and some of its unsecured lenders on the other.

The company had given preferential treatment to the secured creditors, including the bank loan holders, but the bondholders were given short shrift.[35] The latter, as subordinated lenders, were the most impacted by the Greek company's value deterioration. And if the bonds were quoted below par, then logically it meant that the equity portion, held by Weather Investments, had to be worthless.

But the Sawirises and their PE co-investors weren't willing to hand over the keys to the parties sitting immediately ahead of them in the capital structure. Thanks to the pre-pack process, they could come across as the good guys trying to save jobs. In the 21st century version of capitalism, lenders are not always granted priority over the shareholders, no matter what their loan agreement states. One bondholder, Bertrand des Pallières, the chief executive of SPQR Capital, bawdily engaged in hyperbole:

> *"The pre-pack was used [by the Sawiris] to buy their own company without some of its debts. England is known for its good laws, but this is turning it into a bordello for companies to go bust in."*[86]

What made the matter worse was that the subordinated lenders had actually submitted a higher offer, putting forward a bid worth €450 million, comprised of €200 million in equity and the acquisition of the company's €250 million fully drawn credit facility. But they had failed to get enough creditor support for the deal before a lock-up period ended on 30 November. Ultimately, a UK court had found in favour of Weather in its attempt to restructure the telecoms operator's balance sheet. Bondholders were rooting for litigation. Among them, Mike Hodges, Chief Investment Officer of Aladdin Capital, objected:

> *"With the Weather deal now going ahead the company and management team that got Wind Hellas into this situation in the first place will be repurchasing what was a €3 billion company for €50 million and basically using our money by gaining the value of our written off debt."*[87]

Such were the latter-day methods applied by financial investors to preserve their interests. To remain in control, the shareholders had arranged for the purgative restructuring to be initiated by the company itself, citing a pressing need for liquidity rather than as a result of creditor actions.[38] Weather argued that its management expertise in the telecoms sector – rather than simply its status as financial owner – added real value to the lower bid.

Litigation claims would multiply. For now, the company was moving forward, initiating the relocation of its headquarters back to Luxembourg, a management reshuffle, and the fresh issuance of another payment-in-kind note. In December 2009 Nassos Zarkalis, previously head of fixed-line service provider Hellas On-Line and commercial director with Vodafone in Greece, became chief executive officer of WIND Hellas. The new boss was expected to engineer an urgently needed turnaround. And the company's shareholders were not quite done with the debt restructuring. The month of Zarkalis's appointment, WIND Hellas issued a long-dated loan totalling €950 million.

Amazingly, for a company that had just defaulted on part of its debt, WIND Hellas attracted strong interest from the credit markets. Several participants, however, took offence at the timing of the offer and at the intention for the proceeds of the fundraise to be upstreamed to Weather to help the owners effectively finance their acquisition of the newly restructured mobile operator. To those who did not have any qualms about backing a company and the private equity owners that had so blatantly ridden roughshod over bondholders, one market participant countered that it reeked "of poor taste", adding "I wouldn't get involved in this deal on principle, and I have spoken to a number of other investors that feel the same way."[39]


## Walk like an Egyptian

Quickly, WIND Hellas's hopeless reputational and commercial setbacks developed into a financial rout. Following the pre-pack, Hellas II was wound down and Weather Finance III, another entity of the group structure, became the new holding company, filing and reporting financial accounts. But this fresh and hopeful restart did not matter if the underlying operating company did not perform according to plan. In early March 2010, the group's subordinated bonds dropped to the low 40s on the back of weak trading; they were quoted at a 70% discount by the end of the month.[40]

In tandem with WIND Hellas's woes, Greece experienced its own debt crisis, triggered by the turmoil of the global recession and structural weaknesses in the national economy. Flat in 2008, the country's GDP sank 4.3% the following year. In late April 2010 credit rating agencies proceeded to downgrade government bonds to junk status. This provoked a crisis of confidence, which wasn't helped by revelations that successive governments had manipulated economic statistics for the better part of a decade to boost the country's 1999 application to join Europe's monetary union, the eurozone. In May 2010 the Greek Government's budget deficit was revised and estimated to be 13.6%.

About the only piece of good news in these disclosures was that Greece did not have the worst budget deficit: it was the second highest in the world relative to GDP behind Iceland at 15.7%.[41] Trying to salvage the situation, the government raised €13 billion in the bond markets. But the combination of poor economic data, revelations of shady budget reporting and multiple debt issuances led the sovereign bond yields to rise, increasing the cost of risk insurance on Greece's credit default swaps compared to the other eurozone countries.

While the country was sinking into a super-jumbo debt crisis jeopardising its membership to the eurozone, WIND Hellas slipped into fathomless misery. The pre-pack restructuring at the end of 2009 had wiped out subordinated debt, reducing leverage from 9 times to 5.5 times EBITDA.[42] Six months later the group's unsecured bonds traded 85% to 90% below par while secured loans changed hands at 50 cents on the euro.[43] Over that period, the mobile operator's performance had followed the country's economic path. WIND Hellas was once more against the wall.

By June 2010 the company and its lenders were back at the negotiating tables – €55 million of debt payments were due in the last week of the month, but the business only had €35 million in the bank. Despite attempts to strengthen the company's balance sheet, WIND Hellas struggled as the country sank in a deep financial morass. In the face of the Greek Government's austerity measures, consumer spending caved in, forcing the mobile telephony market into a highly competitive price war. In the first quarter of 2010, WIND Hellas's revenues had dropped 18.5% as its subscribers tightened their belts.[44]

Despite the €125 million of fresh equity put in by the financial owners in late 2009, lower capital expenditure, and annual savings in the order of €80 million in coupon payments after slashing debt by almost €1.5 billion, WIND Hellas's cash flows were still no match for the compounding impact of remaining loan commitments. One way for Weather's investors to get the secured lenders on their side during the previous year's cleansing restructuring had been to pay consent fees – almost €55 million had gone towards these commissions.[45] Yet, Weather's capital injection made to protect its ownership was now worthless.

This time around, payoffs would not be sufficient to win approval from creditors. To prepare the ground for another pre-pack, as further illustration of jurisdiction shopping, in July 2010 WIND Hellas transferred three of its subsidiaries to Britain.[46] In a desperate move, that same month the company put itself up for sale after agreeing a standstill with its lenders.[47] By the 15 September deadline six bids were received, including from investment firm Argo Capital, Greek broadband provider On Telecoms, Norwegian group Telenor, US fund Saban Capital (which was one of the secured bondholders), and even one tabled by the insatiable and unshakable Egyptian entrepreneur Naguib Sawiris who was eager to retain ownership.[48] Also in the list of interested parties was Greek technology group Info-Quest, the former owner of Q-Telecom until the sale to TIM Hellas in 2006.

# TIM/WIND Hellas

Whatever bid won the day, the business needed immediate action. According to management, WIND Hellas was likely to book €180 million of EBITDA for 2010 compared to €317 million the prior year.[49] But none of the offers submitted were considered generous enough. In charge since the company's default in the summer, the bondholders decided that they would no longer be pushed around.

On 18 October 2010 Weather Finance III announced that some of the company's creditors had been chosen as preferred bidder. A consortium of the secured lenders had tabled its own debt-for-equity swap. Representing 57% of the secured bonds, distressed debt investors Mount Kellett, Taconic, Providence Equity, Anchorage Capital, Angelo Gordon, and Eton Park made a €420 million cash injection in exchange for 90% of WIND Hellas's stock. The remaining 10% went to the bondholders not willing or able to participate in the funding round. In return, WIND Hellas would be released from its obligations in respect of €1.2 billion in secured loans and €355 million in unsecured notes.[50]

After failing to turn around the business, the private equity backers and the Sawirises had been told to take a walk. Agreed by more than three-quarters of the secured debtholders,[51] this second financial restructuring in less than 12 months marked a new, debt-free era for WIND Hellas. Although the senior management team, including chief exec Zarkalis, stayed put, the board of directors was significantly revamped and beefed up with industry veterans and members of the Greek business community.

With the need to file five separate bankruptcy claims, the WIND Hellas scenario proved to be one of the most technical and convoluted restructurings in Europe.[52] Although widely adopted in the US, the 'loan-to-own' policy followed by the six distressed debt specialists was a fairly new development in Europe. The many corporate zombies spawned by the 2008 financial crisis had forced lenders to be more aggressive and pro-active. Creditors had come to realise that, despite all

247

THE GOOD, THE BAD AND THE UGLY OF PRIVATE EQUITY

their braggadocio and so-called sector expertise, PE owners rarely cared for the priority rights of third parties when trying to sort out past mistakes. After getting burnt in 2009, private debt investors had taken matters into their own hands, creating a new holding company, Largo Limited, this one based in tax haven Guernsey, to replace the disgraced 'Weather' label.

**Figure 8.2 – TIM/WIND Hellas's revenue and EBITDA margin from 2007 to 2010**

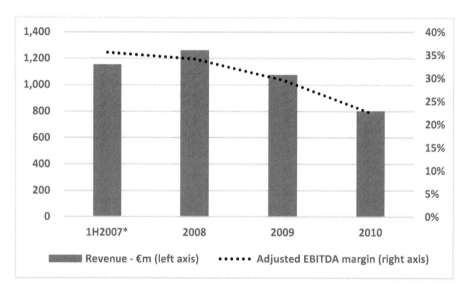

Notes: *TIM Hellas changed its name to WIND Hellas on 29 May 2007 – \*Last twelve months to June 2007 – Source: Company filings and author's analysis*

Purged of the last vestiges of private equity ownership, WIND Hellas closed a difficult period that had seen revenue and EBITDA margin lose 35% and 12 percentage points respectively in the past two years, as seen in Figure 8.2. WIND's breakdown in Greece signalled the end of the Sawirises' yearning to build a successful telecoms empire. After losing control of the Greek operations, for $6.8 billion they announced the sale of the remaining Weather group – Italy's WIND Telecom and the 51.7% stake in Orascom – to VimpelCom, a global operator in emerging markets controlled by Russia's Alfa Group and Norway's Telenor.

Weather was valued at $8 billion upon the merger with VimpelCom,[53] about half the equity valuation in 2008. Becoming minority shareholders in the amalgamated VimpelCom, the Sawirises accepted that, in an environment where credit financing was out of fashion, they needed to join investors with deep pockets in order to fund their ambition for world domination. The combined group created the world's fifth largest mobile telecoms carrier by the number of subscribers, with revenues of $21.5 billion and EBITDA of $9.5 billion.[54]

## Between Scylla and Charybdis

In the summer of 2011, Vodafone disclosed that it was in merger discussions with WIND Hellas to strengthen its Greek subsidiary Panafon.[55] The fact that CEO Zarkalis was a former Vodafone employee should have helped to reach an agreement, but talks eventually floundered. Vodafone's shareholders did not see the economic logic of expanding the group's exposure to a faltering market. In 2010 Greece's GDP had fallen 5.5%, its worst performance since 1974, the year when the country emerged from military dictatorship, although 2011 was to rewrite the country's records books: that year the economy sank more than 9%. And despite the country's desperation, regulators would have hesitated to approve the merger between the country's second and third largest operators. Still, it showed that WIND Hellas was not the only telecoms group in turmoil – before the end of the year, Vodafone would write down €450 million from the value of its Greek business.[56]

THE GOOD, THE BAD AND THE UGLY OF PRIVATE EQUITY

Thanks to the energetic stance taken by its lenders, WIND Hellas survived in a market landscape that remained extremely challenging. For proof, in 2012 national GDP fell a further 7.3%. Eventually, the business found a new trading level, with EBITDA margin hovering in the 18% to 19% range (see Figure 8.3).

While the company was going through the worst of economic environments, the subordinated bondholders that had been bullied out of the capital structure during the November 2009 refinancing intensified their campaign for retribution. They were going to receive outside help.

In December 2011, two years after going into administration, WIND Hellas's previous holding company Hellas II started liquidation proceedings.[57] The liquidators were about to go after the previous private equity owners, and they would not do so quietly, publicly bad-mouthing and questioning the actions of Apax and TPG during the months preceding the 2007 sale to the Sawirises. Indeed, the aspects of this story that are most interesting to study, at least from a private-equity anthropological standpoint, relate to the business customs that came to light during the Hellas II liquidation process. After a lengthy forensic post-mortem, in March 2014 the liquidators decided to sue Hellas II's former PE shareholders for "fraudulent conveyance and unjust enrichment," describing their €1 billion dividend recap in 2006 as "one of the very worst abuses in the private equity industry" comparable to the sack of Troy.[58] The fact that the bolt-on acquisition of Q-Telecom had been codenamed 'Project Helen' – after the queen of Sparta whose abduction is reported as the reason behind the Trojan War in Homer's Iliad – added a mythological dimension to this drama.

## A Greek tragedy

When completing its leveraged buyout back in 2005, the company was already having a tough time. Recall that EBITDA had fallen by more than 10% in 2004. Operating cash flows had collapsed by a third. This was despite the fact that Athens had hosted the summer Olympics that year – roaming charges from foreign visitors as well as higher usage from local subscribers had been a boon. Heightened competitive pressure had seen the operator's subscriber base erode two years on the trot, falling from 2.5 million to 2.3 million subscribers between 2002 and December 2004. While all mobile operators were experiencing a migration of prepaid customers to contract tariffs, TIM Hellas had seen some switch to its cheaper and already much larger competitors: Cosmote and Panafon. It was not a reassuring trend. Contract subscribers are usually higher-margin ones. They are also more loyal, bringing in sustained market share. In the three years leading up to the buyout, although revenues had risen steadily, the company's EBITDA margin had lost ten percentage points (as seen in Figure 8.1). These are not characteristics that one typically associates with LBO candidates. Stability, growth and predictability are preferable factors to face stringent debt-related commitments. The Greek company could best be described as a turnaround candidate.

A leveraged acquisition of TIM Hellas was risky, unless you were not planning to hang around to see the corrosive consequences of debt on a low-growth business facing margin erosion. Following the merger with Q-Telecom six months after the buyout of TIM Hellas, Apax and TPG had managed to deliver one-off benefits, pushing EBITDA margin above 35% in the first half of 2007 compared to less than 30% in 2005. But between 2001 and 2005, profit margin had shed eight percentage points in the face of price competition. While the market consolidation engendered by the combination of the third and fourth mobile operators was likely to reduce price pressure, the fact that mobile services were fast maturing meant that Cosmote and Panafon were likely to keep the pressure on, if only to protect their market shares. Within three years of its acquisition by Weather, WIND Hellas had seen EBITDA margin lose 10 percentage points. That sort of profit attrition is the equivalent of a death warrant for any debt-lashed corporation. WIND Hellas was stuck in near rigor mortis.

Weather and WIND had already been aggressively levered up by the Sawirises before they piled the Greek operator onto the structure in 2007. The effects of a refinancing performed in the loose and heedless manner of the times did not provide the telecoms group with sufficient room to manoeuvre when the forbidding clouds of the financial crisis presented themselves in late 2008.

If we had to decide who is to blame for WIND Hellas's eventual lender-led restructuring, we would have to condemn our modern version of unregulated capitalism. You cannot expect financial investors to assign limits to leverage if regulation does not establish a clear position on what is acceptable and what isn't. The Sawirises had insatiable ambition. At the time, everyone who was anyone wanted to lead the market consolidation. Deutsche Telekom's T-Mobile, Britain's Vodafone and France Telecom's Orange were leading the charge in Europe. Naguib Sawiris needed debt to fund his project, if only to match this trio's firepower. In 2005 the Sawirises' empire already sat atop €10 billion in loans.[59] Five years later it had crumbled.

Another lesson learned relates to market structure rather than capital structure. To protect cash flows in the telecoms sector, market leadership is very important. The world's second largest mobile telephony operator offers valuable advice. In December 2016 Vittorio Colao, CEO of Vodafone, explained that his company's goal was to be number 1 or 2 in all its geographies. He surmised: "The gap versus No. 3s is not only stable, but even increasing. It's about really creating a two-tier market."[60] The top two players in each geography are able to differentiate themselves through superior networks and services, guaranteeing better cash flow preservation and visibility.

This view was supported by facts. In Greece, Cosmote had EBITDA margins close to 40% while Panafon's were in the mid-30s.[61] As the third operator in a small European market, WIND Hellas did not have the tools to differentiate its services, which made it vulnerable to cash flow erosion, which in turn threatened its survival in light of its aggressive financial gearing. Outmanoeuvred by bigger rivals and afflicted by the long-term effects of debt as well as the tug of war between its owners and lenders, the company's EBITDA margin fell below 25% in 2010 (see Figure 8.2).

## LBO blowback

For the lenders that expressed their anger through the medium of several lawsuits, at issue was the role of Apax and TPG in this mayhem. As part and parcel of the private equity fee-based model, the two firms received consulting fees worth €2 million per annum. In addition, they earned €15 million for business advisory services rendered in connection with debt placement and preparation of business and strategic plans at the time of the 2005 buyout.[62]

When the PE duo exited two years later, the Greek telecoms group was carrying 20 times more debt than before the buyout, courtesy of the late-2006 dividend pay-out to its financial sponsors.[63] As covered earlier, that was the subject of the lawsuit eventually filed in September 2015 against Apax and TPG by liquidators appointed to Hellas II, the group's parent company gone bankrupt three years after the dividend distribution. The liquidators were seeking recovery of the money on behalf of creditors, contending that the company did not have sufficient earnings to cover the pay-out, and arguing that it was a fraudulent transfer. In their opinion, the balance sheet was not just stretched, it was stressed.

At first sight, the point seems nonsensical, even tendentious. Not only are PE-induced dividend payments rarely, if ever, covered by the profits of the underlying company, but in many cases such distributions force the company into a net liability position (meaning that its assets are not sufficient to cover its liabilities, because these dividend recaps are funded with bank debt or corporate bonds). We already visited this matter with the Bhs story in Chapter 7.

However, a more pertinent claim made by the liquidators was related to the equity instruments used by the two private equity firms to acquire TIM Hellas. Those securities – known as convertible preferred equity certificates, or PECs – were meant to follow strict redemption rules set out by Luxembourg law. Cashed out at a huge premium – 35 times their par value – under Luxembourg law these certificates do not grant any right to dividends in the absence of distributable earnings at the company. Making such payments even more cumbersome, before any distribution is made the company must secure an independent valuation.[64] To top it all, tax authorities in various jurisdictions were investigating whether appropriate taxes had been paid on this mammoth distribution. Up to €200 million of withholding tax could be due if the PECs were treated as equity (as they would be in the US and other jurisdictions) instead of debt (as is allowed in Luxembourg).[65]

A second litigation case concerned the fiduciary duties of the former directors of the telecoms company, which affected directly the financial sponsors since several of their representatives held board seats at the time. As a line of defence against both claims, the private equity duo maintained that Hellas II was sound when sold in 2007 and that the company's subsequent implosion was a consequence of the country's economic crisis. Yet, various emails exchanged between professionals at the two buyout firms show that some of the investment executives were nervous that the sheer size of the €1.4 billion recapitalisation would put the company at risk. One TPG executive had opined to his Apax counterpart that their actions were "putting the business under huge pressure". The firms' response was that such communications were taken out of context.

# TIM/WIND Hellas

Speaking of "duplicitous and catastrophic plunder," the liquidators likened Apax's and TPG's conduct to "a state-of-the-art Trojan horse designed to financially infiltrate TIM Hellas and Q-Telecom and then systematically pillage their assets from within by piling on debt in order to make large distributions to equity owners".[66] Adding to this barrage of reproaches, former bondholder and creditor SPQR Capital's des Pallières bitterly complained:

> *"This case reveals the private equity industry at its very worst. Apax and TPG loaded up Hellas with debt and used the proceeds to hand themselves huge distribution payments. This was immoral and illegal, as we will tell the Luxembourg court. You cannot pull 1 billion out of a company that has no reserves. It was a greedy and cynical manoeuvre that left creditors and the company itself stranded,"[67]* before adding *"It would open the door to the wholesale looting of companies."[68]*

But it turns out that you can pull that much money out of a company with no equity buffer. On 23 December 2015 the three judges of the District Court of Luxembourg ruled that Apax and TPG had done nothing wrong, rejecting all the claims brought against them.[69]

Yet it wasn't the end of the matter. Civil litigation had been launched against the two defendants in the US. In September 2016 a New York appeals court ruled that Wilmington Trust, an indenture trustee for Hellas Telecommunications noteholders, could bring claims against the former private equity owners. Wilmington was seeking $565 million over defaulted bonds, accusing Apax and TPG of pocketing the proceeds from the indenture. TPG's co-founders David Bonderman and James Coulter alongside Apax's former CEO and chairman Martin Halusa were named as defendants.[70] Almost a decade after taking place, the controversial dividend recap was a gift that kept on giving.

## Disconnected

While TIM Hellas's creditors and liquidators struggled to bring Apax and TPG to account for their alleged sins, perhaps they can take solace in the fact that both fund managers delivered poor results from the vintage funds raised ahead of the financial crisis. Apax Europe VII and TPG Partners V, raised in 2007 and 2006 respectively, both showed an annual rate of return of 5%, thereby failing to meet the industry's standard guaranteed return of 8%.[71] Believers in the almighty free markets will appreciate that, in this purest form of karmic justice, Apax and TPG executives did not earn the right to share in capital gains with their institutional investors by failing to exceed the 8% hurdle rate.

As we saw, Italian group WIND was already saddled high with debt before it acquired TIM Hellas as an add-on. Its owner Weather Investments fitted the LBO mould perfectly by raising the largest ever payment-in-kind loan in Europe. By September 2009 the parent company that controlled both the Italian and Greek activities, had €4.2 billion of senior bank debt and €700 million of lower-ranking loans. At the end of that year, Weather had to use the balance sheet of WIND's Italian business to sustain the weaker Greek activities.[72]

The company was suffering from an acute case of 'debtache': a strong headache caused by an excess of debt injection. In fairness, the business had operated in the most hostile of economic contexts. Between 2008 and 2015 the Greek economy saw its GDP shrink from $355 billion to approximately $200 billion, a 44% drop in seven short years. The government was forced to sell assets at bargain prices. Even the jewels of the country's industrial base had required state support. In November 2008 OTE had been partly bailed out by the state and by German operator Deutsche Telekom, each of them taking a 25% stake in the country's leading telecoms group. Deutsche Telekom increased its stake to 30% in 2009, then to 40% five years later as the Greek Government's need for liquidity kept on rising.

In a modern capitalist economy, a company the size of WIND Hellas seldom stays debt-free for long. In the last quarter of 2016, WIND Hellas's Luxembourg-based parent company Crystal Almond launched a roadshow for a €250 million five-year secured high-yield note. But while management and owners had changed, the borrower's reputation among the banking and hedge fund community remained tainted. Given such a background, any debt issuance was bound to receive a frosty reception.

The market's interest was indeed tepid, but with reduced litigation risks investors were willing to give the Greek company another go, even if the capital controls introduced by the Greek Government in June 2015 added uncertainty – 'would cash flows generated by WIND Hellas be freely accessible to repay debt commitments?' was just one of the questions the issuer would not be able to answer categorically. The public debt offering went ahead. To attract the punters, the company was forced to offer a double-digit coupon. Existing shareholders also had to contribute €25 million of fresh equity to motivate prospective lenders.

Following the bond issuance, WIND Hellas was armed with a very reasonable leverage ratio of 1.2 times net debt to EBITDA.[73] Having seen a healthy stabilisation of its profits in the past four years, and even an uptick in revenue as displayed in Figure 8.3, the business was back from the dead. Though its low production of cash was unlikely to turn it into a proper LBO candidate for a while.

## Figure 8.3 – WIND Hellas's revenue and EBITDA margin from 2013 to 2016

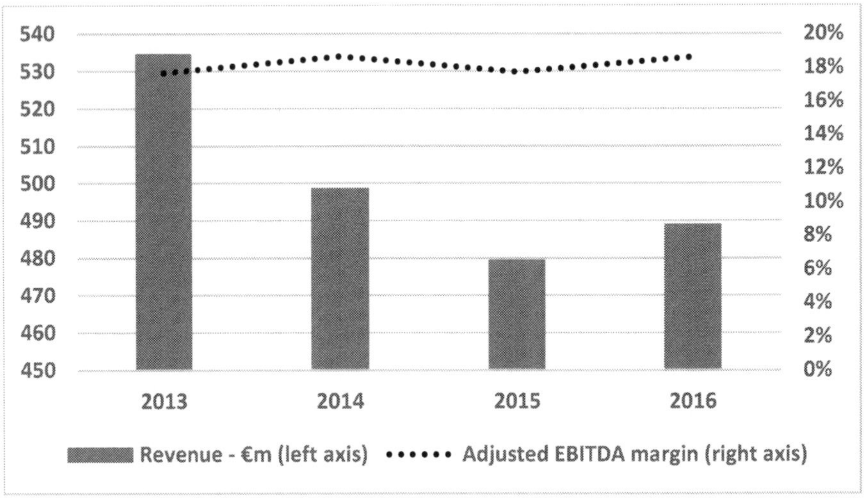

*Source: Company filings and author's analysis*

## Why it's all Greek to some

There is no denying that, for many years, TIM Hellas suffered from the debt overhang, regardless of the skin-deep transformation it underwent under PE ownership. While the senior executives focused their attention on managing down leverage, they were not in a position to take advantage of market opportunities or to adapt to an unprecedented economic debacle. As SPQR Capital's des Pallières pointedly noted:

> *"The private equity industry always pitches how constructive it is as an investor force to create jobs and growth. But there are private equity funds that get rich by breaking companies and making others poor – whether they are creditors, states or employees."*[74]

The surreal quarrel between the lenders – out of pocket to the tune of €1.4 billion – and the group's former owners shows that many parties involved on this transaction couldn't get their head round the modern techniques used by financial sponsors to wring value out of an investment.

The irresistible influence of financiers like the Sawirises, Apax and TPG had even led accountants Ernst & Young to make a serious error of judgment. In June 2015 one of their partners was 'severely reprimanded' and fined by the Institute of Chartered Accountants over a 'serious conflict of interest' caused by their 2009 appointment as administrators to Hellas II, which also happened to be an Ernst & Young audit client.[75] Already in 2011 Ernst & Young had lost their mandate as liquidators, after a High Court had ruled that several avenues of inquiry did "not appear to have been the subject of close critical evaluation by the administrators, such as in relation to the role of Ernst & Young Luxembourg as auditors of the accounts of Hellas II." In response, the High Court had reversed a decision by the accountancy firm to dissolve Hellas II, and instead ordered that an independent insolvency practitioner be appointed.[76] It wasn't Ernst & Young's finest hour. Then again, few parties involved in this fiasco appeared in the best light.

The TIM Hellas situation is an unintended consequence of our decision to deregulate the economy and rely on the market participants to behave in such a way that they can anticipate how their actions will be perceived by the moral construct of their times. Whether we side with financial sponsors, creditors, advisers, management or, to a broader extent, with society in our appraisal of the TIM Hellas transaction, we need to acknowledge that business ethics is not codified and evolves over time. Hence the need for regulation to help guide economic players in their actions.

# THE AMPLIFICATION EFFECT OF LEVERAGE

*When, in the 1980s, the financial world actively campaigned for increased market liberalisation, it produced the intended result: brisk economic growth, through the expansion of the credit markets. But the unexpected consequence of this debt injection was a rise in market volatility. As macroeconomists George Akerlof and Robert Shiller wrote: "The rise in leverage feeds back into asset price increases, encouraging more and more leverage. The same process works in reverse in the downward direction as asset prices fall."[97]*

*Twice-bankrupt TIM Hellas shows how this scenario pans out at the microeconomic level. In 2005-07 the leverage upward cycle enabled Apax and TPG to recap aggressively. In 2008-10 the feedback loop culminated in loan write-offs, a debt-equity swap, and the ultimate loss of ownership by Weather Investments. Private equity sometimes contributes to heightened corporate vulnerability.*

# CHAPTER 9

# Private Equity's C-words: Collusion, corruption and conflicts of interest

> *The following thumbnail studies cover major scandals that plagued the sector in recent times. All claims were settled out of court, enabling the defendants to walk away without admitting guilt. Yet, these stories offer a fantastic window to the well-tried methods and stratagems adopted by fund managers in their quest to maximise returns.*

Private equity is a niche of the financial services industry that has been left unsupervised ever since its emergence in the 1970s. This mode of operation suits fund managers down to the ground. As the previous chapters showed only too well, beyond the victories and failures PE transactions easily veer towards the novelistic.

Not only have regulators chosen to pay little heed to what forward-looking buyout firms get up to, but LP investors' unquestioning demand for high-yield products guarantee that bargaining power shall stay on the supply side.

Although, in most Western economies, the political will has failed to catch up with public opinion, academic research and a vast section of the media, it is now accepted wisdom that private equity has serious unwelcome side effects. The short-term sweating of assets, tax avoidance, excessive leverage and structural under-investment by portfolio companies are widely condemned, even if left unpunished. But the argument that capitalism has an unethical streak is not news. In the interest of economic growth, this plight has been accepted as a necessary evil.

What is more of a concern is a rich lode of scandals and alleged wrongdoings uncovered by regulators in the aftermath of the 2007-08 crisis. A century earlier, a banking crisis had occurred, hurting the image of the financial community in a way not dissimilar to what happened a decade ago. As one commentator puts it: "After the 1907 panic, bankers were regarded as rogues, swindlers and incompetents."[1] Similar views were expressed after the recent financial crisis. This chapter won't dispel the sentiment that bankers are not the only financiers erring on the wrong side of the moral divide.

## Collusion and anti-competitive behaviour

Unlike the mono- or duopolistic world of Silicon Valley titans, the private equity industry is extremely competitive. There is little difference between the investment skills of executives at various firms, which is why the way to win deals is primarily based on price.

At the top-end of the deal spectrum, only a small number of firms can close multi-billion-dollar LBOs. The ability to execute mega buyouts has created a new breed of superinvestors. As they formed part of a very exclusive elite, over the years the top brass got to know each other and to work together. In fact, many got so close that they even collaborated outside the office.

In December 2015 Joshua Harris, one of Apollo's co-founders, partnered with David Blitzer, who had spent years leading Blackstone's European activities before moving back to the US to head the firm's tactical opportunities unit. That month, the two individuals acquired a controlling stake in English Premier League football club Crystal Palace. Harris and Blitzer were already controlling shareholders of the professional ice hockey team New Jersey Devils, bought for $320 million two years earlier. Both were alumni of the Wharton School in Philadelphia, which probably explains why in the summer of 2011 they had purchased the professional basketball team Philadelphia 76ers for $280 million. Buying sports teams that are down on their luck was a way to spend the capital gains they had accumulated over the years.

Such close ties would be unlikely in any other industry. It is hard to imagine Bill Gates and Steve Jobs, or Mark Zuckerberg and Tim Cook, partnering up to invest in their favourite pastime, assuming they shared the same interests. Still, flashy investments by the high priests of private equity into sluggish sports teams is not what intrigued the financial regulators. The rise of club deals in a quickly maturing industry led to another age-old issue with capitalism: accusations of collusion and deal-rigging.

## A brief history of anti-trust practices

Our generation is particularly familiar with the recent, often decades-long, anti-trust cases fought tooth and nail by the US and EU competition authorities against technology companies Microsoft, Intel and Google. Since the dramatic experience of the late 19$^{th}$ century, governments have sought to maintain a level playing field in all sectors of the economy.

The best way to understand anti-competitive behaviour is to review the reasons behind the introduction of anti-trust laws. In 1890 the US Congress passed the Sherman Antitrust Act to protect consumers from unfair pricing practices applied by monopolistic businesses illegally restricting free trade or supply. What drove the American Government to propose such a law was the consolidation of various industries in the second half of the 19$^{th}$ century.

263

Between 1860 and 1890 hundreds of small short-line railroads were bought and integrated into giant systems by tycoons who now form part of the capitalist folklore: James Hill, Jay Gould and Cornelius Vanderbilt among others.[2] In parallel, magnate Andrew Carnegie launched his career in the railroads before amassing a fortune in the burgeoning steel industry during the last two decades of the 19th century.

Both the steel and railroad sectors were eventually broken up by government intervention, but the case that received the most press coverage was undoubtedly the dissolution in 1911 of Standard Oil into 34 separate companies. That oil production and distribution company had been established in 1870 by John D. Rockefeller who eventually managed to corner the US oil market by signing secret agreements with his competitors. As the century drew to an end, Standard Oil controlled about 90% of oil production and refinery facilities in America. The company was eventually sued under the Sherman Act, which led to the group's deconglomeration.

## The private equity illustration

Back when it all started, PE fund managers preferred to complete acquisitions without collaborating with rivals, if only to demonstrate their unique dealmaking prowess and differentiate themselves from the rest of the pack. It also enabled them to have total control over the destiny of their investee companies. If they were going to partner, PE firms had to make sure that their allies had similar interests. Strategies had to be aligned, value-maximising programmes had to blend. That approach required consensus building, which takes time and energy, and is far from certain to deliver the intended results.

As the industry gained in acceptability and confidence, it started taking on much bigger acquisition targets. In the 1980s, other than the very unusual and poorly performing $25 billion buyout of RJR Nabisco by

KKR, the largest buyout was the $5 billion acquisition of consumer goods conglomerate Beatrice by the same KKR. In the 1990s the largest LBO was that of Borden (again by KKR), bought for $2 billion in 1994. Partnering with other PE firms did occur, but only occasionally. That all changed during the bull run of the early noughties.

Between 2001 and 2005 the average size of an LBO transaction rose from less than $400 million to close to $1 billion.[3] Many transactions worth several billion dollars were engineered in the years leading up to the financial crisis, partly because the credit boom helped valuation multiples expand from 6 times EBITDA in 2001 to close to 10 times six years later.[4] Pricier transactions forced acquirers to partner up. Approximately 15% of buyouts completed in 2005 were club deals.[5]

There are two main reasons mentioned by buyout firms for clubbing together. The first one is about risk diversification. Proper risk management requires to limit the impact that a single deal could have on the performance of an investment vehicle. If TPG had closed the Univision buyout on its own, it would have had to invest $3.7 billion in equity instead of the $837 million it put up as part of the Broadcasting Media Partners consortium. Given that the TPG V fund had $15 billion of capital commitments, to allocate Univision's entire $3.7 billion equity ticket to that fund would have made it disproportionately exposed to the success of that single transaction. In view of what happened to the broadcaster in the ensuing decade, diversifying the investor base by partnering up with Madison Dearborn et al was certainly the prudent thing to do for TPG (and its LP investors).

Even if a fund manager does not feel the need to spread the portfolio risk across a large number of transactions, in some situations it might not have sufficient capital to acquire a very large corporate target. Partnering up therefore becomes the only option. After three decades of intense rivalry, the top cadres of the industry naturally got to know their counterparts at other firms. Their mutual respect gradually morphed into trust, which allowed them to consider working together on a broad scale and quasi-systematic basis, even out of the office in the case of Harris and Blitzer.

## False start

In October 2006, reports of an antitrust investigation of private equity clubbing arrangements by the US Department of Justice appeared in the *New York Times* and the *Wall Street Journal*.[6] A civil lawsuit had also been filed in federal court against 13 private equity groups, alleging that they conspired to fix deal prices.[7] The DoJ examined prominent transactions for possible anticompetitive behaviour. Several of the largest US buyout firms, including Carlyle, Clayton Dubilier and KKR, were notified that their practices and involvements in auctions going back three years were being investigated.

The emergence and widespread adoption of PE consortia to bid on specific companies could limit competition and artificially depress the price of takeover bids. The injured parties in this case were the selling shareholders. At a time when LBOs had reached record levels, both in size and numbers, the integrity of the corporate world was at risk. Recent multibillion-dollar transactions had seen Toys "R" Us and Freescale Semiconductors fall into the hands or become targets of private equity consortia. If rigged, these auctions could have a trickle effect on the rest of the M&A market.

The letters that the Justice Department sent the various private equity groups asked for information on a voluntary basis. They were neither subpoenas nor civil investigation demands, simply requests for information. Antitrust lawyers believed that proving collusion would be extremely difficult since most auctions concerned companies that had opted to sell rather than forced, distressed sellers.[8] Private equity firms were armed with deep pockets. The battle promised to be long and arduous.

# Private Equity's C-words

In the meantime, other claims were investigated by judges across the country without much success. In February 2008 Francisco Partners and Vector Capital were cleared of wrongdoing when an antitrust class action suit against them was dismissed by a federal district court.

In late 2005 the board of directors of IT service provider WatchGuard had set up an auction process to sell the company. Interested parties were solicited to participate. As many as 50 potential suitors expressed some level of interest. As the auction progressed, both Francisco Partners and Vector submitted formal bids. By late June 2006 Francisco's bid was at $4.60 per share, and Vector's bid was at $4.65 per share.

On 26 June 2006 Vector withdrew from the bidding, and Francisco soon after lowered its bid to $4.25 per share. WatchGuard's board ultimately accepted that bid on 25 July. Three weeks later, Vector announced that it had reached an agreement with Francisco for a 50% ownership stake in WatchGuard and would pay half of the purchase consideration accordingly.

The district court considered that it was reasonable for private equity firms to join forces to compete with larger rivals. The court also took the view that the two defendants did not possess combined resources enabling them to abuse their market power. The large universe of interested suitors that could have bid for WatchGuard proved that there was sufficient price competition. Finally, the court added that WatchGuard's shareholders could have rejected the bid had they believed it to be too low.[9] This last point shows how little the court understood about the world of mergers and acquisitions.

When a company initiates a sale process, it hopes that there is real appetite for its assets. Failing to find a buyer would send a message that the company is damaged goods. It certainly would not be a good sign to deliver to the marketplace. It might even invite existing and potential suppliers and customers to reconsider their relationship with the business; they might be concerned that the breakdown of the transaction was due to issues hidden by management. An aborted auction would also destabilise the company's corporate strategy; it would undermine staff morale and likely lead to the departure of key employees. Finally, it would make any subsequent relaunch of a sale process, months or years down the line, an uphill struggle. Every bidder involved the second time around would remember that the company failed to find a buyer during the first auction. That would invite potential acquirers to be cautious and to reduce their bids accordingly.

In summary, although the court was indeed right to point out that 'WatchGuard's shareholders could have rejected the bid had they believed it to be too low', such a decision would have damaged the company's prospects in many different ways. Knowing all this, PE firms have an incentive to play hardball whenever they sense that they have the upper hand in the negotiations, and to lower their bid once they are granted exclusivity status.

*Second bite*

Thus, club deals offer the palatable benefit of reducing deal pricing. From there, it is only a small step to restrict competition by agreeing to stay out of each other's way. An 'If you scratch my back, I'll scratch yours' kind of arrangement.

The distinction between collaboration and collusion is a difficult one to make, which is why PE firms can easily deflect a regulator's accusatory arguments. Nevertheless, if Microsoft and Apple or Alphabet and Facebook chose to partner on many of their corporate projects, it would be equally normal for regulators to investigate such practices.

Eventually, the scope of the antitrust lawsuit against the world's largest private equity firms was expanded to include many of the mega buyouts completed at the peak of the credit bubble, in 2005-08. Eleven firms were accused of an overarching conspiracy to rig the market for multibillion-dollar takeovers. In September 2011 Judge Edward

Harrington of Federal District Court in Massachusetts ruled that the plaintiffs – former shareholders of the acquired companies, led by the Police and Fire Retirement System of the City of Detroit – could seek information about several large deals, including the largest buyout ever, the $44 billion takeover of energy group TXU co-led by Goldman Sachs, KKR and TPG.

The plaintiffs claimed that the club deals in vogue at the time were an illegal attempt by PE firms to collude and drive down the prices of buyouts they completed jointly. Other transactions subject to the investigation included Toys "R" Us, Harrah's Entertainment (that had merged with Hilton's former casino operations Caesars Entertainment shortly before the buyout),[*] and Univision (which might explain why Blackstone and other interested parties withdrew from Televisa's bidding consortium, turning the latter's defeat into a humiliating walkover). Bidders involved in these auctions were required to turn over internal documents and e-mails to the plaintiffs.

Unable to offer direct evidence of an agreement between defendants not to compete, the plaintiffs argued that such arrangement could be inferred by the various collaborative practices employed by the bidding clubs. They also offered a few brief e-mails of executives of the defendant firms to show that the latter were acting in concert rather than independently.

The defendants labelled the lawsuit "a far-fetched theory by doing nothing more than describing routine M&A activity, and labelling it anticompetitive", but this unwelcome distraction forced them to spend in excess of $100 million in legal fees.[10] Keen to protect their reputation, the defendants made sure that the judge issued a broad protective order to keep all the evidence from public view. Some of the accusations brought forward by the plaintiffs portrayed a corrupt deal culture where sham bids and secret allocations of deals among the

---

[*] For a full review of the Caesars and TXU buyouts, refer to *The Debt Trap* (2016)

largest PE firms were established practices. The correct interpretation of communications between colleagues, peers or competitors is justly open to debate, which is why it is worth reviewing some of them. Readers will reach their own conclusion.

In September 2006 Blackstone's president Hamilton James e-mailed his colleagues about a conversation he had with KKR's Henry Kravis. Both firms were in the final stages of a bidding contest for technology giant Freescale Semiconductors when James wrote: "Henry Kravis just called to say congratulations and that they were standing down because he had told me before they would not jump a signed deal of ours." As the *New York Times* reported, two days later James sent an e-mail to Kravis's cousin and co-founder George Roberts: "We would much rather work with you guys than against you. Together we can be unstoppable but in opposition we can cost each other a lot of money."[11]

Another intriguing exchange refers to the decision by Blackstone not to bid for hospital owner HCA in the summer of 2006. Blackstone's Neil Simpkins emailed colleague Joseph Baratta: "The reason we didn't go forward [with a rival HCA bid] was basically a decision on not jumping someone else's deal," to which Baratta replied: "I think the deal represents good value and it is a shame we let KKR get away with highway robbery, but understand decision."[12] According to a *Fortune* article published at the time of HCA's relisting in March 2011, KKR's co-investor Bain Capital stood to make over $4.3 billion on the original $1.1 billion equity ticket. "A very good deal", the *Fortune* journalist observed. Fittingly, the same journalist specifically stated that Bain's returns could not be labelled 'highway robbery', as the *New York Post* had implied in a separate article.[13] Back then, Baratta's internal communication in relation to the 2006 bidding process had not yet been made public.

KKR had expressly asked its competitors to "step down on HCA", leading two Texas Pacific Group executives to write: "All we can do is do [u]nto others as we want them to do unto us. It will pay off in the long run even though it feels bad in the short run."[14] The industry's clubby elite had favoured collaboration to hostile rivalry. As another TPG official wrote: "No one in private equity ever jumps an announced deal."[15] Over the years, the top echelons at the largest PE groups had hatched an esprit de corps where friendly cooperation seemed more natural than ruthless competition. They had little abiding interest in hurting returns by paying more for assets than strictly necessary. The 11 defendants had tried nearly a dozen times in four years to get the suit tossed, to no avail. A federal judge in Boston eventually decided in 2013 that there was enough evidence on eight of the original 27 deals that had been targeted by the lawsuit.[16]

Pooling their money together to make larger acquisitions was understandable. Staying out of each other's way in a sort of gentlemen's agreement was not. The judge accepted the claims made by the plaintiffs that behind the acquisitions closed in the heydays of buyout dealmaking were stealth agreements between the major PE groups to divide the big deals among themselves and tamp down valuations artificially. One emailed comment by a Goldman Sachs employee that there was a 'club etiquette' not to outbid each other led the judge to believe that the evidence excluded "the possibility of independent action".[17] The plaintiffs had sought punitive compensation of $10 billion but the buyout firms faced up to $36 billion in liabilities if potential damages were trebled under the Sherman Act.

In the end, all the defendants fell in line and settled out of court, if only to avoid having to disclose embarrassing facts about some of their most controversial practices. As an industry lawyer put it: "It's too ugly. The emails may not prove what they are supposed to prove but they are just too embarrassing." In August 2014 Blackstone, KKR and TPG paid $325 million to settle price-fixing claims. Carlyle agreed to stump up $115 million the following month. Bain Capital, Goldman Sachs and Silver Lake had already settled, paying $54 million, $67 million, and $29.5 million respectively.[18] The prospect of going to trial and be left holding the bag for enormous liabilities was the catalyst to settle, even if it cost close to $600 million in fines...plus legal fees.

Consortia are certainly not a new thing. In Ancient Rome, political alliances were a common occurrence to extend one's power base. Think of the 'Gang of Three', set up by Julius Caesar, Crassus and Pompey to ensure political order through bribery and intimidation. That one lasted over a decade. Octavian, Marc Antony and Lepidus also formed a triumvirate to rule immediately after Julius Caesar's assassination. Their collaboration was very fruitful, including Cicero's murder and the empire's expansion until their eventual falling-out, which turned into an open civil war.

Thus, to expand their financial clout and deal-doing empires, private equity fund managers applied an ancestral practice: they joined forces, the way drug cartels or members of the Organization of the Petroleum Exporting Countries do whenever they wish to manipulate markets via price fixing. It is difficult to blame them for partnering up. As they jockeyed to participate in the biggest debt bubble in living memory, cooperation became the norm. It was a great recipe to improve returns by reducing pressure on asset values.

In the case of Toys "R" Us, most analysts considered that the KKR-Bain bid had exceeded price expectations.[19] Would their individual bids be even higher had they failed to cooperate? It is hard to speculate. But if we answer yes, it would simply mean that the toy retailer would have filed for bankruptcy earlier than in September 2017. It is not clear that the group's employees and lenders would have benefited from even more reckless bidding.

History teaches us that anti-competitive behaviour is more likely to be defeated by other market participants than by governments or regulators. But it will take time for rivals to have a real impact. Although it might appear laughable today in view of the weak market position of the photo film specialist, throughout its history Kodak was the subject of significant anti-trust pressure: first in the 1920s (in private-label film distribution), then in the 1950s (when forced by the US Government to license the colouring process for its films), and again in the 1990s (in the distribution and repair of copier-duplicators). It took the emergence of digital photography, followed by camera phones, in the 21st century for Kodak's dominance to be dealt a humbling and fatal blow. Unless financial regulators show more determination, it could take decades for the market power of global alternative fund managers to be reined in. In the meantime, the latter will continue to produce monopoly profits.

## Corruption – 'pay to play' dirty

Institutional investors, in particular pension funds, are anxious to earn solid returns on the pots of money they manage. To find the right opportunities, they use intermediaries called placement agents. On the other side of the table, financiers running hedge funds, real estate funds and private equity firms, are equally keen to access the vast amounts of capital (we are talking trillions of dollars) held by pension funds and other institutions like insurers, banks and endowment funds.

When the Dodd-Frank Act was passed by the Obama administration in 2010 as a response to the financial crisis, it aimed to put an end to irregularities that had taken place in the selection process of investment advisers by government agencies. Among the reforms introduced was a rule designed to address pay-to-play abuses involving campaign contributions made by certain advisers to government officials able to influence the selection of managers of public pension funds (and of other government assets).[20]

For a commission – paid by the private equity firm seeking to drum up investors – a placement agent could peddle a PE firm's latest vintage fund. In North America, two out of every five fundraising processes used such matchmakers.[21] The new rules prohibited investment advisers, including PE fund managers, from providing services to any state government entity for two years after the advisers or any of their associates had made a political contribution. Otherwise, such commissions would be treated as alleged kickbacks or bribes paid to public officials.

New York State Attorney General Andrew Cuomo led the charge to make sure that companies that failed to abide by the rule were punished. But bribery investigations also unfolded in Kentucky, New Mexico, California and other states. Several big names of the private equity industry ended up being dragged into this new crusade. Among a long list of prestigious cases was a business originally backed by Washington, DC-based Carlyle: energy specialist Riverstone agreed in 2009 to pay $30 million to resolve its role in the pension fund investigation run by Cuomo. Riverstone's founder David Leuschen had to pay an additional $20 million to settle his personal role in the case.[22] That same year, and for a similar $20 million pay-out, politically-connected Carlyle settled its own role in the ongoing corruption investigation. Cuomo's team had uncovered that, over the previous six years, Carlyle had made more than $13 million in payments to an indicted political fixer who arranged for the firm to receive business from a New York pension fund. The firm had paid this intermediary through shell companies and had subsequently received more than $730 million in New York state pension funds for five different projects.[23]

Another well-known firm under review was media expert Quadrangle. Eventually it had to repay $7 million to the New York Common Retirement Fund. As part of its settlement, it publicly put the blame on one of its senior partners, Steve Rattner, by releasing the following statement:

> *"We wholly disavow the conduct engaged in by Steve Rattner, who hired the New York State Comptroller's political consultant, Hank Morris, to arrange an investment from the New York State Common Retirement Fund. That conduct was inappropriate, wrong, and unethical."*[24]

## Private Equity's C-words

It was an awkward moment for the Obama administration since Rattner had joined its ranks as lead adviser to the Presidential Task Force on the Auto Industry shortly before Cuomo had launched his investigation.

Although the pay-to-play scandal never reached the public profile of the foregoing collusion allegations, by December 2010 the Cuomo investigation "had secured agreements with twenty-one firms and four individuals, garnering over $161 million for New York and the pension fund." The Cuomo investigation also led to eight guilty pleas,[25] demonstrating that several of the parties caught up by Dodd-Frank knew that their conduct was not beyond reproach.

Arguably, the biggest scalp was not claimed by Cuomo but by his peers across the country. In July 2014, the largest public pension fund in America – California Public Employees' Retirement System (CalPERS) – saw its former CEO, Fred Buenrostro, plead guilty to conspiracy to commit bribery and fraud. Heading CalPERS between 2002 and 2008, he admitted to numerous offenses, including receiving cash, casino chips and other goodies from former CalPERS board member Alfred Villalobos, who was also indicted.

The scheme (which had begun in 2005) to steer CalPERS investments to certain private equity firms, had allegedly involved payments by fund managers of up to $50 million between 2005 and 2009 for the services of Villalobos (a former deputy mayor of Los Angeles) as a CalPERS placement agent.[26] In one particular instance, Villalobos had received $14 million in fees after helping Apollo Global Management land a $3 billion capital commitment from CalPERS. Although Villalobos denied claims of impropriety, we might never know the full story for he committed suicide in January 2015.[27] Following the scandal, CalPERS made significant changes to its governance, but perhaps it is not surprising that two years later the group entered talks to reorganise and outsource parts of its private equity activities.[28]

## Conflicts of interest – shortcomings of the agent-principal relationship

Completing the triptych of the industry's ugly side is an issue common to all principal-agent relationships: conflicts of interest.

The priority of LP investors should be to line up the private equity fund managers' incentives and interests with their own. This section shows that it is easier said than done. There is extensive academic research that proves that, despite their incredibly generous remunerations, fund managers do not always act in the best interest of their investors.

It is very tempting for middlemen to keep a bigger share of the pot if they can get away with it, a normal occurrence when they are left unsupervised. Over time, private equity firms developed a vast array of innovative techniques to do just that, at the risk of turning their business into an institutionalised game of 'phishing for phools', to use the phrase of economists George Akerlof and Robert Shiller.

Hence the manipulation of the internal rate of return, the yardstick against which the performance of all fund managers is assessed, as previously explained. For instance, in July 2014 Blackstone used a $2.25 billion line of credit called a margin loan – borrowing money from a few banks while pledging its 628 million Hilton shares as collateral – to accelerate the return of capital to its LP investors while the PE firm was still scrambling its way out of a seven-year-long equity position in Hilton. The early restitution of cash helped boost returns on Blackstone's equity in the hotel group without creating any tangible value for the underlying business. Other ways to finesse performance include quick flips and dividend recapitalisations, both discussed in Chapters 7 and 8.

Another example of conflicts of interest saw some PE firms massage their reported returns on existing funds to sway prospective LP investors' decision to commit capital to future funds.[29] By stating higher future returns than they can realistically achieve, fund managers can fool potential investors.

But the scandal that kept the Securities and Exchange Commission busy in the wake of the financial crisis is the overcharging of fees. At an even broader level, the larger private equity groups have been attacked for charging expenses and inventing new fees whenever they feel like it.

The rule of engagement common across the asset management industry is to deliver, at almost any cost, superior returns to investors. Two ways to achieve this feat are to maximise capital gains and to minimise cash leakage (which explains why investments are generally expertly managed through offshore structures to avoid heavy tax levies from governments). However, one factor that has a negative impact on returns is the portion of fees charged to investors by parties that manage their money. This sort of leakage is difficult to monitor.

Most people usually accept that asset managers should be allowed to split capital gains with their investors, even if the 20% share that PE firms keep for themselves seems perversely high when one considers that a significant element of their performance is due to luck or factors outside their control (such as the very loose monetary policy adopted by central banks between 2009 and 2017).

Blackstone generated over $15 billion in performance fees in the ten years to 2016, in a sign that it delivered strong gains for its LP investors. Rightly, it kept these profits for itself. Where Blackstone's results are less impressive is in the fact that, over the same period, the firm engendered $20 billion in management and advisory fees.[30] In summary, fund managers make more money by charging a fixed annual commission on assets under management than by providing superior returns to their capital providers.

In the private equity industry, the decision to enter new investment segments is rarely the result of rigorous and careful consideration.

Rather, it derives from a canine appetite for commissions. What transpires is that, gradually and imperceptibly, LP investors were subjected to a growing number of onerous fees. Fund managers created new ways to recharge operating expenses. These were not necessarily collected directly from their investors – otherwise, the latter might have noticed the subterfuge. Instead, PE firms levied due diligence fees, transaction fees, director fees, advisory fees, monitoring fees (and other commissions with similarly fanciful names) directly on their portfolio companies. While, on occasions, fund managers netted off these commissions against the fees they charged investors, the practice was far from universal.

Between 2014 and 2017 the Securities and Exchange Commission fined some of the biggest names in the industry for crafty practices. In June 2015, for instance, KKR was asked to pay $30 million to settle claims that it had failed to disclose properly the way it charged investors fees incurred for unsuccessful buyout bids. The firm had 'misallocated' over 5% of the $338 million in expenses incurred on broken deals between 2006 and 2011.[31] Four months later, it was Blackstone's turn to be fined $39 million after the regulator accused the firm of ripping off investors over portfolio monitoring fees – $29 million of the fine was to revert to Blackstone's LP investors. What happened is that every time Blackstone charged monitoring fees to a portfolio company, it was passing on only half of the fee to its LPs and retained the other half. The fee created a conflict of interest. Every dollar paid to Blackstone reduced the value of the investee by a dollar but increased Blackstone's own revenue by 50 cents.[32]

Then, in the summer of 2016, billionaire investor and soon-to-be President Trump's Secretary of Commerce Wilbur Ross had to pay $2.3 million in damages for failing to disclose fees to investors. In the decade leading up to 2011, investors in his advisory firm WL Ross had overpaid more than $10 million in fees, which the firm agreed to return with interest.[33] But that penalty was small compared to the $53 million that Apollo had to reimburse for misleading investors. The word 'misleading' is to be understood in its broader sense: one of the firm's partners had charged roughly $200,000 in personal expenses (such as the cost of flying his girlfriend to romantic locations) to Apollo's funds and portfolio companies.[34]

Another high-profile case was reported in December 2017 when TPG settled out of court following accusations that it had exacted accelerated monitoring payments between 2013 and 2015 without proper disclosure to its investors. TPG was fined $13 million, including a $3 million penalty and $10 million in disgorgement and interest to investors in three of its funds: TPG Partners V, TPG Partners VI, and TPG Biotech Partners III. In one instance, the firm had accelerated fee payments even though the relevant TPG fund was exiting the portfolio company and TPG would no longer be providing monitoring services.[35] In essence, the firm had collected fees for future advisory services that it would not be providing since it no longer held the company in portfolio. Admittedly, this sort of excess is widespread in private equity, and Blackstone and Apollo were accused of similar practices.

The heavily fee-dependent private equity model had turned the role of fund manager into a sinecure. But the lack of proper disclosures to LP investors had been interpreted by regulators as a breach of fiduciary duties. Yet, the issue is not just of an ethical or governance nature. Fees are to an investment portfolio what tobacco is to the human body. Fees kill returns. They do so slowly, unremittingly, without the victim noticing it. The long-term impact is extremely damaging to the financial health of pensioners and investors. Net of the annual commissions charged by fund managers, the sector underperforms most other high-risk asset classes once the impact of leverage has been factored in. But as illustrated by Blackstone's ten-year income generation, such fees account for more than half of even the most successful PE groups' remuneration.

Investors had no reason to be suspicious. Throughout the 1990s and early noughties, buyout fund managers had delivered strong returns thanks to economic prosperity, a steady and generous flow of cheap credit, and a decent equity market environment. Taking advantage of past performance, which we would later learn was not due to superior skills but to an extravagant use of leverage and financial innovation, fund managers started piling up new commissions. These were easily hidden while the going was good. But when paper gains translated into real losses, fees were harder to conceal.

One might express surprise that institutional investors were so vulnerable to the fund managers' wiles. But consider that some of these investors had over 100 fund relationships (California-based CalPERS and CalSTRS being two examples), and that in addition to their buyout positions they held commitments in hedge funds, venture capital, real estate, infrastructure, public equity and debt markets. Thus, the complexity of their task is easier to comprehend.

Keeping track of all the commissions charged by fund managers via opaque and confusing fee structures is not a priority when the chief focus is on maximising capital gains. For those reasons, and the fact that fund managers are agents, rent-seeking practices settled in through manipulation and deception. Akerlof and Shiller refer to this phishing method as 'reputation mining',[36] whereby agents take advantage of their decades-long reputation to fool their principals.

# A carry-on about nothing?

Corruption, collusion and conflicts of interest received the most media coverage, but private equity has flirted with all sort of controversy. Incidents investigated by the SEC and other regulators are just the tip of the iceberg. Given the increasing complexity of global finance, questionable practices involve many market participants. Far from exhaustive, the following section is meant to discuss the two most prevalent risks that markets are exposed to when private equity firms engineer public transactions, in particular delistings and public offerings.

One of the key trends of the past decade and a half, as leveraged buyouts became a more mature, even saturated field of finance, has been the growing interactions between private equity and public stock and bond markets. This, in turn, led to cases of market manipulation and insider trading. Here are examples related to our case studies.

- *Market manipulation*

When Toys "R" Us tried to relist on the stock exchange in 2010, the financial sponsors carried out the usual beauty parade among Wall Street banks. The $800 million-dollar IPO of a company supposedly worth $8 billion attracted a lot of interest, especially in a year like 2010, in the doldrums of the biggest recession since the 1930s.

So, the banks competed for a role in the float. In December 2014 financial regulator FINRA fined ten Wall Street firms a total of $43.5 million for conflicts of interest. Although by now the SEC had become the private equity's bogeyman due to its sedulous investigations in the sector's intrigues and cabals, FINRA's militancy dragged such hallowed names as Barclays, Citi, Credit Suisse, Deutsche Bank, Goldman Sachs, JP Morgan and Morgan Stanley into a muddy situation.

Here is what FINRA uncovered:

> *"Toys "R" Us asked equity research analysts from each of the 10 firms to make separate presentations to Toys "R "Us's management and sponsors for the purpose of ensuring that the analysts' views on key issues, including valuation factors, were aligned with the views expressed by the firms' investment bankers. Each firm understood that the performance of their analysts at the presentations would be a key factor in determining whether the firm received an underwriting role in the IPO."*

Alas, as part of their crackdown on dodgy equity research following the dotcom craze of the 1990s, financial regulators had enforced stricter rules surrounding the solicitation of analysts, if only to prevent abuse stemming from pressure by investment bankers on in-house equity analysts to provide favourable coverage. The aim was to avoid over-friendly research and over-inflating of stock valuations – the surest ways to manipulate markets. FINRA accused the ten banks involved in the eventually aborted Toys "R" Us IPO of overstepping "the prohibitions against analyst solicitation and the promise of favorable research."

Communication transcripts reviewed by the regulator included an email from a Citigroup analyst stating: "I so want the bank to get this deal!", and an in-house message from a JP Morgan banker stressing that it was important that "analyst vetting supports our views."[37] Incredibly, one of the lines of defence put forward by some bankers being investigated was that the behaviour FINRA cited in this case was widespread rather than isolated![38]

To be clear, in case the reader had any doubt, "in settling this matter, the 10 firms neither admitted nor denied the charges". But the most interesting point to note is that under the regulation in force, only the banks are obligated to abide by the rules separating research and investment banking.[39] Their clients, be they private equity firms or PE-backed companies like Toys "R" Us, can do as they please.

- *Insider trading*

Blackstone's bid for the publicly listed Hilton Hotels Corporation was announced on 3 July 2007. That day was a Tuesday, and it was only a half day of trading ahead of the July 4 celebrations – US stock markets closed at 1pm Eastern Time, with bond markets closing at 2pm.[40] On 2 July, the day before the transaction was announced, Hilton shares were at $33.87. On 3 July they made one of their biggest moves ever, closing almost 7% higher at $36.05, on double the normal volume.[41] What was curious about this move was that it took place *ahead* of the deal announcement.

In October 2009 billionaire hedge fund manager Raj Rajaratnam was charged with 13 criminal counts of fraud and conspiracy. One of the claims against him included a tip-off in July 2007 from an analyst at rating agency Moody's that the Hilton chain was to be taken private. Rajaratnam bought thousands of Hilton shares and made a $4 million profit when Blackstone's bid was reported.[42] Although pleading innocence, in May 2011 Rajaratnam was found guilty of all charges; he was later sentenced to 11 years in prison. His partner in crime, Moody's analyst Deep Shah, was declared a fugitive and believed to be hiding in India.[43]

Illegal insider trading is widespread and not specific to PE-engineered delistings. We already discussed the issue during the Mergermarket case study, when stating that about a quarter of M&A transactions show unusual pre-announcement movements and, in many cases, stock prices ahead of public disclosures do not follow random fluctuations as the law of normal distribution would suggest (see Chapter 2).

What is little discussed is a practice that is, de facto, legalised insider trading: the right, based on inside information, of private equity owners to time the exit of portfolio companies that they have floated. Even after an investee has gone through its IPO, private equity shareholders usually retain the right to sit on the board until they have disposed of their entire stake in the business. What that allows PE professionals to do is decide when the appropriate time to exit is. We saw that Blackstone's Jonathan Gray sat on the board of Hilton as long as his employer retained a stake, even a very small one, in the hotel group. If a fund manager attends board meetings and learns that trading is improving, he can delay the sale of his stake in the company. Conversely, if results are flagging, the PE owner can accelerate the disposal of shares. Performance rarely improves or deteriorates suddenly; operating indicators generally provide sufficient forewarning.

## No smoke without fire

The liberal media and misguided politicians seem shocked by the recent and sudden rise of populist parties. Ten years after the onset of the financial crisis, no real reforms have occurred. This contrasts greatly with the measures taken in the 1930s following the Great Crash. In 1932 the US Senate launched a full inquiry into the causes of the 1929 Crash. The Pecora Committee, named after the chief counsel for the investigation, eventually led to the separation of commercial and investment banking under the 1933 Glass-Steagall Act and to the establishment of an independent enforcement agency, the Securities and Exchange Commission.

This time around, government guarantees and taxpayer-funded bailouts in 2009 swept all the mistakes committed by overpaid financiers and corporate executives under the carpet. Market fundamentalists who used to argue that the state should not be allowed to meddle in commerce urged governments to save the system from complete meltdown in some form of ideological hocus-pocus.

Due to the increasing complexity of the global financial system, regulators are kept busy trying to control the banking sector (capable of bringing the world economy to a halt, as we saw in 2008) and the asset management industry (overseeing $70 to 80 trillion of assets worldwide). By comparison, the combined $5 trillion managed by the private equity, real estate, private debt and venture capital segments are puny, and not worth spending time on. That leaves a lot of freedom to LBO fund managers. Their fee-maximising and fundraising practices took place with limited supervision, thanks to the low-toned incrementalism of monitoring policies. We cannot therefore claim to be surprised by allegations of covert behaviour or collusion. Power corrupts, and the industry's growing pile of capital commitments has granted the largest private equity groups quasi-unlimited powers. Via the cut and thrust of free-market policies instituted in the past decades, capitalism slowly degenerated into a rent-seeking economic model.

## PRIVATE EQUITY AND ETHICS

*Cases of moral myopia are common in the history of capitalism. If that is evident in public markets, no one should be surprised that an under-regulated arena like private equity suffers from the same ailment.*

*The stories visited in this chapter illustrate an alarming fact. Despite well-grounded suspicion of pathological misconduct, self-regulation grants the tacit right for fund managers to test the limits of what is permissible without fearing much retribution other than the odd fine.*

*Ancient Rome defended the invasion of foreign territories to promote civilisation while its detractors argued that it generated havoc – inspiring the phrase "they create desolation and call it peace."[44] Similar misgiving is expressed about the PE industry's potpourri of value-creation techniques, often leading to job losses and extensive cash diversion to dividend-hungry investors or yield-seeking lenders. Accusations of collusion and corruption will not help change the perception that, like the Romans before them, modern fund managers will stop at nothing in their quest for world domination and economic gains.*

# EPILOGUE

## A matter of underperformance

*"All my life I've been considered by my fellow men to be a cautious, boring, dull sort of fellow. I have often heard myself described as a safe pair of hands…While others might have been hurt, even insulted, by such epithets, I was flattered. If you set yourself up as a fit and proper person to take care of other people's money, then, in my opinion, these are the very qualities that should be expected of you."*

**Be Careful What you Wish for, The Clifton Chronicles, Jeffrey Archer**

Private equity is one of the symbols of modern capitalism. Unbeknownst to them, citizens have entrusted a galley of indomitable, self-appointed fund managers with their retirement and personal savings. In return, the fund managers enjoy a monopolistic hold on these assets, and so for a long period, typically ten years-plus. During that time, these professional investors are entitled to dispose of other people's money as they see fit.

What we also witnessed in the first decade of the $21^{st}$ century is the result of vast sections of the financial community gaining unrestrained and quasi-unlimited access to credit. Like any trend destined to beget offspring until the lode has dried up, leveraged buyouts had dire consequences.

The issue is not just that many underlying portfolio companies, such as Toys "R" Us, never recovered from their leveraged adventure. Neither is it that a panoply of takeover artists like 3i had to scale down their operations and retreat pell-mell into core activities, not just once but on several occasions, in an attempt to survive. The real trouble is that, since the financial crisis, no proper change has been introduced to monitor and regulate this quickly expanding M&A activity. If anything, because regulators and legislators were busy reining in the influence of too-big-to-fail banks, the private equity industry has experienced a boom.

We should not infer from the various case studies that deals like Bhs, TIM Hellas and Univision were deliberately sabotaged. Rather, their respective ordeal was the result of inadequate grasp of market structure, economic cyclicality, and innovative but hazardous debt products. We saw in Chapter 9 that there is a higher judgment in the court of public opinion in terms of the morals of the industry's practices. Yet there is a bigger issue.

One of the problems at the core of investment failures comes from the fact that two generations of fund managers received the wrong education and incentives. Classical economic theory presupposes that people only act for economic motives. What free marketers believe is that the mercenary pursuit of self-interest in the end benefits all, in some sort of magic, perfect equilibrium. In this land of make-believe, regulation is fittingly unnecessary, even hurtful. The best government disposition toward the market is one of compliant tolerance, not active interference. It is what business is all about: the belief that investors are deemed rational. But if that is the case, what can explain the differences in outcome between the good, the bad and the ugly?

First, we need to recalibrate our views on the role of investment craftsmanship as an interpretation for performance, acknowledging the importance of chance. Besides, underneath all the fancy titles, business degrees and qualifications, humans are emotionally driven. That is partly why mistakes are so prevalent; not just in business but in all walks of life. The financial crisis of 2008 has shown that investors are irrational and markets are inefficient (more on that last point later). Both markets and investors can frequently and easily be manipulated by price-setting monopolies or parties benefiting from information asymmetry. While, in principle, fund managers are expected at all times to act in the interest of their investors, in reality they are the victims of significant psychological shortcomings.

Rightfully, there isn't just one cause or motive behind the numerous mistakes observed in private equity investing. But broadly speaking, the reasons fall into two main categories. Some are driven by flawed human nature, others by institutional vulnerability.

# HUMAN AND ORGANISATIONAL FAILINGS

The last financial crisis, as all previous ones, showed that markets are not so much swayed by economic indicators as by human psychology. One of the main reasons why investors can fail is behavioural. Once deeply ingrained, bad habits are hard to correct and often lead to post facto justification. There exist many pet theories to explain human behaviour. As just discussed, in the 1960s and 1970s most economists took for granted the view that humans, and therefore investors, were rational creatures. But a set of renegades eventually developed a very different ideology.

## Overconfidence and intuitive decision-making

We started this book emphasising the overly optimistic nature of many investors, including PE fund managers. Psychologist and winner of the Nobel Prize in economics Daniel Kahneman has argued that many investment decisions are emotional judgments and choices. Investors with considerable experience try to find an intuitive solution, based on

## THE GOOD, THE BAD AND THE UGLY OF PRIVATE EQUITY

either expertise or heuristics, the latter being a practical method not guaranteed to be optimal or perfect but sufficient for fast decision-making.

When this convenient and speedy method of thinking fails, investors revert to more deliberate thought. Unfortunately, because of widespread overconfidence among the investing community and a default tendency towards what Kahneman terms laziness, methodical reasoned thinking is not that frequent. It is usually overtaken by 'gut feeling.' The danger occurs when fund managers turn investments into routine decisions. To quote Kahneman: "Laziness is built deep into our nature."[1] An unguarded moment can lead to a monumental mistake.

Overconfidence is behind the decision by Madison Dearborn and Providence Equity to commit capital to Univision not from just one but from two investment vehicles, despite the pronounced risks of overexposure and the conflicts of interest arising from using funds committed in different years by distinct investors. What happens, for instance, when LP investors in a fund raised in 2005 want their money back while those in the vehicle raised in 2007 remain unstintingly devoted?

Overconfidence explains why 3i kept launching new initiatives in product areas and countries where it had no prior experience (e.g., technology, infrastructure, Japan, Brazil) instead of sticking to its knitting.

Overconfidence also contributed to Philip Green's decision to recapitalise Bhs instead of reinvesting all spare cash into the business to tackle the threat of fast fashion and online retail. Though greed – the desire to bag winners early before the economic tide turns – and the lack of regulation to prevent this sort of imprudent recapitalisations are also to blame, as we saw in the TIM Hellas story.

Rushed intuitive thinking is not the sole reason behind private equity investors' poor choices. Unlike day traders, LBO fund managers go

## Epilogue

through a decision-making process that lasts weeks if not months. Intuitive decisions are frequent, but investment errors are also drawn from other sources.

## Luck, or lack thereof

Across the industry, there is an obsessive fixation on the internal rate of return, or IRR, as the scorecard of investment performance. We saw in Part One that, when it comes to the latter, it is not easy to separate success due to luck from the factors derived from skills. To quote Kahneman:

> *"Luck plays a large role in every story of success; it is almost always easy to identify a small change in the story that would have turned a remarkable achievement into a mediocre outcome."*[2]

The case studies show that many investors with good track records during periods of stable and uneventful economic growth, like the 1980s and 1990s, failed spectacularly as soon as economic conditions deteriorated. Providence Equity, TPG and 3i were able to raise huge funds on achievements derived by the credit-fuelled economic growth of 2002-07, but their luck eventually ran out and they had to scale down their ambitions.

## Herding and groupthink

Beside Kahneman's strong arguments against intuitive thinking, human psychology also influences decision-making in other ways. Economists have long argued that market participants rarely make truly independent judgments. Private equity firms are no exception.

If their competitors invest in a particular sector, fund managers assume that their rivals have done their homework. They conclude that the sector is worth investing in. Herding has deep psychological (and cultural) roots. Kahneman describes in *Thinking, Fast and Slow* that our brains operate through a process called associative activation. Once we have read or learned that a deal in sector X was particularly successful, we have an emotional, cognitive and even physical reaction that is associatively coherent. Going forward, whenever they will be considering deal opportunities in sector X, investment committee members will experience a completely automatic positive response beyond their control. They will have internalised the relation between the sector and strong performance.

This copycat mentality is likely to be a communitywide trait, hence what I termed in the past the 'imitation game'. Herding is provoked by the unconscious association of two ideas – 'sector X' and 'success' – as representations of reality. Note that the reverse is also true. Many years ago, I had one of my prospective deals in Belgium rejected by my senior partners because one of their troubled portfolio companies was headquartered in that country. Talk about irrational behaviour!

Of course, this is made worse by the lack of appropriate training. Incompetence and ignorance make herding more prevalent. If an investor does not know what he is doing and has not bothered to learn from past mistakes, he can reassure himself by copying the methods applied by his peers, who themselves copy other participants, assuming all along that the latter know what they are doing.

This phenomenon of 'following the herd' is amplified by the lack of diversity among investors. Many have argued that investment errors, not just in private equity but in many asset classes, are partly driven from the homogeneity of the investor community. While this argument has been used by advocates preaching for better gender equality, in truth it applies to all facets of diversity. Because of homophily – the common habit of individuals to associate and bond with similar people – PE firms recruit the same kinds of individuals from a long list of parameters, be they of an ethnic, cultural, social, educational or professional nature. We are all driven by the desire to belong and the need for approval, therefore limiting our will to object. This leads to what psychologists call 'groupthink', the practice of making homogeneous, unchallenged decisions within a team that fails to offer different viewpoints.

## Who's the daddy?

Many members of the investment community suffer from the Alpha Male Syndrome. Convinced of their own brilliance, they see any suggestion that they might be wrong as a challenge to their top-dog status. This hierarchical ascendancy makes dissent a very risky proposition. It is likely the reason why, in 2008, few of his colleagues would have dared question Philip Yea's judgment when gearing up 3i's balance sheet, a move that eventually forced a distressed recapitalisation and the firm's demotion from the FTSE 100 index.

Ultimately, in asset management it is up to senior executives to make investment calls (the equivalent for the exclusive right to reproduce in monkeys). Next time you believe your boss is wrong, try telling him... remember, it is all about survival (this does not apply to the same degree if your boss is a woman as the Alpha Female Syndrome tends to be more subdued).

This is a major issue. As Kahneman rightly points out, it is easier to spot other people's mistakes than our own. If others fear to disagree, bad decisions can and will occur. In turn, our need for acceptance creates unhealthy internal politics. As all primates, human beings are social animals. The way this notion translates in the investment world is by the formation of coalitions within firms. Many investment professionals have witnessed how team members support a transaction sponsored by another colleague, sometimes irrespective of its merits, just because that same colleague supported one of their deals in the past. This can hardly lead to the best outcome and certainly is not in the best interest of LP investors.

## Fear and greed

The fear of missing out is common to all aspects of human life. I might want to buy a smartphone on its first day of sale if I feel that the item will be out of stock shortly thereafter due to unusually high demand. In the world of finance, FOMO is made worse by the fact that executives lack discipline. Weak controls, such as the absence of a walk-away price, can have detrimental effects when irrational behaviours kick in. The risk of losing a deal to a rival fund manager leads private equity firms to cut corners in order to close a transaction.

It is equally common for a senior executive to acquire a prized asset for bragging rights. I witnessed instances where a colleague would submit a slightly higher bid, say $1 billion, because a lower valuation (e.g., $950 million) would not qualify as a large buyout. Closing bigger transactions boosts the PR image of a firm and the ego of an investment professional.

## Anchoring

While intuitive thinking is not as prevalent in private equity as in day trading, in part because the period of due diligence gives a chance to bring analytic thinking into play, another psychological phenomenon has a strong influence. Sellers of businesses usually set the price of their asset by leaking it to the press or stating it at the outset of the sale process via their M&A advisers. This greatly affects the bids submitted by potential buyers, as they all tend to cluster towards the asking price or drop out immediately if they realise that they will not be able to meet the seller's expectations. This anchoring issue is amplified by the

Epilogue

presence of aggressive bidders (some of them desperate to deploy capital) in many competitive auctions.

## Incompetence and negligence

There is no formal training programme at most private equity firms. Fund managers are expected to learn on the job, through trial and error. Due to the lack of proper training, but also a hard-wired tendency to take mental short cuts as stated earlier, negligence is a notable reason behind failure. It partly relates to the idea of laziness discussed by Kahneman.

Negligence can take many forms. One concrete, tangible example prevails in private equity. For any fund manager, financial innovation is a very tempting proposition, because its influence cannot be easily stripped off when trying to assess what elements of returns are derived from true operational improvements and which are due to financial gimmickry. It is much easier to create value by borrowing tax-deductible, covenant-lite loans than it is to work out ways to enhance a portfolio company's operational structure and strategic positioning. Structural efficiency gains take time to deliver. The benefits of leverage are instantaneous. This exaggerated need for immediate (or at least short-term) results is a key source of negligence, and the reason behind failed deals like TIM Hellas and Toys "R" Us.

## Monetary stimulus

One cannot speak of the importance of human psychology in the investment industry without commenting on financial rewards. Humans, like animals, respond to stimuli. Behaviours are hugely dependent on incentives. Because it is easier for fund managers to become rich by collecting fees than by waiting many years to determine whether investment decisions will deliver capital gains, Chapter 9 demonstrated how they chose to optimise that side of their remunerative equation by turning it into an annuity.

Similarly, because quick flips and dividend recaps have a pronounced, positive impact on an investment's rate of return, industry participants have learned to give them priority over slower to implement but lasting operational improvements.

# ADDRESSING HUMAN AND ORGANISATIONAL FAILINGS

With over 180 identified cognitive biases,[3] there is significant behavioural risk associated with any human activity, whether investment-related or not. One way to address the many frailties of human decision-making is by 'nudging' people towards the best options. This 'libertarian paternalistic' approach is the one suggested by another Nobel laureate in economics, Richard Thaler.

## Nudging

As just described, irrational behaviour is extensive and, in the case of investment decisions, often expensive. If we follow the arguments presented by Thaler and his co-author Cass Sunstein in their book *Nudge*, one way to cure fund managers' collective optimism, or at least tone down their overconfidence, is by reminding them of bad (and ugly) stories like the ones described in Parts Two and Three. It was the chief reason behind my decision to publish this book.

To limit gut decisions to a minimum, private equity fund managers must embrace a systematic due diligence process, irrespective of the transaction being considered. Young executives typically need time to make up their mind about an investment opportunity because of their lack of experience. They need to engage what Thaler calls their reflective system (deliberate thought, to use Kahneman's terminology). Accomplished professionals trust their guts a lot more, not always with the best outcomes.

My analysis of the Mergermarket opportunity, back in 2006, told me that it was a great deal. This conclusion was partly helped by my due diligence experience with data publishers on past transactions. My colleagues at GMT Communications followed their instinct, reacting negatively to a young upstart with a limited track record. These seasoned executives had a strong knowledge of traditional media companies like newspaper publishers; their grasp of Web-based business models was not as robust. Mergermarket was a new-media company, growing fast and disrupting the newspaper model. It is difficult to convince people who have invested in an industry for twenty years or more that they should not make decisions on instinct but should instead go through a deep, analytic thought process.

Through nudges, fund managers would not be forbidden from acting as they please; they would be encouraged to behave in a certain way. The best approach to achieve this would be to change incentives, or to enforce disincentives. A few examples include:

- Holding fees (i.e., bonuses) in escrow for a number of years to claw them back in situations when a fund manager underperforms. At present, only capital gains are partly placed in escrow, allowing fund managers to become very rich just by charging annual commissions.
- Investors could request the right to withdraw, reduce or even increase their capital commitments according to the ongoing performance of a vintage fund or the behaviour of a fund manager.
- Investors in various vintage funds of the same fund manager could even make their commitments dependent on past, present and future performance. That would give the incentive for fund managers to remain disciplined.

Thaler and Sunstein also recommend self-control strategies to resist temptation. One way to rein in the fund managers' predisposition to turn into hit-and-run merchants enamoured of quick flips and serial refinancings would be for their LP investors to apply a different target investment return to deals that use aggressive financial engineering, acknowledging that many of these overindebted businesses become zombie companies (Univision) or eventually head for Chapter 11 (Toys "R" Us).

Operational and strategic improvements should be rewarded unless they damage the long-term viability of the underlying company or lead to bankruptcy – in which case governments should be able to claw monies back based on the various costs to society, to plug pension holes and cover unemployment benefits, for instance.

Similarly, governments could penalise the exorbitant use of debt by removing the tax shield on interest for companies with debt ratios above a certain threshold. US regulators have guidelines for banks to limit leverage assigned to buyouts to 6 times EBITDA. Why not make interest taxable above that ratio? It is already the case in certain jurisdictions if leverage exceeds a certain proportion of the capital structure.

Governments could also apply a much higher tax rate for the portion of capital gains generated through quick flips or partial exits in the first two years of the holding period. Again, that might dissuade fund managers from acting recklessly and should encourage them to create value over the longer term.

Nudging seems innovative, but the idea of influencing behaviours is not new: in the 1950s and 1960s, this approach was called social engineering. It did not quite deliver on its promises, in part due to the lack of reliable monitoring devices back then. Recent improvements in data mining and analytical tools give more credence to these policies.

# Epilogue

## Better firm structure and training

Beside behavioural techniques, the industry should make organisational improvements. Because of human fallibility, it is best for fund providers (LP investors) if they commit their capital only to firms that adopt a collegial approach to decision-making. Since any one leader (like all human beings) will be subject to biases, he or she risks guiding the firm down dangerous paths. There were several examples of PE firms under the overbearing influence of one strong individual (as sole founder or CEO) that made major blunders in the years leading up to the 2008 financial crisis. Corporate structures dominated by one individual should be shunned by investors keen to follow best practice. But that's just the start.

The kinds of ideas disseminated by social scientists have been studied and appropriated by hedge fund managers. The latter have introduced training to take into account the impact of human psychology in mistakes made by individual traders.

The world of behavioural economics has yet to permeate the PE industry. It is seen as too fluffy, even irrelevant. Plus, it is easier to ignore when you only get benchmarked against your peers and stock indexes every few years, rather than monthly in the case of hedge fund traders. In private equity, it takes at least 5 years for internal rates of return to be considered remotely meaningful, and not to include a disproportionate element of unrealised performance.

Yet, even in the PE sector teams can be trained to communicate in a more disciplined manner. Exposing ourselves to diverse opinions reduces tunnel vision. One way to avoid groupthink, for instance, is prescribed by Kahneman. Before an issue is discussed by a committee, each member should write down his/her position and read from that script. The standard practice of open discussion gives too much weight to the opinions of those who speak early or assertively. Following Kahneman's suggestion makes opinions independent of each other.

## Robots to the rescue

The transactions and fund managers reviewed in this book make a compelling case that value creation in private equity is not a given. It is still frightening to consider how many otherwise smart individuals waste their intellect in trying to make investing more tortuous than necessary by coming up with clever tricks, constantly aiming to derive marginal gains instead of choosing a nobler path. As noted, the most excessive profit-centric deeds can be explained by greed and, occasionally, a serious lack of ethics. Partly due to the absence of risk-monitoring processes, many failures have a more troublesome cause: irrationality.

What can strike as counterintuitive is that, frequently, investment decisions are made according to emotional factors, including office politics, personal and promotional considerations, competitive jealousy (internally and externally), deadlines related to investment timetable or upcoming fundraising, and many others. This is not new.

A solution that is likely to be available to all fund managers within the next decade is artificial intelligence (AI). To investment experts who strongly believe in the superiority of the human brain, this idea will seem far-fetched. Still, robots have proven more reliable than humans for complex human activities like information gathering and indexing (search engines) and autonomous transportation (self-driving trains). Many hedge funds have already espoused trading algorithms to take out the downside and unreliability of human psychology, in particular its emotional angles, fatigue, intellectual constraints and fraudulent behaviour.[4] On that last point, AI is financial regulators' best hope to tackle insider trading and other misdeeds. In his book *Principles*, seasoned hedge fund manager Ray Dalio acknowledges the benefits he gained by complementing human imagination with computerised modelling. Forecasting and decision-making are more accurate through a combination of the two.

# Epilogue

Observers will point out that trading is a quick-thinking game whereas PE investing takes place at a slower pace, which should help to eliminate most, if not all, of trading-related shortcomings. Private equity is influenced by a combination of analysis and intuition. It requires judgment and depends on parameters that differ from those of public markets. For a start, the lack of liquidity requires caution. In a way, this is where algorithms' inability to make gut decisions can play a role. It complements feelings with reason, handling the predictable and repetitive factors of deal-doing.

While I am not as naïve or idealistic as many Silicon Valley venture capitalists and entrepreneurs in thinking that technology can address all of humanity's ailments, I take the view that, in private equity, automation and fact-based software can take out many of the pitfalls associated with political and emotional games at the investment committee level, biased fact-searching during the due diligence phase, and emotions prevalent even in the slow-mo world of networked deal-doing – fear and greed being front of mind. Interestingly, this is a view shared by one of the largest LP investors in Europe, British insurer Standard Life, in an article published in September 2013.[5] After many long and fruitful years of collaboration, most fund managers are reluctant to disagree with their senior colleagues or to shoot down their deals. It is human nature. A robot would have no such qualms; it would offer executives rational arguments for or against investment opportunities championed by grey-haired deal operators.

The AI potential goes beyond desk-top analysis. Research indicates that algorithms can also counter human psychological shortcomings and cope with intricate judgments and resolutions. Hong Kong-headquartered VC firm Deep Knowledge Ventures announced in May 2014 that they had appointed a computer algorithm as equal member of the board of directors. While acknowledging that their robot could not match humans for intuitions, its logical and unbiased approach was a great complement to the contribution of human board members.[6]

Few if any private equity firms use adequate risk-management tools. Investing in a haphazard way is not appropriate when handling third-party money. Robots would help standardise decision-making and flag out risks like disruptive innovation as deal-breakers, sparing LBO managers blushes by staying clear of controversy if they can prove that their decisions were partly based on algorithmic calculations.

## POOR ACCOUNTABILITY AND REGULATION

Better training and nudging work well to correct or anticipate management mistakes. They can have a positive impact on decision-making. While I am a strong believer in Hanlon's razor, whereby we should not seek to attribute to graft or wickedness what is appropriately explained by ignorance or negligence, it is evident that nudging is wholly inadequate to tackle malicious deeds of the sort described in Part Three.

Critics of private equity argue that the main issue with LBO fund managers is one of misaligned interests. We, the pensioners and savers, have no say about how our money is being run by asset managers. We, the principals, exercise no adequate control over fund managers. While this is undoubtedly true and is a problem common to many principal-agent relationships, I would contend that the issue is compounded by the growing complexity of financial markets and the decision – taken by overwhelmed legislators and regulators – to offer a light-touch solution to the central function of oversight. In certain circles, capitalism takes for granted the warped logic that human beings are entrepreneurial, productive and reliable whereas institutions, and particularly governments, are for the most part sclerotic, inefficient and corrupt. Let us call this noble but quixotic market fundamentalist view the Ayn Rand school of thought, in reference to that post-war libertarian philosopher, an uncompromising advocate of free markets.

# Epilogue

A real matter of contention is the widespread belief in the efficient market hypothesis (EMH). It was formulated in the 1960s and became gospel in most economics and finance classes in the ensuing decades. In short, with EMH markets reflect all or most relevant information. In turn, this information is widely available and already reflected in asset prices. That makes markets unpredictable as prices randomly fluctuate in response to new information.

EMH betokened the arbitrary faith in unrestrained capital markets. The latter and their participants should be left to their own device. The emerging 'science' of economic modelling eventually percolated into the political arena. Congruent with the whimsical idea that efficient markets hold perfect information is the conviction that there is little to fear from markets since unexpected events are likely to have a limited and easily defined impact on prices. If EMH holds and investors are fully informed, then there is no need for market regulation. This philosophy – for to call it science is a stretch – acted as a preamble to economic policies. In tandem, in the 1980s the Reagan and Thatcher administrations promulgated new doctrines celebrating the power of markets to self-govern. The obvious corollary was deregulation.

The latter led to financial innovation and the unabated expansion of the fund management industry from the 1980s onwards. The barriers to entry were greatly lowered, generating a boom in institutional asset management, irrespective of the principles posited by EMH that implied the impossibility of beating markets over a prolonged period. Indeed, the theory suggests that no investor can expect to regularly deliver better returns than the market on a consistent basis. That makes it difficult to explain how, in this context, the asset management industry was able to grow exponentially in the past three decades.

At first sight, the efficient market theory and active management of financial assets are antithetical – if markets are efficient, then there should not be opportunities for fund managers to make a living out of active price discovery. Passive investing should represent the bulk of trading volumes, with only limited space for price arbitrage. Instead, passive funds manage just one-fifth of aggregate investment portfolios globally.

Market pundits believed that the relationship between information, investment decisions and market performance could be modelled out with almost surgical precision. This idealism can be endearing, even enthralling for some, but it is best not to set much store by it. Given the history of capitalism, well-provided as it is with market gyrations provoked by emotional reactions to random events, it was evident that the EMH assumptions bore little resemblance with what could be observed in the real world. But this sort of contradiction never stopped economists and government officials from endorsing far-reaching policies. It is surprising that it took until the noughties for alternative economic frameworks to gain acceptance.

## Market inefficiency calls for regulation

Gradually, two sets of evidence undermined EMH. First, the long list of bubbles and crashes corroborated the argument that markets are somewhat inefficient, or at the very least do not 'fully' reflect all available information to all participants. Importantly, market efficiency and investors' rational expectations were disproved by mathematician Benoit Mandelbrot, who explained that price changes in financial markets do not follow a normal distribution but show practically infinite variance. Nowadays, only the most ardent of libertarian ideologues and academics would object to this view.

Second, a very small number of asset managers succeeded in delivering top-flight performance on a consistent basis. Bizarrely, but not surprisingly given the point we made earlier about humans' heuristics of overconfidence, it led many investors to believe that *they* could also beat the market. Hence the massive inflows of money allocated to alternative asset managers, in particular hedge funds and private equity.

# Epilogue

As announced in the Prologue, most hedge fund managers believe that they can generate alpha persistently, even in the face of contradictory data. Most PE fund managers believe that they can be permanent top-quartile performers. But this book, as well as a growing list of academic research papers, offer sufficient evidence that it is emphatically not the case.

The frequency of market swings, increased volatility, as well as the catalogue of corporate shenanigans that plagued the markets in the past three decades – from Michael Milken's insider trading in the 1980s, to Enron's accounting fraud in the noughties, and the more recent Bernard Madoff scandal – have put a dent on the Randian dogma and the religious notion that self-regulation is the appropriate methodology to monitor financial markets.

Even if we accept that the rationality assumption of laissez faire advocates is outlandish, other factors play a part in the financial sector's poor results observed in recent years. Do I need to point out that investment discipline and accountability have always been central to dependable and superior performance? Let me point it out anyway.

In a market economy, just like in a democratic system, behaviours and results are very much conditional on the participants being held accountable for their actions when all-too-fallible plans miscarry. Many of the worst practices described in this book derive directly from the exploitation of limited liability, a concept that enabled capitalism to flourish, but that can have profound consequences when abused. What we learned from the Bhs and TIM Hellas stories is that, in a capitalist system, failure is always somebody else's fault. Pushing the argument to its legitimate extreme, the free market default philosophy postulates that success has many fathers whereas failure is an orphan.

Managing other people's money at no or limited personal cost if things go wrong cannot yield satisfactory results; unless you naively hope that all fund managers will hold the moral qualities of Jeffrey Archer's fictional character quoted at the start of this Epilogue. As economics

Nobel Prize winner Joseph Stiglitz pointed out, self-regulation is an oxymoron. Although it functions as a byword for the PE industry's boundless rent-seeking success, it is not the appropriate solution to monitoring an increasingly complex financial sector. Self-governance has demonstrated its shortcomings in many human activities outside the inbred world of asset management. Here are some familiar examples.

# Foul play

Football (soccer in America) is indisputably the most popular sport on the planet. Every week, millions of fans follow the performance of local and foreign teams. The English Premier League's TV rights for the three seasons going from 2013-14 to 2015-16 totalled £3 billion.[7] Passions run high among fans, and riches await teams that can win their national league or a European championship.

But the most anticipated and prestigious tournament of the game is, without the shadow of a doubt, the World Cup. Held every four years, its final between France and Croatia on 15 July 2018 attracted a TV audience of over one billion people and millions of online and mobile viewers. On each occasion, the tournament is organised by a different country. It is an opportunity for the host nation to market itself to the world. Countries compete aggressively to win the bidding contest. Yet the cost of hosting the tournament can be astronomical. In anticipation of the 2014 edition, Brazil spent a reported $12 billion renovating and building stadia, upgrading public transportation and marketing the event – the equivalent of 61% of the country's education budget.[8] For a country as poor as Brazil, if feels like an extravagance. But for the organisation in charge of coordinating this beauty pageant, it is a bonanza.

The Fédération Internationale de Football Association (FIFA), a self-regulated body headquartered in Zurich, Switzerland (with the familiar

# Epilogue

tax benefits), is responsible for the country nomination process. Given the global phenomenon that is football, FIFA is a sizeable organisation. Its accumulated profits exceeded $1.5 billion in 2014. The World Cup that year brought in $4.8 billion, including $2.4 billion in TV rights (a point briefly discussed in the Univision story). That compared to only $358 million in prize money, so the tournament is a sure winner for the organisation, no matter which team ends up triumphing.[9]

Being a self-governed body, FIFA is a law unto itself. What that entails is that any dispute does not go to civil courts but is resolved through the organisation's own mechanisms. FIFA is run like any independent country. It operates according to its particular rule of law and elects its president according to its own statutes. Rather like many dictators of banana republics, in the past FIFA presidents have been so difficult to dislodge that they are frequently only replaced if they die in office or resign out of exhaustion – Frenchman Jules Rimet held office for thirty-three years until his retirement in 1954 at the tender age of 81, and Brazilian João Havelange stayed in office for twenty-four years before bowing out a month after his 82nd birthday. Between 1904 and October 2015 FIFA only had eight presidents. Three of those actually died in office. So, when the Swiss Sepp Blatter won a fifth mandate in May 2015 to begin his eighteenth year in command, it was very much business as usual as far as FIFA's modus operandi is concerned.

The Association's president is all powerful. It is not uncommon for the incumbent offering himself for re-election (oddly enough, only men seem to be candidates) to magically stand unopposed. With the regularity of a Swiss clock, other possible candidates tend to withdraw before the elections or after the first round. Unlike presidential elections taking place in many countries, FIFA's ballots do not invite outside observers to monitor the process. The choice of the World Cup host country is made by the executive committee. As anyone could predict, this sort of governance encourages side deals and covert alliances. Understandably, in view of the commercial interests at stake, over the years FIFA has had its fair share of bad press. None, however,

## THE GOOD, THE BAD AND THE UGLY OF PRIVATE EQUITY

reached the degree of outrage raised by the decision taken in 2010 to award the 2022 World Cup to Qatar, a Middle Eastern nation state of less than 2 million people whose national football team had never managed to qualify to take part in a previous World Cup tournament.

Shortly thereafter, stupefaction was replaced by claims of corruption. During the year 2012, controversy emerged among allegations of vote-buying. After orchestrating a two-year internal investigation, in November 2014 FIFA released the conclusions in a report that gave the organisation a clean bill of health. The report was immediately discredited when its author resigned and divulged that the public version contained "numerous materially incomplete and erroneous representations."[10] Various independent investigations unearthed backhanders being paid for several past World Cup host selections. Every bidding process since the Italia 1990 World Cup was implicated in some form of financial irregularity. As for the decision to award the 2022 edition to Qatar, it turns out that the executive committee's plebiscite had allegedly been swayed by the intervention of then French president Nicolas Sarkozy after a meeting with Qatar's crown prince.[11] Under pressure, Blatter was forced to resign a month after his re-election and was handed a six-year ban from participating in FIFA activities.

Of course, FIFA should not be singled out. It would be wrong to assume that it is the only sports federation to be run in such a medieval and nefarious manner. The International Olympic Committee (headquartered in tax-friendly Lausanne, Switzerland) and the International Association of Athletics Federations (IAAF), based in Monaco (another tax shelter), operate under a self-regulated model that leaves much to be desired. In 2015 the World Anti-Doping Agency (WADA) issued a report revealing that police were investigating the IAAF's former President Lamine Diack over allegations that he had taken bribes to cover widespread doping offences by Russian athletes.[12] For track and field athletes to be accused of doping was nothing new. Several memorable drug-cheat cases include Ben Johnson (a Canadian stripped of his gold medal shortly after the 1988 summer Olympics), American male athletes Marion Jones and Justin Gatlin, and a long list of Jamaican runners, from Sherone Simpson to Yohan Blake.

No sports organisation has been marred by scandals as much as the Union Cycliste Internationale (UCI, or International Cycling Union), also based in tax-light Switzerland. Routinely undermined by doping claims whenever major events like the Tour de France generate superhuman performances from riders (including those of seven-time Tour winner Lance Armstrong), the UCI was accused of proactively seeking to hide evidence. Armstrong was part of a system. Many recent winners of the Tour had been found guilty of doping offences. Armstrong pushed the system to its logical conclusion: if everyone cheats, let's cheat better and more than the rest of the peloton.

## No master but God

To many fans, football is a religion. They attend every weekend feature. Like pilgrims, they faithfully travel to other cities for away games. They worship key players like idols. So, it is not much of a stretch to draw parallels between FIFA and the Catholic Church.

The latter is one of the most potent and far-reaching of institutions: it has over one billion devotees globally. Importantly, it operates according to its own laws since it is headquartered in the Vatican, an independent state, with all the benefits that come with such a status. In the pope, the Church has one of the most influential heads of state of any country – his 'election' is as opaque and undemocratic as that of FIFA's president. Candidates are also exclusively men.

The Catholic Church has its own army and never used to shy away from the use of force to expand its fan base, as even a cursory study of its history, from the Crusades to the Inquisition, will attest. Nowadays, it tends to favour soft power. In recent decades, as it gradually lost some of its prestige and audience in the West and the media became less reverential, the Catholic Church has faced public embarrassment, some of it related to sexual misconduct by members of the clergy. A surprisingly large number of its representatives have betrayed the trust of the faithful.

Another set of offences that is a lot more relevant, given the theme of this book, concerns the trials and failings of the Vatican's financial operations, in particular those surrounding the Institute for the Works of Religion, more commonly known as the Vatican Bank. Money laundering, links with Mafia families such as the Gambinos in the US and the Spatolas in Sicily, as well as fraud and corruption – including the collapse of Banco Ambrosiano, and the murder of that bank's chairman Roberto Calvi in 1982 – have all made front page news. Despite arrest warrants ordered by justice departments in various countries, officials of the bank have repeatedly been blessed with diplomatic immunity or protection from the pope.[13]

The Vatican Bank's troubles over the last forty years are evidence enough that letting a self-governed institution operate a bank without proper supervision can be lethal. While regulators have no oversight on how the Vatican Bank functions, the latter can still negatively affect the global financial system and breach international laws by laundering money, funding arms dealers, financing military coups or subsidising organised crime, as Eric Frattini chronicles in his book *The Entity*.

## ADDRESSING ACCOUNTABILITY AND REGULATORY FAILINGS

If self-governance had shown its shortcomings in so many areas of public life, why did governments think that it would be a good idea to apply a similar model to the economically strategic area of finance? The stories covered in Chapter 9 should concern us all. The troubles encountered by 3i and many of its peers also demonstrate that markets

# Epilogue

are inefficient and investors, even institutional ones, far from rational. This sort of environment requires proper regulation. Otherwise, we risk leaving the gamblers in charge.

## Monitoring and disclosures

It is not possible to make recommendations on regulation and legislation without first understanding the reasons behind the decision to let private equity self-regulate. The main justification is that fund managers serve a set of financial customers deemed 'sophisticated', implying that they have sufficient experience and knowledge to weigh the risks and merits of an investment opportunity. One of the main implications is that it restricts the ability of sophisticated investors to seek redress before the financial regulator.

We will ignore the consequences that such a sweeping waiver can have on the behaviour of agents that are entrusted with third-party funds. Again, the case studies in Parts Two and Three provide clear examples of how the fractured financial regulatory system of the 1990s and noughties let fund managers make a fortune, not thanks to capital gains and superior performance, for those were often temporary or illusionary, but on a litany of fees.

Rather, the issue that is most troubling is that, by certifying retirement-plan managers, banks and insurers as sophisticated, governments and regulators ignored a key fact. The actual end-customer of fund managers is the pensioner, the bank account holder and the insured, not the institutions where these individuals have chosen to park their savings. For that reason alone, self-regulation seems wholly inadequate. If an LP investor picks the wrong private equity fund manager, the injured party is not the institutional investor itself but the individual pensioner or saver.

For that reason, disclosures of private equity activity must improve to encourage better behaviour. That would also help the outside world supervise this growing business segment. Corporate governance advocates commonly quote Louis Brandeis, Supreme Court Justice of the United States, who tellingly uttered the following words in 1933, during the Great Depression caused by the market crash of the late 1920s:

> *"Sunlight is said to be the best of disinfectants; electric light the most efficient policeman."*[4]

# Regulation

As it turns out, the efficient market hypothesis and the assumption about investors' rational expectations were spurious. We saw that these faulty theories convinced economists, policy makers and business people that regulation could only damage the economy. But it had another side effect, one that proved crucial in the development of the private equity trade.

Long-term market efficiency evokes predictability. As we saw, the latter is one of the key parameters that encourages the flow of credit in an economy, since it provides more certainty around the solvency of the borrowers and the cost of debt. Leveraged buyouts became ever more prevalent because, if markets were efficient, the economy could be considered more predictable than it truly is. The 2008 financial crisis has shown the shortcomings of such a theory.

Yet regulation is not only needed to reflect the unpredictable nature of markets. It also serves as a stick with which to beat bad behaviour. If a meaningful number of market participants collude to rig deal pricing, bribe government officials to gain an unfair advantage, or abuse the trust of their investors by charging them hidden fees, markets can hardly be called efficient, can they?

Fund managers have shown very little desire to learn from past mistakes. This attitude is not just derived from deep insecurities or an intrinsic inability to learn. It also comes from the fact that they face limited downside. They do not get punished other than by being fined inconsequential and negligible penalties. And they scarcely ever lose complete access to capital: for every pension fund manager or university endowment refusing to back the next vintage fund, PE firms onboard new investors among the plethora of family offices and sovereign wealth funds.

One of the problems with self-regulation is that it assumes that 'nudging' is a panacea; that it suits all situations. While nudges undoubtedly work to influence irrational decision-making, they are useless in cases of misbehaviour, where the refusal to reform traps millions of people in fee-sucking retirement plans.

## Legislation

Members of the legislative body also need to act. Some claim that the reason government representatives or lawmakers do not step in is because they are in the pockets of high finance, including wealthy fund managers – they call this plight 'regulatory capture'. If so, we should hope that cases of corruption are rare occurrences. Because to halt the sorts of practices discussed in Chapter 9, legislation is a necessity. Unlike overstretched balance sheets, collusion and conflicts of interest are not accidental, unfortunate missteps. They are structural flaws.

The predicament for politicians is striking a balance between what is condoned or rightly encouraged and what is condemned or even outlawed. The year after criticising Philip Green in April 2016 for being "just the sort of capitalist to give capitalism a bad name", government official David Davis carried the flag of unrestrained free markets during his Brexit negotiations with the European Union. It is easy to forget that Philip Green simply adopted techniques universally applied by PE firms. As one journalist imperiously remarked, Bhs's downfall was "a story of political failure as well as a product of commercial mismanagement."[15] To punish and bully entrepreneurs – often with more indignation than conviction – yet leave fund managers unchallenged in order to preserve the power of London's financial district is unlikely to yield meaningful results. No British politician criticised Bain Capital or KKR when, in early 2018, the UK arm of distressed retailer Toys "R" Us filed for bankruptcy with a pension shortfall of £25 million. Without structural reforms and unfailing legislation, behaviours will not change.

There is a lot of frustration among regulators, the public (witness the rise of populism) and experts (economists Joseph Stiglitz and Thomas Piketty among others) that not enough is being done to change the mentality and corporate culture of high finance. But mentalities take a long time to adapt. Think that it took until the 1980s, a century after the invention of the automobile, for seat belts to become mandatory in most Western nations. The main obstacle to the introduction of seat belt laws was the suggestion by freedom advocates that it would infringe on personal liberties. People should be free to choose whether to wear seat belts or not, irrespective of the costs to society.

Our very modern obsession with free markets is an impediment to apply restrictions to, and protection against, the irresponsible use of leverage and excessive fees. Market fundamentalists claim that economies should not be tempered with, that they operate better without government interference. What the scandals surrounding various sports federations demonstrate is that institutions should only be granted the right to self-regulate if they abide by strong governance standards. Contrary to what libertarians will have us believe, socialism is not the sole alternative to rampant free markets. A better option is a mixed economy, a healthy blend of free enterprise and supervision.

If, as suggested in the various case studies, people are at the core of poor decision-making and of its corollary – underperformance – then individuals must either be taken out of the investment equation (by using artificial intelligence) or closely supervised. The status quo is no longer tenable. It is up to legislators and investors to prime private equity executives into more socially and economically responsible behaviours.

# Watchdog without a bite

To learn from past errors, individuals must apprehend two things. First, that their mistakes are indeed mistakes. Second, that those have negative consequences, which implies that the culprits must change their attitude. Because regulators have repeatedly refused to intervene to punish or correct errors committed, accidentally or voluntarily, by fund managers, the latter have reached the erroneous conclusion that their detrimental conduct can go on.

This reaction is not as irrational as it appears. If they do not get disciplined for actions that lead to value erosion – and are told instead that it is all part of capitalism's desirable and indispensable processes of creative destruction and constant reinvention – it follows that fund managers have no reason to apply self-control or corrective measures.

If properly regulated, capitalism has the potential to turn into a combined harvester, threshing fertile crops of economic prosperity reaped by the many. When left to their own device, competitive markets resemble a steamroller crushing every obstacle in its path, bringing rewards mainly to those in the driver seat. Self-regulation is a wonderful lever for those seeking to nurture and further their individual wealth. Yet it bears repeating that self-regulation is self-contradictory. There is little evidence that it brings much benefit to many market participants, be they workers, pensioners, investees or governments.

Too often, when tolerated, regulation is considered a necessary evil. Instead, it should be treated as a bulwark against potential excesses of financial innovation. Although regulatory oversight can sometimes appear arbitrary, the lack of it leads to endemic abuses and externalities. As economists Akerlof and Shiller explain: "competitive markets by their very nature spawn deception and trickery."[16] The stories in Part Three prove their point.

Lastly, perhaps more poignantly, what is intriguing about the way private equity operates is that, unlike other cases of substance abuse, it is not the fund manager that dies of a debt overdose or falls into a zombie-like state. Rather, it is the portfolio company that has been force-fed the loans. This is where the lack of accountability acquires an ethical dimension. Our economic policies ought not, as a matter of necessity, breed a lack of morals or impede social conscience. If our market economies persist in granting investors free reins to structure a company's balance sheet aggressively while not holding them accountable for the long-term effects of their investment model, the bona fide performance of private equity will remain unknown.

There are too many behavioural and institutional factors behind the industry's failings for the participants – investors, regulators and legislators – to find an easy solution. Yet giving up is not an option. As American abolitionist Wendell Phillips once said: "Eternal vigilance is the price of liberty; power is ever stealing from the many to the few." What applies to society is also true in business. Self-regulation and human psychology have shown their shortcomings only too well. It is high time to introduce proper governance and vigilance to the world of finance.

# ACKNOWLEDGEMENTS

This book was meant to be part of *The Debt Trap*, published in late 2016. There were concerns that the book would turn into an encyclopedic volume, running over 700 pages long. The decision was taken to develop separately the topics covered in this volume, but the completion of the whole project would not have been possible without the extraordinary support of a number of people.

In addition to contribution from industry specialists, many of my students at various business schools supplied valuable advice, sometimes unknowingly, to improve the format and content of the narratives.

Thanks to those who read and gave feedback on early drafts of the manuscript, including Frederic Chiappini, Marc Denjean, Ariane Hofmann-Maniyar, Dharmesh Maniyar, Stephen Perrin and Nathalie Romang. They took the time to review various sections and versions and provided me with helpful recommendations and corrections. Other contributors chose to remain anonymous due to their continuing involvement in finance. I thank all these people for making a difference in the quality and delivery of the end product.

Finally, I am indebted to a great many more friends for their encouragement.

# ABOUT THE AUTHOR

Sebastien Canderle was educated in France and the United States. He has more than 20 years of work experience in the consulting and financial sectors in New York and London, including as an investor for various private equity firms. He is the author of *Private Equity's Public Distress* and *The Debt Trap* and has been a business school lecturer in private equity for many years. His writings have appeared in Economia, the Financial Times, Hedge, MoneyWeek, Naked Capitalism, Pension Pulse, Real Deals, ValueWalk and other publications. He is a fellow of the Institute of Chartered Accountants in England and Wales and received his MBA from the Wharton School.

# INDEX

3i, 9, 81, 119, 121, 123-56, 288, 290, 291, 310
    FCI, 120, 121

    FFI, 121

    ICFC, 120, 121, 125, 127, 135, 149, 151

ABC, 93, 104, 105
ABN AMRO, 68
Acuris. *See* Mergermarket
Akerlof, George, 260, 276, 280, 316
Allders, 203
Alliance Boots, 172
Allianz Capital Partners, 80
Alphabet, 268
Altegrity, 117
Amazon, 102, 108, 109, 164, 166, 173, 180, 182, 183, 187
Amber Day, 193, 194, 196, 199
Amsterdam Stock Exchange, 167
Anchorage Capital, 247
Angelo Gordon, 247
Anselmo, Rene, 87
Apax, 9, 229, 233, 235, 237, 238, 239, 240, 241, 250, 251, 253-56, 259, 260
    Esprit Telecom, 233

Inmarsat, 233

Intelsat, 233

Rue21, 229

Apollo Global Management, 21, 74, 80, 159, 160, 213, 262, 275, 278, 279
Apple, 70, 184, 268
Arcadia, 194, 196-205, 207, 210-12, 214, 217-19, 224-27
Asda, 197
Atlee, Clement, 119
Azcárraga Jean III, Emilio Fernando, 116
Azcárraga Milmo, Emilio, 115
Azcárraga Vidaurreta, Emilio, 87, 115, 116
Bain Capital, 9, 80, 89, 159-62, 170, 172, 175, 185, 186, 229, 270-72, 314
Bally Entertainment, 14
Banco Ambrosiano, 310
Bank of England, 1, 120, 121, 155
Bank of Scotland, 196, 197, 200, 201, 212
Baratta, Joseph, 270
Barclay, David and Frederick, 194
Barclays Bank, 153, 281

Baugur, 196, 204
BC Partners, 53-6, 60, 61
Bear Stearns, 22, 30
Bertelsmann, 73
Best Buy, 184
Bhs, 192-9, 201-20, 222-4, 226,
    228, 229, 254, 288, 290, 305,
    314
    Duff & Phelps, 223

    pension deficit, 216, 221,
    225, 226

    PricewaterhouseCoopers,
    226

Blackstone, 9, 13, 15, 17-27, 30-
    42, 80, 83, 89, 111, 132, 147,
    167, 262, 269, 270, 271, 276-
    9, 282, 283
Blatter, Sepp, 308
Blitzer, David, 262, 266
*Bloomberg*, 25, 41, 47, 54
Bloomberg, Michael, 48
BMG Rights, 73
Bollenbach, Stephen, 14, 15
Borrows, Simon, 143, 144, 148
Brandeis, Louis, 312
Brandon, David, 175, 176, 181
Brexit, 313
British Growth Fund (BGF), 154,
    155, 156
British Home Stores. *See* 3i
British Telecom, 233
British Venture Capital
    Association (BVCA), 127
Broadcasting Media Partners, 89,
    99, 265
Brown, Gordon, 153
Buenrostro, Fred, 275

Buffett, Warren, 85, 141
bullet loan, 79
bullet repayment, 7
Bureau van Dijk (BvD), 44, 45
Burger King, 161
Burton, 196, 207, 219
buyout bubble, 21, 115, 135
Caesars Entertainment, 15, 117,
    269
CalPERS, 9, 117, 118, 275, 280
CalSTRS, 9, 117, 118, 280
Cameron, David, 153, 221
Candover, 44, 45, 139
Carlyle, 62, 82, 83, 89, 147, 266,
    271, 274
Carnegie, Andrew, 264
Cascade, 89
CBS, 89, 93, 101, 105, 112
Cerberus Capital, 159, 160
Chappell, Dominic, 213, 215,
    217, 221, 223-6
    Retail Acquisitions, 209,
    213, 215, 216, 221, 222,
    226, 228

Chapter 11 filing, 72, 115, 162,
    179, 180, 182, 185, 215, 229,
    298
Citi, 281
Clayton Dubilier, 266
Clear Channel, 91, 117
CMBS (convertible mortgage-
    backed securities), 24
Colao, Vittorio, 252
Cook, Tim, 263
Cosmote, 232, 238, 240, 251, 253
Costco, 182
covenant-lite, 79, 91, 95, 101,
    171, 173, 175, 295
Creasey, Clay, 174

## Index

credit bubble, 87, 140, 268, 272

Credit Crunch, 18, 20, 21, 30, 95, 96, 136, 137, 143, 144, 146, 155, 167, 204

Credit Suisse, 159, 281

Crow, Bob, 221

Cuomo, Andrew, 274, 275

CVC, 62

*Daily Mail*, 222

Dalio, Ray, 300

Davis, David, 222, 313

Debenhams, 195, 203, 204, 210

Deep Knowledge Ventures, 301

delisting (also take-private), 17, 20, 26, 159, 170, 196, 200, 235

Dell, 1

Deutsche Bank, 102, 281

Deutsche Telekom, 252, 256

Diageo, 134, 138

Dodd-Frank Act, 273, 275

Dollarama, 161

Domino's Pizza, 161, 175

Dorothy Perkins, 196, 207, 219

dotcom bubble, 128, 129, 146, 233

Dreams, 208

Eagle, Angela, 222

efficient market hypothesis (EMH), 303, 304

EMI Music, 73

Enron, 72, 305

Equity Office Properties, 20

Ericsson, 233

Etilasat, 237

Eton Park, 247

Euronext, 232

Evans and Wallis, 207

Eyler, John, 161, 166, 184

Facebook, 70, 73, 268

Falco, Randy, 100

FAO Schwarz, 158, 161, 168, 176, 184, 186

fear of missing out (FOMO), 294

Federal Communications Commission (FCC), 94, 112

Fédération Internationale de Football Association (FIFA), 306, 307, 308, 309

financial crisis (2008), 6, 24, 30, 52, 57, 71, 80, 81, 83, 115, 118, 137, 138, 142, 143, 152, 153, 171, 185, 187, 204, 208, 216, 240, 247, 252, 256, 262, 265, 273, 277, 284, 288, 289, 299, 312

Financial Times, *52*, *213*

Financial Times Group, 50, 51

FINRA, 281, 282

First Chicago Corporation, 115, 116

*Fortune*, *270*

Four Seasons, 23

FOX, 93, 105

France Telecom, 252

Francisco Partners, 267

Frattini, Eric, 310

Freescale Semiconductors, 266, 270

Fuller, Richard, 221

Galavision, 88

Game Group, 184

Gamestop, 184

Gates, Bill, 89, 263

Gateway, 124, 125

General Electric, 70, 89, 96

general partner, 9

general partner (GP), 9

Getty, Paul, 30

GIC (Government of Singapore Investment Corporation), **9, 61, 62**

Gillette, **70**

Glass-Steagall Act, **284**

GMT Communications Partners, **44, 45, 46, 49, 55, 62, 297**

Goldman Sachs, **102, 159, 201, 222, 269, 271, 281**

Google, **54, 70, 73, 263**

Gordon Brothers, **216**

Gould, Jay, **264**

Gray, Jonathan, **24, 35, 283**

Great Depression, **170, 312**

Great Recession, **20, 24, 27, 30, 31, 52, 80, 85, 99, 110, 114, 118, 142, 152, 168, 169, 170, 182, 186, 204**

Green, Cristina, **205**

Green, Philip, **193, 195, 196, 198-201, 204, 205, 207, 208, 213, 215, 217, 220-9, 290, 313**

   Alan Sugar, **222**

   Etam, **203**

   Evans, **219**

   Harrods, **198**

   Kate Moss, **217**

   Lord Grabiner, **197**

   Mark One, **197**

   Olympus, **194, 216**

   Operation Socrates, **199, 201**

   Outfit, **219**

   Owen Owen, **194**

   Pension Protection Fund, **217, 222**

   Pensions Regulator, **217, 225**

   Revival Acquisitions, **200**

   Shoe Express, **194**

   Taveta, **205, 207, 209, 210, 211, 212, 218, 219, 220, 224, 226**

   Tony Blair, **224, 225**

   Warehouse, **194, 197**

   Xceptions, **194**

Green, Terry, **195, 196, 215**

groupthink, **291, 293, 299**

Guinness, **134**

Gymboree, **229**

Habitat, **192**

Hallmark Cards, **115, 116**

Hamleys, **204**

Harrah's Entertainment, **15, 269**

Harris, Joshua, **262, 266**

Hasbro, **164, 179, 182**

HCA, **172, 270**

Heinz, **1**

Hertz, **1**

Hill, James, **264**

Hilton, **viii, 6, 13-42, 60, 70, 72, 84, 269, 276, 282, 283**

   delisting, **17, 20, 26**

## Index

Hilton Grand Vacations (HGV), 24, 35, 36, 38

Hilton Worldwide. *See* Hilton

Hilton, Barron, 14, 15, 16

Hilton, Conrad, 13, 14

Hilton, Paris, 13, 16

Hispanic Broadcasting, 88

HNA, 35, 38

Hobson, Andrew, 102

homophily, 67, 292

House of Fraser, 204

HSBC, 153

Hunter, Tom, 194

Iceland (food chain), 204

Intel, 263

Interamerican, 231

International Association of Athletics Federations (IAAF), 308

Investcorp, 132

IPO (initial public offering) also listing, flotation, 17, 20, 21, 24, 25, 26, 28, 32, 33, 35-7, 40-2, 62, 100, 102, 103, 112, 114, 123, 126, 128, 129, 137, 139, 148, 152, 167, 169-72, 176, 181, 196, 281, 282, 283

IRR (internal rate of return), 26, 62, 239, 276, 291

J.Crew, 218

James, Hamilton, 270

Jobs, Steve, 263

JP Morgan, 22, 281, 282

Kahneman, Daniel, 289, 290, 291, 292, 293, 295, 297, 299

Kaplan, Stephen, 22, 26

Karen Millen, 204

Kay, Christopher, 161

KB Toys, 158, 161, 185, 186

Kimco Realty, 159, 160

KKR, 9, 21, 73, 74, 80, 83, 89, 111, 132, 159, 160, 162, 163, 167, 170, 172, 185, 197, 265, 266, 269-72, 278, 314

Kmart, 158

Kodak, 272

Kravis, Henry, 270

La Forgia, Robert, 25

La Quinta, 17

Larcombe, Brian, 132, 141

Lazarus, Charles, 157

LEGO, 164, 184

Lehman Brothers, 21, 30, 137, 167, 237, 240

Leighton, Allan, 195, 215

Leonard Green & Partners, 217

Leuschen, David, 274

limited partner (LP investor), 9, 61, 81, 82, 83, 117, 237, 261, 265, 276-9, 294, 297, 299, 301, 311

Littlewoods, 203

Lloyds Bank, 153

London Stock Exchange (LSE), 123, 126

LXR Luxury Resorts, 17

Macmillan Gap, 120

Macy's, 183

Madison Dearborn, 89, 91, 117, 240, 265, 290

Madoff, Bernard, 305

*Mail on Sunday*, 195

Mandarin Oriental, 23

Mandelbrot, Benoit, 304

Marks & Spencer (M&S), 194, 197, 199-203, 205, 206, 208, 210, 213, 214

Marriott, 20, 32, 39, 41

Matalan, 203

Mattel, 164, 179, 182

323

May, Theresa, 228
Mergermarket Group, 6, 43- 62, 70, 71, 77, 84, 109, 283, 297
Metro-Goldwyn-Mayer, 117
Microsoft, 263, 268
Midland Bank, 123
Milken, Michael, 305
Mint (hotel), 23
Miss Selfridge, 194, 196, 204, 219
Mizuho, 143, 147
Moody's, 55, 61, 95, 99, 101, 103, 161, 168, 283
Morgan Stanley, 102, 237, 281
Morrisons, 197
Mothercare, 192, 193
Mount Kellett, 247
Myners, Paul, 200
Nasdaq, 129, 232
Nassetta, Christopher, 17, 27, 30, 41
NBC, 89, 93, 105
Nelson, Jonathan, 90
Netflix, 100, 102, 108, 109
New Look, 194, 203, 210
New York Common Retirement Fund, 274
*New York Post*, *270*
New York Stock Exchange (NYSE), 33, 88, 160, 167, 171
*New York Times*, 26, 266, 270
Nordstrom, 218
OBO (owner buyout), 191, 195, 197, 227
Omnicom, 94
Orascom Telecom, 239, 249
OTE, 232, 256
Panafon (Vodafone), 232, 238, 240, 249, 251, 253
Park Hotels & Resorts, 36, 37, 38
Patricof, Alan, 233

Peacocks, 203
Pearson, 50-3, 55, 58, 60, 62
Pecora Committee, 284
Perenchio, Andrew Jerrold, 87, 88, 90, 93, 94, 115, 116
Permira, 159
PIK (payment-in-kind) loan, 234, 238, 244, 256
Piketty, Thomas, 314
Primark, 203, 214
Promus, 14
ProSiebenSat, 90
Providence Equity, 9, 89-91, 97, 112, 117, 118, 237, 238, 247, 290, 291
Quadrangle, 274
Queen, Michael, 141, 143
RAC, 62
Rajaratnam, Raj, 283
Rand, Ayn, 302
Rattner, Steve, 274, 275
Reagan, Ronald, 303
Retail Acquisitions
    Grant Thornton, 222

    Olswang, 222

Reuter, Paul Julius, 48
revolver. *See* revolving credit facility
revolving credit facility, 7, 53, 61, 91, 96, 168, 170
RevPAR (revenue per available room), 18, 19, 25, 28, 40
Riverstone, 82, 274
RJR Nabisco, 76, 264
Roberts, George, 270
Rockefeller, John D., 264
Rodriguez, Ray, 93, 98
Rose, Stuart, 200

# Index

Ross, Wilbur, 278
Rothschild, Nathan, 48
Rowlands, Chris, 153
Royal Bank of Scotland, 68, 153
Russell, George, 129
Saban Capital, 89-91, 94, 95, 246
Saban, Haim, 90
Safeway, 197
Sarkozy, Nicolas, 308
Saunders, Robin, 194
Sawiris, Naguib, 235, 238, 246, 252
Schwarzman, Stephen, 17, 24, 26
Sears, 158, 194, 196, 201, 216
SEC (Securities and Exchange Commission), 277, 278, 284
Securities and Exchange Commission (SEC), 281
Selecta, 80
Shah, Deep, 283
Sheraton, 33
Shiller, Robert, 260, 276, 280, 316
Silver Lake, 271
Simpkins, Neil, 270
Slim Domit, Carlos, 89
Slim, Carlos, 88, 89, 108
Smith, Keith, 213
Standard & Poor's, 61, 91, 95, 96, 161, 241
Standard Chartered, 153
Standard Life, 301
Starwood, 23, 32, 33
Stevenson, Lord, 200
Stiglitz, Joseph, 306, 314
Storch, Gerald, 166, 173, 174, 182
Storehouse, 192, 193, 195, 209, 216, 217, 226
*Sunday Telegraph*, 218

*Sunday Times*, 222
Sunstein, Cass, 296, 298
Taconic, 247
Target, 158, 164
Technologieholding, 129
Telecom Italia Mobile (TIM), 231, 232, 233
TeleFutura, 88
Telemundo, 92, 96, 98, 105, 107, 110
Televisa, 88, 89, 95-100, 103, 107, 109-13, 116, 269
Tesco, 197
Thaler, Richard, 296, 298
Thatcher, Margaret, 124, 149, 152, 303
Thomas H. Lee, 89, 90, 91, 117
TIM/WIND Hellas, 30, 78, 79, 232-42, 244-60, 288, 290, 295, 305
  delisting, 235

  Ernst & Young, 259

  Q-Telecom, 235, 236, 238, 246, 250, 251, 255

  STET Hellas, 231, 232

  TCS Capital, 234, 235, 239

  Troy GAC, 233, 234

Time Warmer, 101
Topman, 196, 204, 207, 217, 218, 219
Topshop, 196, 202, 204, 207, 214, 217, 218, 219, 227
Towerbrook, 229
Toys "R" Us

delisting, 159, 170

Toys "R" Us, 1, 73, 75, 78, 79, 157-62, 164-70, 172-7, 179-87, 266, 269, 272, 281, 282, 288, 295, 298, 314
    Babies "R" Us, 157-9, 164, 166, 167, 169, 170, 181, 184

    Global Toys Acquisition, 162

    Imaginarium, 158, 164

    Kids "R" Us, 157

TPG (Texas Pacific Group), 9, 89, 90, 91, 97, 98, 102, 112, 117, 233, 235, 237-9, 250, 251, 253-6, 259, 260, 265, 269-71, 279, 291
Trump Organization, 14, 103, 191
Trump, Donald, 103, 107, 114, 191, 227, 229, 278
Turkcell, 237, 238
Union Cycliste Internationale (UCI), 309
UNITE HERE, 114
Univision, 71, 73, 78, 87- 118, 265, 269, 288, 290, 298, 307
Urcelay, Antonio, 174, 175
Uva, Joe, 94, 100
Vanderbilt, Cornelius, 264

*Vanity Fair*, 227
Vatican Bank, 310
Vector Capital, 267
Venevision, 89
Villalobos, Alfred, 275
Vodafone, 232, 244, 249, 252
Vornado Realty Trust, 159, 160, 162, 167, 170, 185
Waldorf Astoria, 14, 23, 33
Walker, Simon, 222
*Wall Street Journal*, 266
Wallis, 194, 219
Wal-Mart, 158, 159, 164, 166, 182, 187, 195
Wasserstein, Bruce, 124
WatchGuard, 267, 268
Weather Investments, 238-44, 246-9, 252, 256, 260
Welch, Jack, 70
Westin, 33
WestLB, 194
WIND Telecomunicazioni, 235, 239
Wood Mackenzie, 44, 45, 58
Woolworth, 192, 196, 216
working capital facility. *See* revolving credit facility
World Anti-Doping Agency (WADA), 308
Yea, Philip, 132, 140, 141, 152
Zara, 200, 214
zombie company, 77, 113, 118, 180, 247, 298, 316
Zuckerberg, Mark, 263

# NOTES

## Prologue

[1] The End of Alchemy, Mervyn King (2016)
[2] Casey Research, 2012; Institute of International Finance, 2017
[3] Polaris Wealth Advisers, Polaris Educational Series, 2015 Market Commentary, March 2015
[4] Axios, 21 November 2017, quoting research from MIT Sloan School of Management Professor Antoinette Schoar

## Chapter 1 - Hilton

[1] Hiltonfoundation.org, history page
[2] Hilton Hotels Corporation, annual report 1948
[3] Hilton Hotels Corporation, annual report 1978
[4] Hilton Hotels Corporation, annual report 1999
[5] Hilton Hotels Corporation, Forms 10-K for the fiscal years ended December 31, 2005 and December 31, 2006
[6] DealBook, New York Times, 3 July 2007
[7] Reuters, 26 December 2007
[8] Financial Times, 3 July 2007
[9] Scotland on Sunday, 8 July 2007
[10] United Press International, 3 July 2007
[11] DealBook New York Times, 21 June 2007; CNNMoney.com, 22 June 2007
[12] Independent, 5 July 2007
[13] New York Times, 9 August 2007
[14] Daily Telegraph, 14 August 2007
[15] Financial Times, 3 July 2007
[16] Hilton 2006 annual report
[17] Financial Times, 13 November 2007
[18] GlobalCapital, 25 January 2008
[19] Financial Times, 4 February 2008

THE GOOD, THE BAD AND THE UGLY OF PRIVATE EQUITY

[20] Times, 11 March 2008
[21] Times, 7 November 2008
[22] Daily Telegraph, 22 November 2008
[23] Ibid
[24] GlobalCapital, 11 August 2009
[25] DealBook New York Times, 12 December 2013
[26] GlobalCapital, 28 October 2009; Wall Street Journal, 29 October 2009
[27] Wall Street Journal, 20 February 2010; Financial Times, 7 October 2010
[28] DealBook New York Times, 12 December 2013
[29] Wall Street Journal, 23 April 2009; Reuters, 15 January 2010; New York Times, 24 December 2010
[30] Independent on Sunday, 20 March 2011
[31] Financial Times, 25 February 2012
[32] International Financing Review, 5 to 11 January 2013; Financial Times, 1 April 2013
[33] International Financing Review, 3 to 9 August 2013
[34] GlobalCapital, 11 September & 14 November 2013; International Financing Review, 21 to 27 September 2013 & 14 November 2013
[35] Reuters, 11 December 2013
[36] New York Times, 12 December 2013
[37] Hilton 2016 annual report
[38] Hilton Worldwide Holdings Inc. IPO prospectus dated December 11, 2013
[39] Ibid
[40] International Financing Review, 12 September 2013
[41] New York Times, 12 December 2013
[42] Irish Independent, 14 May 2015
[43] Hilton Hotels Corporation, Form 10-K for the fiscal year ended December 31, 2006; Hilton 2008 and 2010 annual reports
[44] Hilton Worldwide Holdings Inc. IPO prospectus dated December 11, 2013
[45] Ibid
[46] International Financing Review, 7 to 13 December 2013
[47] Financial Times, 19 August 2013
[48] Ibid
[49] Travel Weekly, 30 June 2014; International Financing Review, 14 to 20 June 2014
[50] International Financing Review, 4 November 2014; PERE News, 6 November 2014
[51] Dow Jones Institutional News, 11 May 2015; International Financing Review, 11 May 2015 & 12 to 18 August 2017
[52] Hilton website, 11 February 2015; Daily Mail, 8 April 2015
[53] The Deal, 11 March 2016
[54] The Blackstone Group L.P., Form 10-K for the year ended 31 December 2015

55 CreditSights, 2 & 8 August 2016; International Financing Review, 20 to 26 August 2016

56 Wall Street Journal, 24 October 2016

57 Financial Times, 21 April 2016

58 International Financing Review, 12 to 18 November 2016

59 CreditSights, 14 November 2016

60 Times, 27 February 2016; Park Hotels & Resorts website

61 Hilton Worldwide Holdings Inc., Form 10-K for the year ended 31 December 2016

62 International Financing Review, 4 to 10 March 2017

63 Law360, 2 June 2017

64 International Financing Review, 10 to 16 June 2017

65 Law360, 15 June 2017; International Financing Review, 17 to 23 June 2017

66 seekingalpha.com, 20 September 2017

67 International Financing Review, 30 September to 6 October 2017

68 BusinessWire, 6 November 2017

69 Hilton 2016 annual report

70 The Economist, 11 February 2017

## Chapter 2 - Mergermarket

1 Informed Options Trading prior to M&A Announcements: Insider Trading? By P. Augustin, M. Brenner, M. Subrahmanyam (2014); Equities.com, 19 June 2014; Times, article on insider deals, 19 January 2018

2 Financial Times, 15 July 2017 – FTMoney supplement - Comment by Stuart Veale, Managing Partner of Beringea, which manages ProVen VCT funds

3 Dealbook, New York Times, 8 August 2006

4 https://exithub.com/bc-partners-portfolio-company-mergermarket-reported-to-sell-infinata-for-under-20m/

5 GlobalCapital, 16 January 2014; International Financing Review, 18 to 24 January 2014; Financial Times Group Limited accounts for the year ended 31 December 2013; multiple based on information in Mergermarket Topco Limited consolidated financial statements for the 54-week period 16 December 2013 to 31 December 2014

6 Moody's Investors Service, 15 January 2014

7 Private Equity Wire, 30 June 2014; AVCJ, 22 September 2015; Unquote, 12 November 2015; Private Equity Wire, 6 January 2016; Sunday Times, 23 April 2017; Unquote, 24 May 2017

8 Mergermarket Limited – annual reports and financial statements for the years ended 2005, 2008 and 2014

# THE GOOD, THE BAD AND THE UGLY OF PRIVATE EQUITY

[9] International Financing Review, 29 July to 4 August 2017
[10] Operating EBITDA and cash EBITDA differed due to adjustments for foreign exchange and deferred income. Multiples also depended on last-twelve-months or forward data. Financial Times, 30 June 2017; Mergermarket Topco Limited consolidated financial statements for the year ended 31 December 2016
[11] Moody's, 5 July 2017; GlobalCapital, 20 July 2017
[12] PEHub, 11 April 2017

## Chapter 3 - Blueprint

[1] Benjamin Franklin, *Poor Richard's Almanack*, 1736
[2] Merrill Corporation, 19 January 2018
[3] Guardian, 7 July 2010; Private Equity News, 8 July 2010; http://carlylecapitallawsuit.com/
[4] Financial Times, 30 November 2009
[5] Financial Times, 28 August 2016 & 8 February 2017

## PART TWO – The Bad

[1] Letter to the Shareholders of Berkshire Hathaway Inc., 2 March 1990

## Chapter 4 - Univision

[1] Los Angeles Times, 28 April 2006; Univision Communications Inc. form 10-K for the year ended 31 December 2006
[2] Univision Wikipedia page
[3] Univision Communications Inc. form 10-K for the year ended 31 December 2006
[4] Thomas H. Lee press release, 27 June 2006
[5] Univision Communications Inc. Form 10-K for the Fiscal Year Ended December 31, 2006
[6] MarketWatch, 27 June 2006
[7] New York Times, 21 June 2006
[8] Financial Times, 22 June 2006
[9] U.S. Equity News, 28 June 2006; International Financing Review, 1 to 7 July 2006
[10] Univision press release, 29 March 2007
[11] New York Times, 15 December 2006
[12] Los Angeles Times, 30 March 2007
[13] Financial Times, 27 December 2006
[14] 2008 Preqin Global Private Equity Review
[15] GlobalCapital, 16 February 2007
[16] International Financing Review, 17 to 23 February 2007 & 3 to 9 March 2007

# Notes

[17] GlobalCapital, 2 February 2007

[18] Reuters, 15 February 2007

[19] Financial Times, 28February 2007

[20] MarketWatch, 27 June 2006

[21] New York Times, 9 February 2006

[22] Univision Communications Inc. form 10-K for the year ended 31 December 2006

[23] U.S. Census Bureau

[24] Financial Times, 15 April 2012

[25] U.S. Equity News, 5 March 2007

[26] Financial Times, 28 February 2007

[27] New York Times, 6 July 2006; Wall Street Journal, 7 July 2006; U.S. Equity News, 21 July 2006

[28] U.S. Equity News, 9 April 2007

[29] CreditSights, 30 December 2007

[30] GlobalCapital, 27 July 2007 & 25 January 2008

[31] International Financing Review, 1 to 7 March 2008

[32] International Financing Review, 27 September to 3 October 2008

[33] International Financing Review, 12 to 18 April 2008

[34] GlobalCapital, 23 May & 15 August 2008

[35] GlobalCapital, 21 November 2008

[36] GlobalCapital, 30 October 2008

[37] Fox News, 23 January 2009; San Diego Union Tribune, 23 January 2009; GlobalCapital, 23 January 2009

[38] CreditSights, 25 May 2009

[39] Financial Times, 6 January & 5 May 2009

[40] Los Angeles Times, 9 July 2009

[41] GlobalCapital, 3 April 2009

[42] International Financing Review, 2 to 8 June 2007

[43] International Financing Review, 27 June to 3 July 2009

[44] GlobalCapital, 11 June 2009; International Financing Review, 27 June to 3 July 2009; CreditSights, 28 June 2009

[45] https://www.c21media.net/univision-axes-300-jobs/

[46] Variety, 31 July 2009

[47] Dealbook, New York Times, 14 June 2010

[48] New York Times, 5 October 2010; International Financing Review, 9 to 15 October 2010

[49] Moody's, 6 October 2010; International Financing Review, 23 to 29 October 2010

[50] International Financing Review, 13 to 19 November 2010 & 10 January 2011

[51] Financial Times, 15 March 2011

[52] Financial Times, 30 June 2011

# THE GOOD, THE BAD AND THE UGLY OF PRIVATE EQUITY

[53] International Financing Review, 25 April 2011

[54] CreditSights, 3 May & 15 August 2012; International Financing Review, 4 to 10 February 2012 & 15 August 2012

[55] International Financing Review, 9 to 15 February 2013 & 16 May 2013; CreditSights, 16 May 2013

[56] International Financing Review, 11 to 17 January 2014

[57] Wall Street Journal, 12 June 2014

[58] Univision Holdings, Inc. Amendment No 6 to form S-1, as filed with the Securities and Exchange Commission on October 20, 2016

[59] Moody's, 29 December 2914; Los Angeles Times, 31 December 2014

[60] Financial Times, 11 March 2015; International Financing Review, 14 to 20 March 2015; Univision Holdings, Inc. Form S-1, as filed with the Securities and Exchange Commission on July 2, 2015

[61] Financial Times, 11 March 2015

[62] CreditSights, 13 April 2015; International Financing Review, 2 July 2015

[63] Financial Times, 30 June 2015; New York Times, 3 July 2015

[64] PrivCo, 29 October 2015

[65] International Financing Review, 2 July 2015

[66] Moody's, 7 July 2015

[67] MarketWatch, 7 July 2015; UNITE HERE report, April 2016

[68] Seeking Alpha, 15 July 2015

[69] CreditSights, 28 October 2015

[70] CreditSights, 23 February 2016

[71] Wall Street Journal, 4 December 2015

[72] Univision Holdings, Inc. Form S-1, as filed with the Securities and Exchange Commission on July 2, 2015

[73] Guardian, 19 January 2016; Los Angeles Times, 21 April 2016; Adweek, 18 August 2016

[74] CreditSights, 10 November 2016; Forbes, 16 November 2016; Los Angeles Times, 2 January 2017

[75] Los Angeles Times, 2 January 2017

[76] ZeroHedge, 18 January 2017

[77] Nielsen data, The Economist, 3 September 2015

[78] Univision Communications Inc. form 10-K for the year ended 31 December 2006; Univision Holdings, Inc. Amendment No 6 to form S-1, as filed with the Securities and Exchange Commission on October 20, 2016

[79] Los Angeles Times, 28 February 2009 & 3 April 2014; money.cnn.com, 16 November 2016; Washington Post, 16 November 2016; Media Moves, 8 March 2017; Latin Times, 4 April 2017

[80] New York Times, 22 June 2006

[81] United Press International, 23 June 2006; CreditSights, 27 June 2006

[82] www.portada-online.com, 4 January 2017

# Notes

[83] International Financing Review, 2 July 2015
[84] CreditSights, 27 June 2006
[85] medialifemagazine.com, 27 December 2016
[86] UNITE HERE report, April 2016
[87] UNITE HERE report, April 2016; Fees, Fees and More Fees: How Private Equity Abuses Its Limited Partners and U.S. Taxpayers, CEPR, May 2016
[88] New York Times, 21 November 1987; Chicago Tribune, 31 March 1990
[89] Chicago Tribune, 26 April 1990
[90] New York Times, 9 April 1992
[91] medialifemagazine.com, 27 December 2016
[92] Financial Times, 13 June 2010; CalPERS, Private Equity Program Fund Performance Review, as of December 31, 2016; California State Teachers' Retirement System, Private Equity Portfolio Performance, As of September 30, 2017; 2017 Preqin Global Private Equity & Venture Capital Report
[93] CalPERS, Private Equity Program Fund Performance Review, as of December 31, 2016
[94] New York Times, 24 April 2015

## Chapter 5 – 3i

[1] Times, 14 July 1931
[2] Times, 24 January 1945
[3] Times, 1 February 1945; Times, 20 March 1948; Times, 21 October 1963; Times, 10 February 1975
[4] International Private Equity, by Eli Talmor and Florin Vasvari
[5] Times, 29 October 1974; Times, 10 February 1975
[6] International Private Equity, by Eli Talmor and Florin Vasvari
[7] Times, 13 October 1983
[8] Times, 5 July 1983
[9] Times, 19 May 1987
[10] Times, 3 April 1986; Times, 7 July 1987
[11] Times, 14 March 1988
[12] Ibid
[13] Times, 19 May 1988
[14] Times, 9 April 1992
[15] Times, 5 October 1992
[16] International Private Equity, by Eli Talmor and Florin Vasvari
[17] Times, 9 February 1994
[18] Times, 6 & 19 July 1994
[19] Times, 8 September 1994
[20] Times, 18 February 1995

THE GOOD, THE BAD AND THE UGLY OF PRIVATE EQUITY

[21] 3i Group plc - Report and accounts for the year ended 31 March 1998
[22] Guardian, 26 January 1999
[23] 3i Group plc - Preliminary statement of annual results for year to 31 March 2000
[24] 3i Group plc - Reports and accounts for the years ended 31 March 1995 and 31 March 2000
[25] 3i Group plc – press release of preliminary statement of annual results for the year ended 31 March 2002
[26] Ibid
[27] Ibid
[28] 3i Group plc - Reports and accounts for the year ended 31 March 2003
[29] Evening Standard, 25 March 2004
[30] 3i Group plc - Reports and accounts for the year ended 31 March 2005
[31] 3i Group plc – annual results investor presentation for the year ended 31 March 2005
[32] 3i Group plc – annual results supplementary information for the year ended 31 March 2006
[33] 3i Group plc – annual results investor presentation for the year ended 31 March 2007
[34] Ibid
[35] 3i Group plc – annual results investor presentation for the year ended 31 March 2008
[36] Ibid
[37] 3i Group plc - Reports and accounts for the year ended 31 March 2009
[38] 3i Group plc – Reports and accounts for the year ended 31 March 2011
[39] 3i Group plc – Reports and accounts for the year ended 31 March 2009
[40] thisismoney.co.uk, 8 May 2009
[41] 3i Group plc – Reports and accounts for the year ended 31 March 2009
[42] 3i Group plc – annual results investor presentation for the year ended 31 March 2009
[43] 3i Group plc – Reports and accounts for the year ended 31 March 2011
[44] 3i Group plc – annual results investor presentation for the year ended 31 March 2010
[45] 3i Group plc – Reports and accounts for the year ended 31 March 2010
[46] 3i Group plc – annual results investor presentation for the year ended 31 March 2011
[47] 3i Group plc – annual results investor presentation for the year ended 31 March 2013
[48] Ibid
[49] 3i Group plc – Reports and accounts for the year ended 31 March 2013
[50] Ibid
[51] Reuters, 2 June 2014

## Notes

[52] 3i Group plc – Reports and accounts for the year ended 31 March 2015
[53] 3i Group plc – Reports and accounts for the year ended 31 March 2017
[54] Times, 9 April 1993
[55] Times, 19 February, 29 April & 20 October 1986
[56] Psychology Today, How We Make the Same Mistakes Over and Over, 31 October 2014
[57] Quote attributed to Benjamin Franklin, Mark Twain and Albert Einstein among others

## Chapter 6 – Toys "R" Us

[1] Guardian, 12 August 2004
[2] New York Times, 13 August 2004, 14 September 2004 & 18 March 2005
[3] New York Times, 13 August 2004
[4] Financial Times, 12 August 2004; Guardian, 12 & 24 August 2004; International Financing Review, 5 to 11 March 2005
[5] Independent, 2 March 2005; Financial Times, 4 & 6 March 2005
[6] Times, 10 March 2005; Financial Times, 11 March 2005
[7] Toys "R" Us, Inc. Form 10-K for the fiscal year ended January 28, 2006; GlobalCapital, 11 March 2005; Financial Times, 18 March 2005; New York Times, 18 March 2005
[8] International Financing Review, 26 March to 1 April 2005; KKR & Co. L.P., Form S-1, 3 July 2007
[9] CreditSights, 17 March & 31 May 2005; Toys "R" Us, Inc. Form 10-Q for the quarter ended June 30, 2005
[10] CreditSights, 22 June 2005
[11] International Financing Review, 25 June to 1 July 2005
[12] CreditSights, 1 July 2005
[13] New York times, 25 May 2004; Financial Times, 29 June 2004; Wall Street Journal, 29 June 2004; Toys "R" Us, Inc. Form 10-K for the fiscal year ended January 28, 2006; Quartz Media, 18 September 2017
[14] CreditSights, 27 March 2006
[15] New York Times, 8 February 2006
[16] GlobalCapital, 13 January 2006; International Financing Review, 14 to 20 January 2006
[17] GlobalCapital, 23 June 2006; International Financing Review, 24 to 30 June 2006
[18] New York Times, 18 July 2006
[19] Financial Times, 26 July 2006
[20] Wall Street Journal, 2 May 2006

THE GOOD, THE BAD AND THE UGLY OF PRIVATE EQUITY

[21] Toys "R" Us, Inc. Forms 10-K for the fiscal years ended January 31, 2004 and February 2, 2008

[22] GlobalCapital, 27 March 2009

[23] International Financing Review, 4 to 10 July 2009

[24] GlobalCapital, 25 June 2009; International Financing Review, 4 to 10 July 2009

[25] GlobalCapital, 19 October 2009; International Financing Review, 14 to 20 November 2009

[26] Les Echos, 31 May 2010

[27] Toys "R" Us, Inc. Form S-1 registration statement to the Securities and Exchange Commission, May 27, 2010; Financial Times, 29 May 2010

[28] Daily Telegraph, 4 July 2010; New York Times, 15 July 2010

[29] International Financing Review, 11 & 17 August 2010

[30] CreditSights, 26 January 2011

[31] Toys "R" Us, Inc. Form 10-K for the fiscal year ended January 29, 2011; CreditSights, 16 February & 7 March 2011

[32] International Financing Review, 19 to 25 March 2011; CreditSights, 14 June 2011

[33] Toys "R" Us, Inc. Form 10-K for the fiscal year ended January 28, 2012

[34] International Financing Review, 24 to 30 March 2012

[35] Sunday Times, 29 April 2012

[36] International Financing Review, 26 July 2012

[37] Wall Street Journal, 9 March 2011

[38] GlobalCapital, 21 February 2013; CreditSights, 3 April 2013

[39] Toys "R" Us, Inc. withdrawal notice to the Securities and Exchange Commission, March 29, 2013

[40] International Financing Review, 3 to 9 August 2013

[41] Toys "R" Us press release, 21 August 2013

[42] Les Echos, 4 December 2013

[43] Ibid

[44] Wall Street Journal, 23 October 2013; FierceRetail, 23 October 2013

[45] Toys "R" Us, Inc. Form 10-K for the fiscal year ended February 1, 2014; Les Echos, 4 December 2013

[46] CreditSights, 11 January 2015

[47] International Financing Review, 27 September to 3 October 2014 & 11 to 17 October 2014

[48] Forbes, 2 June 2015

[49] Financial Times, 15 June 2016

[50] Toys "R" Us, Inc. Form 10-K for the fiscal year ended January 28, 2017; CreditSights, 12 April 2017

[51] Toys "R" Us, Inc. Forms 10-K for the fiscal years ended January 31, 2004, January 29, 2005, January 28, 2006, January 31, 2015, January 30, 2016, and January 28, 2017

# Notes

[52] International Financing Review, 19 September 2017
[53] GlobalCapital, 21 September 2017
[54] New York Times, 19 September 2017; Telegraph, 19 September 2017
[55] Toys "R" Us, Inc. Form 10-K for the fiscal year ended January 28, 2006
[56] CreditSights, 26 January 2011
[57] Market Realist, 19 January 2016
[58] CreditSights, 17 March 2005
[59] CreditSights, 26 January 2011
[60] Oneclickretail.com, The Amazon Effect U.S. Toys Market, 26 January 2017
[61] CreditSights, 8 March 2011
[62] Toys "R" Us, Inc. Form 10-K for the fiscal year ended January 28, 2006
[63] CreditSights, 16 June 2017
[64] Daily Telegraph, 21 January 2014

## PART THREE – The Ugly

[1] Everything Counts, Depeche Mode (1983)

## Chapter 7 - Bhs

[1] Herald Scotland, 25 April 2016
[2] Daily Telegraph, 25 January 2015; Herald Scotland, 25 April 2016
[3] Herald Scotland, 25 April 2016
[4] Daily Telegraph, 4 April 2009
[5] Daily Telegraph, 17 March 2002
[6] Times, 25 September 1992
[7] Daily Mail, 9 July 1999
[8] Times, 28 March 2000
[9] Storehouse plc - Annual report and accounts 2000
[10] Scotland on Sunday, 20 January 2002
[11] Storehouse plc - Annual report and accounts 1999
[12] Independent, 16 July 2000
[13] Daily Mail, 16 September 2000; Guardian, 7 November 2000
[14] Evening Standard, 22 May 2002
[15] Sunday Times, 26 May 2002
[16] Sunday Telegraph, 3 November 2002
[17] Evening Standard, 21 January 2002; Mail on Sunday, 24 February 2002
[18] Sunday Times, 19 May 2002
[19] New Statesman, 16 September 2002
[20] Evening Standard, 14 June 2002

# THE GOOD, THE BAD AND THE UGLY OF PRIVATE EQUITY

[21] Financial Times, 7 September 2002; Taveta Investments Limited – Report for the period ended 30 August 2003

[22] Evening Standard, 19 March 2002; Sunday Times, 7 April 2002; Times, 30 August 2002

[23] Sunday Times, 8 September 2002

[24] Times, 1 November 2002; Financial Times, 1 November 2002

[25] Daily Telegraph, 14 December 2002; Evening Standard, 13 July 2003; Independent, 15 November 2004

[26] Sunday Times, 8 December 2002

[27] Daily Mail, 20 January 2003

[28] Taveta Investments Limited – Report for the period ended 30 August 2003

[29] Times, 24 October 2003

[30] Sunday Telegraph, 26 October 2003

[31] Ibid

[32] Evening Standard, 6 November 2003

[33] Bhs Group Limited – Financial statements, Directors' and Independent Auditors' Reports for the 52 weeks ended 27 March 2004

[34] Independent, 23 December 2003; Herald, 30 March 2004

[35] Daily Telegraph, 29 May 2004; Sunday Telegraph, 30 May 2004; Sunday Times, 30 May 2004

[36] Independent, 2 June 2004

[37] Evening News, 3 June 2004; Western Mail, 4 June 2004

[38] Daily Mail, 18 June 2004; Daily Telegraph, 18 June 2004

[39] Daily Telegraph, 9 July 2004; Financial Times, 4 October 2004; Marks and Spencer Annual report and financial statements 2004

[40] Breakingviews.ie, 30 May 2004; Evening Standard, 8 June 2004

[41] Daily Mail, 16 July 2004

[42] Daily Telegraph, 6 September 2004; Daily Mail, 14 October 2004

[43] Arcadia Group Limited – Annual reports for the years ended 30 August 2003 and 28 August 2004; Daily Telegraph, 22 October 2004

[44] Daily Telegraph, 4 November 2004

[45] Financial Times, 7 January 2005

[46] Independent, 13 October 2005

[47] Taveta Investments Limited – Annual report for the year ended 27 August 2005

[48] Independent, 15 February 2005; Bhs Group Limited – Financial Statements, Directors' and Independent Auditors' Reports for the 52 weeks ended 1 April 2006

[49] Daily Mail, 19 February 2005; Sunday Times, 27 February 2005

[50] Daily Mail, 14 July 2005

[51] Bhs Group Limited, Arcadia Group Limited, and Taveta Investments Limited financial statements and annual reports for the fiscal years 2004, 2005 and 2008

[52] Financial Times, 8 October 2008

# Notes

[53] Herald, 22 October 2008

[54] Financial Times, 4 February 2009; Evening Standard, 5 February 2009

[55] Sunday Times, 8 March 2009

[56] Independent, 27 May 2009

[57] Daily Mail, 16 July 2009

[58] Bhs Group Limited – Financial Statements, Directors' and Independent Auditors' Reports for the 74 weeks ended 29 August 2009

[59] Taveta Investments Limited – Annual Report for the year ended 29 August 2009

[60] Marks & Spencer – Annual reports, 2006, 2008, 2009, 2010

[61] Independent, 13 March 2010

[62] Evening Standard, 18 November 2010

[63] Taveta Investments Limited – Annual report for the year ended 28 August 2010

[64] Times, 30 May 2011; Independent, 11 September 2011

[65] Bhs Limited – Report and financial statements for the year ended 27 August 2011; Financial Times, 24 November 2011

[66] CityAM, 22 November 2012

[67] Sunday Times, 10 November 2013

[68] Bhs Limited – Reports and financial statements for the year ended 30 August 2014

[69] Sunday Times, 25 January 2015

[70] Taveta Investments Limited – Annual Report for the year ended 29 August 2015

[71] Times, 26 May 2000; Daily Mail, 10 July 2002

[72] Storehouse plc - Annual reports and accounts 1999 & 2000

[73] Times, 14 July & 25 September 2006

[74] Bhs Group Limited – Financial Statements, Directors' and Independent Auditors' Reports for the 52 weeks ended 30 March 2002

[75] Guardian, 3 November 2004

[76] Herald, 30 March 2004

[77] Taveta Investments Limited – Annual report for the year ended 28 August 2004; Daily Telegraph, 18 October 2004; Taveta Investments Limited – Annual report for the year ended 27 August 2005

[78] Sunday Times, 11 November 2012

[79] Financial Times, 13 March 2015

[80] Ibid

[81] Daily Telegraph, 12 March 2015

[82] Ibid

[83] Associated British Foods plc - Annual Report and Accounts 2009

[84] Mintel.com, 15 September 2017; Statista

[85] Daily Mail, 3 December 2007

[86] Daily Mail, 13 March 2015

[87] Sunday Times, 24 April 2016

[88] Daily Telegraph, 7 March 2016

# THE GOOD, THE BAD AND THE UGLY OF PRIVATE EQUITY

[89] Observer, 30 May 2004

[90] Bhs Limited – Financial Statements, Directors' and Independent Auditors' Reports for the 52 weeks ended 1 April 2006; Bhs Limited – Annual report and financial statements for the year ended 30 August 2014

[91] Sunday Times, 19 April 2015; BBC News, 7 March 2016

[92] Chappell was first declared bankrupt in 2005 when he failed to pay fees on a property sale, and again 2009 over the unsuccessful Island Harbour Marina development on the Isle of Wight (Daily Mail, 26 April 2016)

[93] Sunday Times, 6 March 2016; Times, 7 March 2016; Financial Times, 8 March 2016

[94] Independent, 1 May 2007; Arcadia Group website, August 2017

[95] Financial Times, 6 December 2012

[96] Times, 28 October 2002

[97] Financial Times, 16 November 2005

[98] Sunday Telegraph, 20 January 2002

[99] Daily Post, 12 April 2008; Evening Standard, 5 September 2008

[100] Daily Mail, 3 March 2006; Sunday Telegraph, 15 July 2007; Daily Post, 14 April 2008

[101] Daily Mail, 29 September 2006

[102] Taveta Investments Limited – Annual Report for the year ended 30 August 2014

[103] Taveta Investments Limited – Annual Report for the year ended 29 August 2015

[104] Sunday Times, 15 November 2015

[105] Daily Mail, 18 September 2015

[106] Daily Telegraph, 25 April 2015

[107] Sunday Times, 12 April 2015

[108] Daily Mail, 14 August 2010

[109] Daily Mirror, 14 August 2010

[110] Financial Times, 27 April 2016

[111] Daily Telegraph, 25 April 2016

[112] Independent, 3 June 2016

[113] Evening Standard, 13 June 2002

[114] Financial Times, 25 April 2016

[115] Evening Standard, 15 June 2016; Independent, 15 June 2016

[116] Evening Standard, 25 April 2016

[117] Taveta Investments Limited – Annual report for the fiscal years 2006 to 2016

[118] Independent, 8 June 2016

[119] Times, 5 January 2006

[120] Guardian, 25 May 2016

[121] Financial Times, 28 February 2017

# Notes

[122] Taveta Investments Limited – Annual Report for the year ended 27 August 2016; Guardian, 27 June 2017

[123] Over the years Green and his family chalked up significant gains from Bhs through property deals and interest payments. Once these are added, Bhs generated almost £590 million (Financial Times, 27 April 2016). On that basis, Green made a net loss of £260 million out of the business over a 15-year holding period

[124] Independent, 13 November 2010

[125] Evening Standard, 6 December 2010

[126] Daily Mirror, 4 June 2016; Daily Mail, 9 June 2016

[127] BreakingNews.ie, 5 December 2012; Daily Mail, 10 June 2016

[128] Newsweek, 16 March 2018

[129] Telegraph, 19 May 2017

[130] USA Today, 16 May 2017; cnbc.com, 12 July 2017; wolfstreet.com, 12 October 2017

## Chapter 8 – TIM/WIND Hellas

[1] TIM Hellas annual report 2004; New York Times, 19 March 2005

[2] GlobalCapital, 21 June 2005

[3] Financial Times, 29 September 2005; Wall Street Journal, 24 November 2005

[4] GlobalCapital, 22 July, 26 August & 23 September 2005; International Financing Review, 17 September to 23 September 2005; TIM Hellas annual report 2005

[5] International Financing Review, 1 October to 7 October 2005

[6] http://www.ekathimerini.com/35442/article/ekathimerini/business/tims-merger-with-troy-gac-hits-an-obstacle

[7] TIM Hellas annual report 2004

[8] TIM Hellas Telecommunications S.A. debt offering memorandum, 28 November 2005

[9] TIM Hellas annual report 2005

[10] New York Times, 7 December 2005

[11] TIM Hellas annual report 2005

[12] Apax Partners press release, 7 February 2007

[13] International Financing Review, 28 January to 3 February 2006

[14] District Court of Luxembourg, Commercial ruling no. 1648/15 of the 15th division, Handed down on 23 December 2015

[15] Financial Times, 5 April 2006; GlobalCapital, 7 April 2006; International Financing Review, 8 April to 14 April 2006

[16] Daily Telegraph, 13 July 2006; District Court of Luxembourg, Commercial ruling no. 1648/15 of the 15th division, Handed down on 23 December 2015; Times, 25 September 2006

[17] ekathimerini.com, 18 October 2006; Gulf News, 26 November 2006; PE News, 4 December 2006

[18] District Court of Luxembourg, Commercial ruling no. 1648/15 of the 15th division, Handed down on 23 December 2015

[19] Times, 7 December 2006; GlobalCapital, 8 December 2006 & 5 January 2007

[20] International Financing Review, 16 December to 5 January 2007

[21] International Financing Review, 6 January to 12 January 2007, 10 February to 16 February 2007 & 25 February to 2 March 2012; New York Times, 15 March 2010

[22] Apax Partners press release, 7 February 2007

[23] Ibid

[24] TIM Hellas annual report 2004

[25] US Bankruptcy Court, Southern District of New York, Memorandum opinion and order granting in part and denying in part defendants' motions to dismiss, Case No. 12-10631 (MG), 29 January 2015

[26] GlobalCapital, 20 July 2007

[27] Sunday Telegraph, 10 February 2008

[28] International Financing Review, 7 June to 13 June 2008

[29] Weather Finance III S.A.R.L. annual report for the year ended 31 December 2009

[30] GlobalCapital, 28 August, 18 & 25 September 2009

[31] International Financing Review, 9 & 17 to 23 October 2009

[32] International Financing Review, 21 to 27 November 2009

[33] Daily Telegraph, 13 November 2009

[34] Thisismoney.co.uk, 6 March 2010

[35] International Financing Review, 21 to 27 November 2009

[36] Thisismoney.co.uk, 6 March 2010

[37] International Financing Review, 28 November to 4 December 2009

[38] International Financing Review, 11 May 2010

[39] International Financing Review, 12 to 18 December 2009

[40] International Financing Review, 6 to 12 March 2010 & 20 to 26 March 2010

[41] Daily Telegraph, 19 February 2010

[42] International Financing Review, 11 May 2010

[43] International Financing Review, 15 to 21 May 2010 & 29 May to 4 June 2010

[44] Independent, 26 June 2010; International Financing Review, 19 to 25 June 2010

[45] International Financing Review, 15 to 21 May 2010

[46] Mail on Sunday, 18 July 2010

[47] International Financing Review, 3 to 9 July 2010

[48] International Financing Review, 25 September to 1 October 2010

[49] International Financing Review, 25 September to 1 October 2010; Weather Finance III S.A.R.L. annual report for the year ended 31 December 2009

[50] Financial Times, 18 October 2010

# Notes

[51] International Financing Review, 23 to 29 October 2010

[52] International Financing Review, 18 December to 7 January 2011

[53] Apax Partners Annual Report 2011

[54] Cellular News, 4 October 2010

[55] Financial Times, 30 August 2011

[56] Financial Times, 8 November 2011 & 6 February 2012; Daily Telegraph, 7 February 2012

[57] Wall Street Journal, 24 December 2015

[58] Wall Street Journal, 13 March 2014; Financial Times, 14 March 2014; The Economist, 20 June 2015

[59] Wall Street Journal, 24 November 2005

[60] Wall Street Journal, 12 December 2016

[61] M2 Presswire, Research and Markets, 22 October 2008

[62] New York Times, 15 March 2010

[63] Ibid

[64] New York Times, 7 September 2015

[65] https://www.thepressproject.gr/article/69714/Wind-Telecom-and-the-largest-capital-drain-in-Greek-financial-history; The Economist, 20 June 2015

[66] Independent, 28 October 2015

[67] Ibid

[68] Observer, 31 October 2015

[69] Wall Street Journal, 24 December 2015

[70] Law360, 16 September 2016

[71] California State Teachers' Retirement System, Private Equity Portfolio Performance, As of September 30, 2017

[72] GlobalCapital, 15 December 2009

[73] International Financing Review, 25 October 2016; GlobalCapital, 28 October 2016

[74] New York Times, 15 March 2010

[75] Financial Times, 16 June 2015

[76] Daily Telegraph, 2 December 2011

[77] *Animal Spirits: How human psychology drives the economy, and why it matters for global capitalism*, George A. Akerlof and Robert J. Shiller (2009)

## Chapter 9 – Private Equity's C-words

[1] Ron Chernow, The Warburgs (1993)

[2] https://www.american-rails.com/railroad-tycoons.html

[3] Bear Stearns, 8 December 2006 presentation by Dan Katsikas

[4] S&P Capital IQ

[5] New York Law Journal, 29 June 2006

## THE GOOD, THE BAD AND THE UGLY OF PRIVATE EQUITY

[6] Wall Street Journal, 10 & 11 October 2006; New York Times, 12 October 2006
[7] StayCurrent, A client alert from Paul Hastings, April 2007
[8] New York Times, 12 October 2006
[9] Dechert, OnPoint, March 2008
[10] New York Times, 10 September 2011
[11] New York Times, 12 October 2012
[12] Pomerantz Monitor, May/June 2013
[13] Fortune, 12 March 2011
[14] New York Times, 12 October 2012
[15] Pomerantz Monitor, May/June 2013
[16] Ibid
[17] New York Times, 15 March 2013
[18] Financial Times, 7 August 2014; Cartelcapers.com, 5 September 2014
[19] International Financing Review, 19 to 25 March 2005
[20] dodd-frank.com
[21] New York Times, 12 May 2015
[22] Wall Street Journal, 4 December 2012; New York Times, 19 June 2013
[23] Abcnews.com, 14 May 2009
[24] Fortune, 7 October 2010
[25] ag.ny.gov, 15 December 2010
[26] sfgate.com, 12 July 2014
[27] LA Times, 14 January 2015
[28] cnbc.com, 7 September 2017
[29] Do Private Equity Funds Manipulate Reported Returns?, G.W. Brown, O. Gredil, S.N. Kaplan, 2013
[30] Blackstone, Forms 10-K for the years ended 31 December 2007 to 2016
[31] Financial Times, 29 June 2015
[32] Bloomberg, 7 October 2015
[33] Reuters, 25 August 2016
[34] New York Post, 24 August 2016
[35] Pensions & Investments, 22 December 2017
[36] *Phishing for Phools: The Economics of Manipulation and Deception*, George A. Akerlof and Robert J. Shiller (2015)
[37] International Financing Review, 11 December 2014
[38] International Financing Review, 21 to 27 February 2015
[39] FINRA news release, 11 December 2014; Dealbook, New York Times, 11 December 2014; Bloomberg, 11 December 2014
[40] CNNMoney, 3 July 2007
[41] Financial Times, 9 July 2007
[42] Guardian, 17 October 2009
[43] DealBook, New York Times, 24 August 2011; Washington Post, 13 October 2011
[44] The Agricola, Tacitus

Notes

## Epilogue

[1] Daniel Kahneman, *Thinking, Fast and Slow* (2011)
[2] Ibid
[3] https://en.wikipedia.org/wiki/File:The_Cognitive_Bias_Codex_-_180%2B_biases,_designed_by_John_Manoogian_III_(jm3).png
[4] Bloomberg, 27 February 2015
[5] The Daily Telegraph, 11 September 2013
[6] Observer.com, 13 May 2014; Wired UK Edition, January 2015
[7] Evening Standard, 2 July 2014
[8] Forbes, 11 June 2014
[9] Business Insider, 20 March 2015
[10] Times, 12 June & 18 December 2014; bbc.co.uk, 13 November 2014; Guardian, 18 December 2014; Independent, 18 December 2014; Wall Street Journal, 18 December 2014
[11] Spiegel, 16 July 2012; Evening Standard, 27 May 2015; Financial Times, 31 October/1 November 2015; Sunday Times, 1 November 2015
[12] Times, 13 November 2015; Observer, 15 November 2015; Time, 23 November 2015
[13] Eric Frattini, *The Entity*, JR Books
[14] *Other People's Money and How the Bankers Use It*, Louis D. Brandeis (1914)
[15] Guardian, 1 May 2016
[16] *Phishing for Phools: The Economics of Manipulation and Deception*, George A. Akerlof and Robert J. Shiller (2015)

Printed in Poland
by Amazon Fulfillment
Poland Sp. z o.o., Wrocław